WATER WAR IN SOUTH ASIA

Brahmaputra Dam and Diversion

WATER WAR IN SOUTH ASIA

Brahmaputra Dam and Diversion

Col. Puneet Raina (Retd.)

NEHA PUBLISHERS & DISTRIBUTORS
DELHI

Publisher
NEHA PUBLISHERS & DISTRIBUTORS
4832/24,Prahlad Lane,S-207 Ansari
Road, Daryaganj, Delhi-110002
Ph.: 43570976, 23278261
Email: nehapubdistributors@gmail.com

Edition: 2016

ISBN: 978-93-80318-87-5

Laser Typesetting
JEE-VEE Graphics, Delhi

Price: 1295/-

Printed
Vikas Computers, Delhi

Preface

Water is an increasingly precious resource. In Asia, the sharing of our rivers and water sources can be a bitterly divisive issue, pitting state against state, country against country. A network of treaties and endless diplomatic wrangling have shaped this process over the years, but whether it's Pakistan and India's mutual dissatisfaction over the Indus Water Treaty, India's opposition to China's proposed diversion of the Tsangpo-Brahmaputra, or Bangladesh's concerns over the division of waters from the Ganga-Brahmaputra-Meghna basin, water sharing is a source of much contention.

China's grand plans to harness the waters of the Brahmaputra River have set off ripples of anxiety in the two lower riparian states: India and Bangladesh. China's construction of dams and the proposed diversion of the Brahmaputra's waters is not only expected to have repercussions for water flow, agriculture, ecology, and lives and livelihoods downstream; it could also become another contentious issue undermining Sino-Indian relations.

Diversion of the Brahmaputra's waters is another – and much more portentous – potential use. Planned diversion of this river's waters from India's water-surplus northeast to drought-stricken western and southern states, though at least temporarily on hold, is the key to India's River Linking Project (RLP). China's diversion plans, on the other hand, are lodged in the mammoth and already underway South-North Water Diversion Project (SNWDP). If currently discussed proposals to include the Brahmaputra in an extended version of the still pending Western Route of the SNWDP were implemented, the consequences for downstream India and, even more so Bangladesh, might be disastrous.

The 2,880 km-long Brahmaputra originates in Tibet, where it is known as the Yarlung Tsangpo. It flows eastwards through southern Tibet for a distance of 1,625 kilometers and at its easternmost point it swings around to make a spectacular U-turn at the Shuomatan Point or Great Bend before it enters India's easternmost state, Arunachal Pradesh. Here it is known as the Siang River. After gathering the waters of several rivers it announces itself as the Brahmaputra in the state of Assam. The river snakes lazily through Assam to then enter Bangladesh, where it is known as the Jamuna. In Bangladesh it is joined by the Ganges (known as the Padma in Bangladesh) and Meghna and together these rivers form the world's largest delta before emptying their waters into the Bay of Bengal.

The relations between India and China are driven, of course, by much more than water; and even water cannot be confidently said to be driving things relentlessly and unalterably in the direction of violent conflict between them. Still, China's dire water circumstances, combined with its impressive economic strength, military power, and uniquely advantageous upper riparian position, give us little reason for optimism when it comes to river sharing agreements with lower riparian countries. There are today no formal agreements at all between China and India in regard to water sharing of the transboundary Brahmaputra; and one should not expect any grand cooperative interstate scheme to develop any time soon in regard to that river. On the contrary, mounting tensions and at least verbal skirmishing between China and India over the Brahmaputra's contested waters seem more likely. There will surely be water woes impacting their relationship, in other words, even if water wars never materialize.

This book contains the fundamental and basic information of the subject and useful for teachers, students and researchers.

—*Editor*

Contents

1

Introduction

CHINA GRAND PROJECTS

Traditionally, the Chinese people's respect for their Emperor increases when the latter is undertakes projects that no human mind can conceive of. After all, the Emperor is the Son of Heaven, and only in Heaven can projects such as the Grand Canal or the Great Wall can be envisioned.

It is also the role of the Emperor to bring Heaven's vision down on earth. If he fails, his Mandate is terminated by Heaven and a Revolution or a Rebellion occurs.

This story began long ago: a Chinese website proclaims: "*The Grand Canal of China is the world's oldest and longest canal, far surpassing the next two grand canals of the world: Suez and Panama Canal. The building of the canal began in 486 B.C. during the Wu Dynasty. It was extended during the Qi Dynasty, and later by Emperor Yangdi of Sui Dynasty during six years of furious construction from 605-610 AD. The canal is 1,795 Km (1,114 miles) long with 24 locks and some 60 bridges.*"

The Great Wall was also 'furiously' constructed under different dynasties, through what the communist Party terms today as 'management contracts': " *The construction of the Great Wall, drew heavily on the local resources for construction materials, was carried out in line with the local conditions under the management of contract and responsibility system. A great army of manpower, composed of soldiers, prisoners, and local people, built the wall. The construction result demonstrates the manifestation of the wisdom and tenacity of the Chinese people."*

The Communists came into power in China in 1949. On October 1, from the rostrum of the Tiananmen Square, Mao addressed the masses assembled to listen to the new Emperor. He told them: *"The Chinese people have stood up"*. A dynasty was born.

The First Generation of this dynasty also had to build a new Canal or a new Wall. Mao's Dream was to catch up with the West and produce as much steel as UK in a few years time. It resulted in the Great Leap Forward and the death of 40 million people. Mao lost his mandate for a few years, but came back with an even greater project: a Great Proletarian Cultural Revolution which also took the lives of a few millions. Deng Xiaoping continued along the same direction with his new economic Revolution: "To become rich is Glorious". In many ways, he succeeded and entered the Pantheon of the Great Emperors. In the next generation, the Premier Li Peng, an engineer by profession, undertook the massive Three Gorges Dam which is to produce 18,000 Mega Kilowatts of electricity.

The New Projects

Four mega projects have been described in an article in 2001 by Zhao Qinghua, the Chinese Ambassador to Bangladesh. To quote him: *"Four gigantic projects to be built in the next five years in China are expected to balance the supply of the nation's water, energy, mineral and human resources, which are vital to a coordinated development of the national economy but unevenly distributed in the vast land....*

The four projects are designed to solve these problems. They are the diversion of southern water to the north, a west east natural gas pipeline, transmission of electricity from west to east and a railway linking Tibet with the rest of the country."

We shall now spend some time on the South to North water diversion project mentioned in *The Draft Outline of the Tenth Five-year Plan for National Economic and Social Development (2001 2005)* and expounded by Zhao: *According to the 10th Five-year Plan, water will be diverted from the south via three channels in the eastern, central and western regions, respectively. The western route draws water from*

Tongtianhe, Yalongjiang and Daduhe, tributaries of the Yangtze River in southwest China, to the upper reaches of the Yellow River to solve water shortage in the northwestern regions. The central route is to fetch water from the Danjiangkou Reservoir on the border between Hubei and Henan provinces to Beijing and Tianjin. The eastern route draws water at Yangzhou on the lower reaches of the Yangtze, flowing through a section of the ancient Grand Canal and lakes northward to reach Hebei and Tianjin.

Upon completion, the project will link up the Yangtze, Huaihe, the Yellow River and Haihe valleys, forming a network of four horizontal and three vertical waterways that allows a rational allocation of the country's water resources nationwide. The project is designed to divert 38 48 billion cubic meters of river water a year, which equal the annual flow of the Yellow River, the second longest in China. It is expected to quench the thirst in the north and break the bottleneck hampering economic and social development in China so as to promote a sustainable social and economic development and benefit future generations, according to the Ministry of Water Resources.

With the relocation of water resources, not only some 20 large and medium- sized cities like Beijing, Tianjin and Shijiazhuang will be relieved of the constraints of water shortage, new economic growth points will rise up along the new waterways, especially in the western regions in a short time."

One can have an opinion on most of these projects and particularly on the gigantism of some of its components, but they are internal problems of China. However one is not: the Brahmaputra diversion!

The Problem of food: can China feed itself?

Let us first see the rationale of these projects.

Two of the most acute problems facing China today are the questions of food and water. These two issues are closely interlinked and, if not solved, are bound to have grave social and political consequences for the country.

The leadership in Beijing has proclaimed: *"China can feed itself in the next century"*, but the mere fact that the problem is oftened at the highest level of the Chinese hierarchy shows that the problem is not solved, that the new emperors are not sure where the solution lies or even if there is a solution.

This has been pointed out in a remarkable book written by one of the foremost world experts in agriculture, the American Lester Brown. His book, *Who Will Feed China* published in the mid-eighties in *the Worldwatch Environment Alert* Series, forced the Chinese leadership to rethink their agricultural strategies a few years ago.

In an article in the *Beijing Review* in September 1996, a reporter admitted: "*The fact that China's population of over 1.2 billion continues to grow by an annual rate of 10 millions have led some to ask if China can feed its people.*" The problem is very simple, again according to the *Beijing Review: "China's total coverage of cultivated land dropped by an astounding 21 millions hectares between 1958 and 1995, while the nation's population grew significantly from 660 millions to 1.2 billion during the same period."*

The theory advanced by Lester Brown is the following: with the growth in population, which will stabilise only in 2045 at 1.6 billion and the increase in industrial development, the arable lands reduce rapidly but the needs of the population increase simultaneously. The result will be that China will have to import more and more grain from outside increasing the rise of the price of grain on the world market. A point will be reached when the planet will not be able to produce enough grain for the world demand or the poorer nations will not be able to buy their food.

Today everyone admits that 90 million extra human beings on the planet every year is beyond the limits that the planet can produce or give to her children. Due to the size of the country, China's problems immediately take greater proportions. It is obvious that a problem affecting 1.2 billion people, is very different to when it concerns a smaller country. To give a practical example, if the entire Chinese population would today drink two extra bottles of beer, it would require the entire annual grain production of Norway in order to produce these additional bottles.

According to global statistics, the conversion of agricultural land into other uses (factories, residential areas, airports, roads, fly-overs, etc...) has provoked the loss of 52% of Japan's grain harvested areas, 46 of Korea's and 42% of Taiwan's. China's development is not different from these three countries though it started later.

Another problem which is a direct consequence of the rapid economic development is that the affluence of the population has risen tremendously during the past two decades. Deng Xiaoping had asked his people to become rich. It may be a fine motto for someone who had just come back from political exile, but when it translates into national realities, becoming richer has many unpleasant consequences. First of all people change their culinary lifestyle; before buying a flat or a vehicle, an individual will try to improve his diet. And traditionally Chinese people are not vegetarian as in India. The Chinese love to eat pork, eggs or chicken. To produce these animals more grain is needed and the problem of food grain becomes further compounded. The forces which were (and still are) at play in Japan, Korea and Taiwan are not different in China. Today the above three Asian countries are importing 71% of their food grain. How can China avoid facing the same problem?

One of the solutions is to increase the yield, but China's yield is already quite high and to succeed where Japan failed is not an easy task.

Eighty per cent of the agricultural lands are irrigated land, one way to get a better production is to increase the irrigation. But the result is a depletion of the aquifers. This problem is even getting more serious as traditional irrigation water is being used for industrial purpose.

Lester Brown concludes his study by citing again the examples of the industrialised Asian countries Japan, Korea and Thailand which in spite of the best conditions have become grain importers. He prophesizes: *"In an integrated world economy, China's rising food prices will become the world's rising food prices. China's land scarcity will become everyone's land scarcity. And water scarcity in China will affect the entire world... It could well lead us to redefine national security away from military preparedness and toward maintaining adequate food supplies."*

A small mercy is the fact that for the past two years China's development growth has been reduced to a more manageable per annum 7-8%.

The Problem of Water

This leads us to the problem of water. We quote from another study of the *World Watch Institute:*

In 1999 the water table under Beijing fell by 2.5 meters (8 feet). Since 1965, the water table under the city has fallen by some 59 meters or nearly 200 feet, warning China's leaders of the shortages that lie ahead as the country's aquifers are depleted. Hydrologically, there are two Chinas — the humid south, which includes the Yangtze River basin and everything south of it, and the north, which includes all the country north of the Yangtze basin. The south, with 700 million people, has one third of the nation's cropland and four fifths of its water. The north, with 550 million people, has two thirds of the cropland and one fifth of the water. The water per hectare of cropland in the north is one eighth that of the south.

The northern part of the country is drying out as the demand for water outstrips the supply. Water tables are falling. Wells are going dry. Streams are drying up, and rivers and lakes are disappearing. Under the North China Plain, a region that stretches from just north of Shanghai to well north of Beijing and that produces 40 percent of China's grain, the water table is dropping by an average of 1.5 meters per year.

Farmers in the north are faced with losses of irrigation water both from aquifer depletion and from the diversion to cities and industry. Between now and 2010, when China's population is projected to grow by 126 million, the World Bank projects that the nation's urban water demand will increase from 50 billion cubic meters to 80 billion, a growth of 60 percent. Industrial water demand, meanwhile, is projected to increase from 127 billion cubic meters to 206 billion, an expansion of 62 percent. In much of northern China, this growing demand for water can be satisfied only by taking irrigation water from agriculture.

What happens to irrigation water supplies directly affects China's agricultural prospect. Whereas less than 15 percent of the U.S. grain harvest comes from irrigated land, in China it is close to 70 percent.

In the competition for water between cities, industry, and agriculture, the economics of water use do not favor agriculture. In China, a thousand tons of water produces one ton of wheat, worth perhaps $200. The same water used in industry will expand output by $14,000-70 times as much. In a country that is desperately seeking economic growth and, even more, the jobs it generates, the gain in diverting water from agriculture to industry is obvious.

Though some may disagree with this pessimistic view of China's future, nobody dares to reject them outright. The fact that the Chinese Government published a *White Paper* entitled *"The Grain Issue in China"* shows the vital importance of the question for the leadership. In this document, Beijing tries to answer the following questions: *"What is the food situation in China? What is the country's grain production potential? Can the Chinese people feed themselves? And how will China improve its grain production? Through scientific analysis the Chinese government, in the manner of seeking truth from facts, now addresses these questions of universal concern."*

The problem can be analysed but not wished away.

From where the waters flow

This led the Chinese experts in Beijing to look around for water. Where did most of Asia's waters flows from? The obvious answer was not far: the Tibetan plateau, the principal watershed in Asia and the source of its ten major rivers. Tibet's waters flow down to eleven countries and are said to bring fresh water to over 85 percent of Asia's population, approximately 50 percent of the world's population.

Three of the world's ten major rivers, the Brahmaputra (or Yarlung Tsangpo in Tibet), the Yangtze and Mekong have their headwaters on the Tibetan Plateau. The other major rivers which originate in Tibet are the Huang Ho (or Yellow River), the Salween, the Arun, the Karnali, the Sutlej and the Indus. About 90% of their runoff flows downstream to China, India, Bangladesh, Nepal, Pakistan, Thailand, Myanmar, Laos, Cambodia and Vietnam.

For us in South Asia, the main concern is the Brahmaputra, the Indus, the Sutlej, the Arun and the Karnali whose waters give life to more than one billion people living downstream. It is roughly estimated that 10-20% of the Himalayan region is covered by glacial ice while an additional area ranging from 30-40% has seasonal snow cover. Himalayan glaciers cover around 100,000 square kilometers and store about 12,000 cubic kilometers of fresh water: the most incredible water tank one can imagine.

The perennial run of the rivers originating from these glaciers also result in a stable flow of water to regions which are dominated by monsoon rainfalls (with rain pouring for only a few months of the year). Consequently, the Tibetan rivers, independent of seasonal precipitation patterns, are an important factor in sustaining hydrological regimes of South Asia.

South-North Water Diversion

As mentioned in the *Draft Outline of the Tenth Five-year Plan for National Economic and Social Development* and explained by Ambassador Zhao, the 'gigantic' project to divert the waters of three major Tibetan rivers (Yangtse, Yellow River and Brahmaputra) to China's drought-stricken north involves the construction of massive canals, aqueducts and tunnels.

In September 200113, *Associated Press* commented: "The sheer scale harkens back to the megaprojects of imperial China and the heyday of communist central planning. But even in the home of the 1,500-mile Great Wall, the scheme is raising eyebrows. Some question if such a gargantuan project is needed - or even wise."

Imagine one route following two-thirds of the northern section of the 1,900-km Grand Canal with 15 enormous pump stations built to push water uphill to Tianjin, a major port near Beijing. Then, a second route going through central China which will require digging a 1100 km long trench towards Beijing. The aqueduct will have to pass under the Yellow River in an 8 km tunnel. The trickiest route will be the third one - cutting through some of Tibet's tallest mountains. Some optimists thought that the plans would stay on the drawing boards for a few more decades. But it is not so.

This study shall concentrate on the third route, mainly the southern most components: the diversion of the Brahmaputra river, the life-giver to eastern South Asia.

The case of the Yarlung Tsangpo

The Yarlung Tsangpo or Brahmaputra as it is known in India, has an immense bearing on the life of hundreds of millions in the sub-continent.

It is the largest river on the Tibetan plateau, originating from a glacier near Mt Kailash. It is considered to be the highest river on earth with an average altitude of 4,000 meters. It runs 2,057 kilometers in Tibet before flowing into India, where it becomes the Brahmaputra. One of its interesting characteristics is the sharp U turn it takes at the proximity of Mt. Namcha Barwa (7,782 meters) near the Indian border.

Like the Nile in Egypt, the Yarlung Tsangpo has fed the Tibetan civilization which flourished along its valleys, particularly in Central Tibet. The two larger tributaries of the Tsangpo are the Kyichu (or Lhasa River) and the Nyangchu. Near Shigatse region, the Yarlung valley is 20-30 km wide. This area with its sand dunes and lakes is the cradle of a two thousand year-old civilization. *China's Tibet*, a Chinese magazine describes the scenery: "*The complex and unique geographic and climatic conditions created by this great river provide Tibet with a wide array of wildlife. Black-necked cranes, Tibetan antelopes, wild Tibetan donkeys, sheep and Tibetan gazelles are among the larger animals found in the river valley.*" In Tibet, the river is often navigable, local people use coracles (made of yak hide and bamboo) to cross it.

The Yarlung Tsangpo enters in India in Siang district of Arunachal Pradesh. When it penetrates Assam, it is joined by two other rivers (the Dihang and Lohit). The Brahmaputra as always been considered as the very soul of the State by Assamese poets and ordinary people alike. Its valley has fertile farmland, with large areas covered with Sal forests, a valuable tree that yields resins. Crops of tea, rice and jute bring wealth to the region. River floods over much of the valley in the rainy season providing natural irrigation to rice growers.

The rare one-horned rhinoceros, extinct in other parts of the world, is still found in Assam, along with tigers, elephants and a large variety of fishes. Around the settlements in the Brahmaputra

Valley many fruit-bearing trees like mango, jackfruit and papaya are easily grown.

Entering Bangladesh, the river unites with the Ganga and is known as the Padma, before becoming the Meghna-Brahmaputra after merging with the river Meghna. Finally it divides into hundreds of channels to form a vast delta which flows into the Bay of Bengal.

The Grand Canyon

But let us come back to the Tibetan plateau. When the Tsangpo reaches its easternmost point in Tibet, it takes a sharp U turn known as the Great Bend. Only recently it has been found that the Yarlung Tsangpo gorge forms the longest and deepest canyon in the world.

For the first time in May 1994, *Xinhua News Agency* mentioned about the length and depth of the canyon: "*Chinese geologists claim that a remote Tibetan canyon is the world's largest, bigger and deeper than the Grand Canyon. The Yarlung Zangbo Canyon, in the vast Himalayan range that encircles China, averages 3.1 miles (5 km) in depth and extends 198 miles (317 km) in length. The Grand Canyon in the southwestern U.S. state of Arizona is, by comparison, a mere 1 mile (1.6 km) deep but 217 miles (347 km) long, with a width of between 4 and 12 miles. The dispatch did not reveal the width of the Yarlung Zangbo Canyon. The canyon was cut during the Pliocene Epoch two million years ago by the Brahmaputra River, which flows from the Tibetan capital of Lhasa before swooping down to the Indian subcontinent. Scientists found that the canyon, located in the Himalayan range, averages 5,000 meters in depth, with the deepest section reaching 5,382 meters.*"

A few years later, it was found that near Mt. Namchakbarwa (7,756 metres), the Tsangpo Gorge is eight times as steep and three times as large as the Colorado in the Grand Canyon.

It is in the Great Bend that China is planning one of the most important components of the 'western route' diversion scheme. This pharaonic project is perhaps the most mind-blowing part "*of the national strategy to divert water from rivers in the south and west to drought-stricken northern areas.*"

The Project

The Tsangpo project will have two components: one will the construction of the world's largest hydroelectric plant that would generate twice the electricity produced by Three Gorges Dam. Today, the biggest power station in the world is located in Itaipu in Brazil: it has a total installed capacity of 12,600 Megawatts. The Three Gorges Dam on the Yangtze River (still uncompleted) will have a 18,200 Megawatts capacity. The hydroelectric plant on the Great Bend of Yarlung Tsangpo will dwarf all these projects with a planned capacity of 40,000 Megawatts.

The second component of the project will be the diversion of the waters of the Tsangpo which will be pumped northward across hundreds of kilometers of mountainous regions to China's northwestern provinces of Xinjiang and Gansu.

For the Chinese leaders, it is enough to know that the Tsangpo river tumbles down over 3,000 meters in less than 200 km. This gives the gorge one of the greatest hydropower potentials available in the world. It makes emperors dream.

For the Tibetans, it is one of the most pristine regions of their country. They consider the area around the Bend as the home of the Goddess *Dorjee Pagmo,* Tibet's Protecting Deity. Many believe that this place, locally known as Pemakö is the sacred realm often referred to in their scriptures: the last hidden Shangrila.

For South Asia and more particularly for India, the enormity of the scheme and its closeness to the Indian border can not be ignored. It is not only the sheer enormity of the project which has to be considered, but the fact that if is accomplished, it will have ominous consequences for millions of people downstream. Their basic need for water and their survival would be endangered. Once Ismail Serageldin, a former Senior Vice President of World Bank said: *"The next World War will be over water."* China's green light for the project could be considered by South Asia as a declaration of war.

History of the project

The gigantic project was first mentioned at a conference in Alaska in July 1986. Projects under the Global Infrastructure Fund

(GIF) were discussed and the *'Himalayan Hydropower project'* was short-listed. At that time, it was envisaged to have a series of 11 dams around the 'Brahmaputra loop'. It included a tunnel through the mountains bringing water to a powerhouse projected to have a capacity of 48,000 Megawatts. The overall capacity of the 'loop' was speculated to be 70,000 Megawatts.

Later, the GIF stopped mentioning the project, engineers in Beijing had not shelved it. On the contrary, its new avatar appeared a few years later, as a single mega power station with an installed capacity of around 40,000 Megawatts.

The project was reported in the *Scientific American* in June 1996. This article giving credence to the Chinese plans. The journal wrote: *"Recently some Chinese engineers proposed diverting water into this arid area [Gobi Desert] from the mighty Brahmaputra River, which skirts China's southern border before dipping into India and Bangladesh. Such a feat would be 'impossible' with conventional methods, engineers stated at a meeting held last December at the Chinese Academy of Engineering Physics in Beijing. But they added that* "we can certainly accomplish this project" *with nuclear explosives."*

The Journal continued: "This statement is just one of the many lately in which Chinese technologists and officials have touted the potential of nuclear blasts for carrying out non-military goals."

It is said that one of the reasons for China's refusal to sign the Comprehensive Test Ban Treaty (CTBT) was because their desire to keep the possibility of experimenting with what is called PNE (Peaceful Nuclear Explosion). The Chinese argument was *"why should promising and potentially useful technology be abandoned."*

The first (and almost only time) that the matter was reported in the Indian Press was in June 1997 when *Outlook* magazine wrote a piece entitled: *"A river runs through it — China proposes to divert the Brahmaputra at source to green the arid Gobi desert."* The magazine wrote: *"The initial report — that the Chinese were planning to raise their food output in the decades ahead — was hardly stop-press material. But as details leaked out, policymakers in India and Bangladesh felt a shiver of apprehension: the Chinese proposed to divert the Brahmaputra river at source, in Tibet, even set off a peaceful nuclear explosion, to serve their purpose."*

At that time, the only thing that a former director, *Asian Development Bank* said was that under international law, no one could stop China and that *"The Chinese government has equal rights to the use of the river."*

However, *Outlook* revealed that "the concern in Assam and Bangladesh is understandable. The Luit - as the river [Brahmaputra] is locally called - figures prominently in the folklore and culture of Assam and the Northeast; has been the theme of countless Bhupen Hazarika songs. The river is crucial to the economy of the entire region, where the concept of irrigation through groundwater sources has not really taken off."

In the coming months, more publicity was given to the dam as well as the diversion proposals. In September 1997, *Agence France Press* in Beijing reported: *"Three experts propose construction of giant dam in Tibet"*. It stated: *"After a long experience of exploration on the site, we believe that the project could begin to be included in the agenda of the concerned department"*. Electricity produced was claimed to be: *"available for export to Bangladesh, Burma and India, [a feature of the GIF plans] and the diverted water could irrigate the northwestern deserts of the country"*.

The project was also mentioned in news briefs in the *China Daily Business Weekly* (21 September 1997) and the *International Water Power & Dam Construction Mon*thly (November 1997).

In January 1998,, the German TV channel ZDF presented a feature on the Yarlung Tsangpo project, in a program entitled *"Die Welt"* [The World]. The Chief Planner, Professor Chen Chuanyu was interviewed. He described the plan to drill a 15 km (9.3 miles) tunnel through the Himalayas to divert the water before the U turn and direct it to the other end of the bend. This would shorten the distance of the approximately 3,000 meters altitude drop from 200 km to just 15 km. He explained that the hydropower potential of 40,000 Megawatt could be used to pump water to Northwest China over 800 km away.

An interesting aspect that we have briefly mentioned is that this area known to the Tibetans as Pemakö was considered to be a sacred area, rarely visited by outsiders. The difficulty of access to this unexplored region must have created one of the greatest obstacles for the engineers in Beijing. At the end of the 90's, the Chinese government decided to permit foreigners to explore the Grand Canyon. The well-known *National Geographic* expedition, with ultra sophisticated materials and highly professional rafters made the first discoveries. Though it resulted in the death of an American kayaker, Doug Gordou in October 1998, it permitted a far greater knowledge in several previously unexplored parts of the gorges. Books and video footage of this expedition (as well as subsequent ones) certainly helped the Chinese planners to get a more accurate picture of the difficulty of the terrain (as well as the potentialities).

The opening of the area to adventure tourism was certainly the step of the preparatory work to find an approach way for dam site.

In the recent years, the Chinese have been more discreet on the project, although a few reports have continued to come in. The correspondent of *The Telegraph* in Beijing wrote in October 2000: *"Chinese leaders are drawing up plans to use nuclear explosions, in breach of the international test-ban treaty, to blast a tunnel through the Himalayas for the world's biggest hydroelectric plant."*

The Telegraph justly warned: *"China will have to overcome fierce opposition from neighbouring countries who fear that the scheme could endanger the lives and livelihoods of millions of their people. Critics say that those living downstream would be at the mercy of Chinese dam officials who would be able to flood them or withhold their water supply."*

According to the London paper, the cost of drilling the tunnel through Mt Namcha Barwa appears likely to surpass £10 billion. The article gives further details: *"At the bottom of the tunnel, the water will flow into a new reservoir and then be diverted along more than 500 miles of the Tibetan plateau to the vast, arid areas of Xinjiang region and Gansu province. Beijing wants to use large quantities of the plentiful waters of the south-west to top up the Yellow River basin and assuage mounting discontent over water shortages in 600 cities in northern China."*

However, it seems that the proposal has drawn flak from several Chinese scientists. Yang Yong, a geologist who had explored the river, stated that the dam could become an embarrassing white elephant amid growing signs that the volume of water flowing in the Yarlung Zangpo could shrink over the years.

But in 2000, before becoming Premier Wen Jiabao had declared: "In the 21st century, the construction of large dams will play a key role in exploiting China's water resources, controlling floods and droughts, and pushing the national economy and the country's modernization forward."

In China, the only pertinent question is perhaps: does a Chinese emperor have any choice other than to take up pharaonic works if he wants to remain emperor?

The Implications

The construction of this multi-billion dollar project is tentatively scheduled to begin in 2009, the year the Three Gorges Dam is supposed to be completed. Based on mean annual flow, the Yarlung Tsangpo, constitutes 33 per cent of the total flow of the Brahmaputra when it enters India. In other words for the sub-continent, it is the largest proportion of stable flow from glacial sources. The implications of a huge storage dam on the Yarlung Tsangpo and the diversion of the waters to northwestern China are multiple and far reaching for Tibet, India and Bangladesh. But most importantly, this project represents a direct threat to the people living downstream in India and Bangladesh.

For Tibet and the surrounding areas

A reservoir for a 40,000 Megawatts capacity dam would create a huge artificial lake inundating vast areas of virgin forest within the canyon and beyond. The reservoir would stretch hundreds of kilometers upstream the Yarlung Tsangpo into the Kongpo region. Rare species of flora and fauna within the canyon (though not yet well documented) will be lost for scientific study. The Chinese authorities themselves admit that the Canyon is the home for more than 60 per cent of the biological resources on the Tibetan Plateau.

Although the population in the canyon is rather small, the indigenous people would suffer great hardship and be forced to leave their ancestral lands. It may not be a problem for Beijing who has 'resettled' more than one million Chinese Hans since the beginning of the construction of the Three Gorges Dam, but for the Tibetans, it would mean the loss of a last sacred place and the home of their Protecting Deity. Furthermore, Tibetans would not benefit in any way from the power produced by the hydroelectric plant, as it would be sold to China's southern neighbours or used to send the water upstream to northwestern China.

Additionally, the water diversion scheme is likely to be a highly inefficient and wasteful exercise with billions of cubic meters of water being lost to evaporation, leakage, percolation, etc... through the 800 km-long canals and aqueducts.

If the project comes to fruition, Tibet and the world would have lost this virgin region and its canyon, a great treasure heritage. The Central Tibetan Administration of the Dalai Lama even suggested recently that the *"Yarlung Tsangpo canyon is a unique and magnificent natural phenomenon with diverse plant and animal life which should be considered as an UNESCO World Heritage Site or similar preserved site of international significance."* But, when the stakes are so high and the ego of the small emperors so big, one can have no doubt that the scheme will be implemented.

The potential use of nuclear devices to create tunnels for the project raises further serious concerns about the environmental impacts of such a project for the region and those living downstream. There will also be a great danger of sending contaminated waters to northwestern China. 28 This is perhaps one of the most important side-effects, not yet addressed by the Chinese scientists.

For South Asia

India and Bangladesh would be at the mercy of China for adequate release of water during the dry season, and for protection from floods during the rainy season. India knows from its own internal problems how difficult it is to solve a water dispute. When it comes to a transboundary question (when the boundary is not even agreed upon), it seems practically impossible to find a workable understanding. The Cauvery dispute in the South or the Ravi-Beas disagreement between Haryana and Punjab are nothing compared to a possible confrontation between India and

China over the use of the Himalayan waters. Precipitation in North India (particularly Assam) and Bangladesh is very high (80%) during the four monsoon months (between June to September), and low (20%) during the remaining eight months. China, seeing her own interests, could withhold water for power generation and irrigation during the dry season and release water during the flood season with the catastrophic consequences for eastern South Asia.

The Arunachal floods

An event which occurred in June 2000 could be an illustration at a very reduced scale of what could happen if the Tsangpo project is one day completed. At that time, the breach of a natural dam in Tibet led to severe floods and left over a hundred people dead or missing in Arunachal Pradesh. It is not difficult to understand that areas downstream in Arunachal or Assam are extremely vulnerable to what takes place upstream in Tibet. At the time of the incident, Rediff.com reported: *"Although news of floods in distant northeast may not be hot for Delhi, the flash floods that hit the border state of Arunachal Pradesh in June has made officials at the Central Water Commission and the MWR sit up and take notice. As officials pour over the technical data, a new dimension that the Chinese Army in Tibet, as part of an experiment, may have deliberately blasted the dam has been added to the already hazy picture.*

According to Nabam Rebia, member of Parliament from Arunachal Pradesh, puzzled by the nature of the floods and the equally mysterious response of China, the Government of India's remote sensing agency hired a Canadian satellite to take a close look at the scene of the breach. Top officials who confirmed this said, "All the technical details and pictures from the area are with us now and confirm that a breach had taken place on a dam on the river Tsangpo leading to flash floods in the northeastern region. According to the official, who had seen the technical data, the flash flood occurred because of a breach in a dam located in an area pinpointed as latitude 30.15 degrees north by 94.50 degrees east, which falls in China controlled Tibet.

A few weeks later, a similar mishap took place on the other end of the Himalaya. The Tribune in Chandigarh reported this strange event: *"Even three days after the disaster, the mystery of the flashfloods in the Sutlej, which wrecked havoc along its 200-km lenghth in the state, remains unresolved."* It added: *"Experts are at a loss to understand where the huge mass of water came from."*

Imagine a 50-ft high wall of water descending into the gorges of Kinnaur in Himachal Pradesh! In a few hours, more than 100 persons died, 120 km of a strategic highway (Chini sector) was washed away and 98 bridges destroyed. The details of this incident were similar to the Arunachal Pradesh's one.

A detailed study carried out a few months later by ISRO scientists confirmed that the release of excess water accumulated in the Sutlej and the Siang river [the Tsangpo] basins in Tibet had led to the flooding. Nearly a year later, the weekly India Today commented: *"While the satellite images remain classified, officials of the Ministry of Water Resources indicate that these pictures show the presence of huge water bodies or lakes upstream in Sutlej and Siang river basins before the flash floods took place. However, these lakes disappeared soon after the disaster struck Indian territory. This probably means that the Chinese had breached these water bodies as a result of which lakhs of cusecs of water were released into the Sutlej and Siang river basins."*

In this context, it is interesting to go back to one event of 1950. In the evening of August 15, a terrible earthquake shook Eastern Tibet. *"This was no ordinary earthquake; it felt like the end of the world,"* wrote Robert Ford, the British Radio operator working in Eastern Tibet. *"Mountains and valleys exchanged places in an instant, hundreds of villages were swallowed up, the Brahmaputra River was completely rerouted and for hours afterwards, sky over the southeastern Tibet glowed with an infernal red light, diffused with the pungent scent of sulphur."* It is a fact that the course of the Brahmaputra changed during those few hours. One may argue that only nature can produce such an upheaval, but nothing is less certain, especially if PNEs are used.

Nehru visited the Indian side of the border and made a long vivid description of the damages and sufferings of the people. On his return from Assam, he made a broadcast to the nation on All Indian Radio: *"It is said that the epicenter of the earthquake was somewhere in Tibet, near a place called Rima, some miles from the Assam frontier. We know nothing of what has happened in Tibet or on the mountainous regions of the border. As a result of the landslides, rivers were blocked up for a while, and when they broke through, they came down with a rush and a roar, a high wall of water sweeping down and flooding large areas and washing away villages and fields and gardens. These rivers have changed their colour and carried some sulphurous and other material which spread a horrible smell for some distance around them. The fish in them died. The remains of villages, animals, including cattle and elephants, and large quantities of timber floated down these raging waters. Paddy fields were destroyed, stocks of grains were washed away and some tea gardens also suffered great damage."* The reading of this broadcast gives a clear idea of what could happen on a much larger scale, if this project is carried out.

The second component of the plan a massive diversion of the river to China's northwest. This would have even more devastating consequences. North India and Bangladesh would be starved of their life line. Nutrient-rich sediments that enrich the soils of these regions would be held back in the reservoir. With no more reaching the river's delta, millions of people would be affected. A water war would ensue.

In a recent interview with the Dalai Lama, he told us: *"I remember that one day in the early sixties, one man from Xinjiang came to see me. He was an ex-minister of the local government belonging to the Ugyur nationality. While we were having some food, (it was not here, it was in my previous residence in Dharamsala), he told me that there is a real danger in the future of China changing the course of the major Tibetan rivers towards the deserts of Xinjiang or Gobi areas.*

The Chinese can do it! If that happens, what will happen to India? At that time, I thought that it was very difficult, but now I think that it is possible. For example, look at the Three Gorges project, the Chinese can undertake such big projects. In fact in Tibet, it is easier, arrangements can be made to divert rivers because [the Tibetan plateau] geographically slopes from higher areas to lower areas.

[To make such diversion] on a few hundred kilometers, from Kongpo in Southern Tibet to Northern Tibet, is not that difficult."

The Dalai Lama who met Mao for the first time 50 years ago, knows well how the minds of the Chinese leaders function. His interview confirms the apprehensions of many experts'.

Another aspect to be considered is that once a project has come on the drawing board, it must to be executed for leaders in Beijing not to loose face, and this, whatever be the cost or consequences. There is also the competition angle. A couple of weeks ago, *The Pradva* in Moscow mentioned diversion the Siberian rivers. Beijing also knows about the Vajpayee government's project to link most of the Indian rivers during the next ten years. They certainly would not like to be seen lagging behind their southern neighbour in terms of grandiose schemes.

[It has to be noted that if the Tsangpo project is implemented, large parts of the scheme of linking the Indian rivers would become redundant.

Last and perhaps most serious: the Great Bend is located in a highly earthquake prone area. A huge reservoir and a few NEPs could provoke new earthquakes even more serious than the one in August 1950. Will men will be wise enough to learn from the past and study Nature's limits and reactions before wanting to alter her?

The Situation Today

In June 2003, the Indian Prime Minister spent 6 days in China. On his return, everyone clapped. At last the past could be left behind and a new era begun for the two Asian giants. Analysts thought that the old dream of Nehru, a true *Hindi-Chini Bhai-Bhai,* could finally manifest. The ancient ideologues of the Long March were dead and gone, a Fourth Generation of young, pragmatic and dynamic leaders had taken over. One could finally speak business.

The Prime Minister was only just back, when the news of Chinese intrusions on Indian soil was flashed by the Indian press. Such an embarrassment for the MEA's officers who had worked for months to draft a Panchsheel type of declaration! Once again, like 45 years ago, the Five Principles had been violated.

Everything could still have passed off without too much fuss. The MEA could have 'diplomatically' handled the situation. But the unfortunate happened: the Chinese Foreign Ministry spokesman declared: *"China does not recognise the so-called Arunachal Pradesh mentioned by the Indian newspaper report"*. A weak Indian

External Affairs Ministry could only feebly respond that the GOI was aware of the 'transgression' of the LAC by a Chinese patrol.

This raises an important question: why did Beijing chose this particular time to kindle the most sensitive issue of the Sino-Indian relationship. Why stir up this question when China had already won a battle over Tibet?

Perhaps, the 'Arunachal' announcement was a diplomatic diversion to hide a far more serious matter for India: the Tsangpo project. On July 17, 2003 the *People's Daily* had published a small item *"China to Conduct Feasibility Study on Hydropower Project in Tibet"* It ran thus: *"China plans to conduct a feasibility study in October on the construction of a major hydropower project on the Yarlung Zangbo River, in the Tibet Autonomous Region... an expert team [was sent] to the area for preliminary work between late June and early July. The Chinese section of the river, 2,057 kilometers long, boasts a water energy reserve of about 100 million kilowatts, or one sixth of the country's total, ranking second behind the Yangtze River. The location for the possible hydropower plant is the U-shaped turn of the river in the southeastern part of Tibet. The river drops by 2,755 meters in the 500 kilometer-long "U" section."* The cat is out of the bag, though very few people have noticed it.

INDIA AND SOUTH ASIA: FROM CONFLICT TO CO-OPERATION

This World Water Day comes in year which has been declared as the "International Year of Water Cooperation" by the United National General Assembly. In addition, the UN has proclaimed the decade 2005-2015 as the International Decade for Action, "Water for Life".

The UN declarations would be welcome if we are able to take credible and effective steps towards water cooperation at every level in an equitable, sustainable way and through local participation. This becomes increasingly relevant when demand for water is increasing due to rising population, urbanisation, industrialisation, increased per capita use and increased losses due to climate change. The available and utilisable supply of water is either stagnant or decreasing due to increased pollution, increased temperatures, changing rainfall pattern, melting of glaciers and over exploitation. Moves towards centralised and undemocratic governance and privatisation of resources are not helpful as they do not promote cooperation, but only further conflicts. The prevailing and emerging situation is a sure fire recipe for increasing conflicts, not cooperation.

At the same time, UN Declaration of July 2010, declaring water as a human right remains only on paper. UN and the governments will clearly need to go beyond mere words and pious declarations.

Water: Some key characteristics Water is not just a commodity for market or an economic good. It is an ecological entity embedded in larger ecology that includes the climate, land, forests, and biodiversity. This includes, but is not limited to: Glaciers, rivers, wetlands, lakes, aquifers, soil, snow and water vapour in the atmosphere. In fact our understanding of the interplay of water in the larger eco-system is still far from complete. When we use water from any source, we should be mindful of its impact in the larger ecosystem. The UN resolution for declaring the 2005-2015 decade was not called "water for life" for nothing. Life here includes not just life of every human being but life on the entire planet.

INDIA AND NEIGHBOURS

On this occasion, it would be useful to take a look at the situation in the region. India and China are locked in one-up man ship in Brahmaputra basin, India and Pakistan are competing in destroying shared rivers, ecology and connected livelihoods through hydropower projects in the Indus river basin while India and Bangladesh are struggling to arrive at an agreement on sharing the Teesta waters. When it happens, this will be only the second water sharing treaty, among the 54 rivers shared by India and Bangladesh.

Considering that the countries in this region share the Himalayan watershed on which numerous big and small rivers and millions of people and biodiversity depend, there is an urgent need to have a Regional Policy for the common good of the people of the region.

Possible Chinese diversion The Chinese government officials have often talked about China's intention of diverting the Brahmaputra (basically Siang River, one of the main tributaries of the Brahmaputra) river to North China, just before the river enters India. China has officially declared its plans to build at least four hydropower projects on the river. The work on the water diversion project is yet to start and China has denied that the project is being taken up. However the Indian government is pushing more big hydro projects in Arunachal Pradesh, claiming that these will help establish India's prior use rights over the waters of these rivers when China does decide to take up its North South diversion project.

Such a push for big hydro in Arunachal Pradesh under the bogey of Chinese plans is only likely to worsen the situation for the people of Arunachal Pradesh and also for downstream areas in India and Bangladesh. This will only create new water conflicts. Moreover, there is no international mechanism that would help India claim its prior user right. The 1997 UN Convention on the Law of the Non-Navigational Uses of International Watercourses could have been of use, but India has yet to ratify the convention. The best course for India is to push China for a water sharing treaty.

In view of the crisis of climate change, this need has become even more acute. Today, there is no such policy and each country is developing multiple projects on its own, and many of the so-called development projects are actually accelerating climate change impacts and conflicts. Hundreds of hydropower projects are either constructed, are under construction or are being planned across the countries in the region. These projects, along with their paraphernalia of roads, townships, mining, tunnelling, blasting, muck dumping, diverting of rivers and dams are cumulatively having huge, though as yet unquantified impact on the glaciers, forests, aquatic and terrestrial biodiversity, communities, water availability and water supply,thereby impacting the climate as well.

Flood forecasting: One of the areas where information sharing is immediately required is in the area of sharing information about forecasts related to floods in the shared rivers. The governments in the region seem to have a number of agreements to share information in this regard, including Pakistan-India, Nepal-India, Bhutan-India, Bangladesh-India and China-India. Unfortunately, the shared information in this aspect is not in the public domain. Such shared information must be in public domain. What use is the flood forecasting related information if it is not shared among the people who are going to face the disastrous impacts of floods?

Transparency and Participation in governance in shared river basins There are elaborate, mostly bilateral inter-governmental mechanisms on governance of water and rivers in a number of cases in the South Asia region. These pertain to the bilateral arrangements of India with Pakistan, Bhutan, Bangladesh, Nepal and China. These arrangements include basin level commissions, minister level committees, officer level committees, project specific commissions and so on. Unfortunately, there is practically no transparency in the functioning of these mechanisms, nor is there any role for any concerned actors outside the government. In governance of rivers, waters and related projects, local people have the right to know what is going on in these committees and commissions.

The need for such public participation was acutely felt in the aftermath of the Kosi Disaster on the Indo-Nepal border in August 2008. During the initial period of this disaster, it was shown how the bilateral Kosi High Level committee had failed to achieve the proper maintenance of the embankment that breached with the flow of water in the river was less than 1.5 lakh cusecs (Cubic Feet per Second) even as the design capacity of the embankment was over 9 lakh cusecs. In the days that followed, it became clear that if there had been some non government people on the Indo Nepal Kosi committees and there was more transparency with representation from local communities and civil society in the committees, it would have helped ensure the maintenance of the embankment and that possibly would have saved it from breaching at least on that particular occasion.

Conditions for water cooperation We need to understand key conditions that would help achieve better cooperation in water sector. Some key conditions in this regard include: Clearly defined priorities for water use, rules of allocation of water to different users, water allocation mechanisms among various sectors, democratic rules of governance of such mechanisms, understanding the importance of ecosystem resources, Conservation of ecosystem resources including Wetlands, forests, rivers, lake, biodiversity; clearly defined and legally enforceable Right to Water and mechanisms to enforce the same. Good governance in this context would include clearly defined norms for key aspects like transparency, accountability and participation. There is need to have legal and institutional set up to achieve these goals.

The weaker sections (tribals, Dalits, women, marginal farmers, coastal and mountain populations) or weaker stakeholders (environment, rivers) have always been losing at the negotiating table. Centralising of authority and decision making being more and more away from local stakeholders creates possibility of more conflicts and conflict resolution becomes more difficult. Local water management can help reduce and also help address conflicts at the local level.

WORLD COMMISSION ON DAMS

Framework for cooperation in water management The report of the World Commission on Dams: *Dams and Development – A New Framework for Decision Making*provides a useful starting point to achieve cooperation in water management. The recommendations of the report are applicable at every level, from community to international level. It would be good if the United Nations recognises the principles in the WCD report in this year of water cooperation and provides some institutional support for their implementation and if countries in the region follow these recommendations for transboundary as well as local rivers.

The Role Of UN

Sixty percent of the world's freshwaters are transboundary. So there should be little doubt that water cooperation is critical to avoid conflicts and ensure effective and sustainable use of shared resources. Over the years, the UN has been coming out with various programs and principles on water resources management.

However, none of them have legal and institutional back up. Its 1997 Convention on the Law of the Non-Navigational Uses of International Watercourses is yet to come into force as it has yet to receive ratification of the required 35 countries. Significantly, India abstained from voting for the convention at the UN and also has yet to ratify it.

Another instrument in this context is the UNECE (UN Economic Commission for Europe) Convention on the Protection and Use of Transboundary Watercourses and International Lakes (Water Convention) is currently the only international legal framework *in force*governing the management of transboundary water resources. It turned into a global convention in Feb 2013, having received sufficient number of ratifications. The UNECE website says in this regard: "This is a ground-breaking development as the Convention was originally negotiated as a regional instrument by countries of the United Nations Economic Commission for Europe. It is also a major milestone of the International Year of Water Cooperation celebrated in 2013… more than 30 countries from outside the UNECE region already actively participate in activities under the Convention. Several countries have already indicated their interest in becoming Parties… will create a strong legal base for present and future Parties to the Convention to join their forces to protect transboundary waters and the benefits deriving from them… Moreover it will strengthen political support to transboundary water cooperation."

At the same time UN needs to ensure that it does not become cause of greater conflicts as is happening now through its funding of destructive hydropower and other projects under the UNFCCC's Clean Development Mechanism. Those projects are happening at the cost of the local communities and their environment and providing completely unjustified, unwarranted and unnecessary funding of project developers, thus fattening the bank balances of the rich and at the same time creating more conflicts.

The world leaders and media have been quoting *ad nauseam* the now infamous quote from the former United Nations Secretary General Boutros Boutros Ghali to the effect that next war may be fought for water. Many would call this unwarranted war mongering, that too from a UN personnel. There is a lot the UN needs to do to achieve greater water cooperation across the world to wash off this image. May the UN succeed in this effort!

THE BRAHMAPUTRA: WATER HOTSPOT IN HIMALAYAN ASIA

Strategic analysts around the world increasingly have their eyes on the Brahmaputra River, a transboundary watercourse that has its headwaters in the Tibetan Plateau of the Himalayan mountain range. In both length and discharge one of the Earth's most formidable rivers, the Brahmaputra (the Yarlung Tsangpo in China) has a lengthy run eastward of about 1,700 kilometers (1,100 miles) through China's Tibetan Autonomous Region before winding south into India's northeast, thence into Bangladesh from where it empties into the Bay of Bengal.

The three riparian states sharing the Brahmaputra – China, India, and Bangladesh– are the world's first, second, and seventh most populous countries. All three face severe problems of water scarcity. All three also face steeply rising demand for increased power – including hydropower – generation. The possibility of serious resource conflict involving these demographic giants stems primarily from Chinese and Indian plans, some already being implemented, to put the river's thus-far relatively unexploited waters to greater use.

Hydropower generation is one such use. The combination of burgeoning populations, rapid economic growth, and intensified global competition for energy resources is driving China and India to put increasing emphasis on hydropower. India, already the world's sixth largest energy consumer, ranks seventh globally (2008) in current hydropower generation. Possessing an estimated 148,700 MW of installed capacity potential, it ranks sixth globally (2010) among nations in economically exploitable hydropower. However, only about 19.9 percent of India's hydropower potential has been developed thus far. Hence, India's river resources loom large today in Indian energy plans. With its untapped potential standing at 95 percent, the Brahmaputra looms largest of all. China also has immense energy requirements. In 2010, it consumed

20.3 percent of the world's primary energy supplies; and in that year it overtook the United States to become the world's largest energy consumer. Its power sector is largely dependent on fossil fuels, coal in particular; but with China's energy consumption bound to grow immensely in coming decades, the need to lower coal- dependence means a massive shift to alternative fuels, including hydropower.

China already has more hydroelectric dams (over 22,000) than any other country in the world. With its installed hydropower capacity reportedly having reached 213,000 MW by the end of 2010, it was by far the world's leading producer of hydroelectricity. It plans to lift the proportion of non-fossil fuel use in the country's energy sector to 15 percent by 2020; and half of that is expected to come from hydropower. That means that China aims to have 430,000 MW of hydropower capacity hardly a decade hence, a better than doubling of its existing capacity. That figure is over two- and-a-half times larger than India's entire power sector could boast for all fuels in 2010, and nearly twelve times larger than India's hydropower output in that year. To put it most graphically, China's hydropower quest is intended to add the equivalent of one new Three Gorges Dam, at 22,500 MW the world's largest, each year over the current decade. Given the overall vast leap in anticipated energy consumption, this converts to a truly major surge in hydroelectric dam building.

China is now predictably casting its eyes on the Brahmaputra's hydropower potential on China's side of the border. According to one close observer, Tibet researcher Tashi Tsering, China has already constructed 10 dams on tributaries of the upper Brahmaputra, with 3 more under construction, 7 more under consideration, and yet 8 more proposed – a grand total, if eventually built, of 28.1. Those dams already built are small in scale and, since none are on the Brahmaputra mainstream, have stirred little interest outside China. However, China's plans apparently include building 5 major dams directly on the Brahmaputra mainstream. Completion of construction on the first of them, the $1.18 billion 510 MW Zangmu hydropower project in the middle reaches of the river, is expected by 2014.

More worrying yet was the possibility that China's aggressive search for promising hydropower dam sites in Tibet might ultimately drive Beijing to focus on the so- called Great Bend in the Brahmaputra, the point in the Himalayas where the river curves south onto India's Assamese plain. It was reported in May 2010 that research had indeed been carried out for a massive project at the bend.2 Tsering, noting the Great Bend's reputation "for having the greatest hydropower potential of any site in the world", with a drop of nearly 2500 meters over the length of the bend, predicted that China was likely to construct a 38,000 MW hydropower station and large storage dam near Motuo.

Such a dam, if built, would dwarf even the massive Three Gorges Dam. Interviewed by *The Hindustan Times,* Tsering said: "If or when the Motuo project is built, China will gain significant capacity to control the Brahmaputra's flow.... Basically, India will become dependent on China for flow of what is now a free-flowing international river".

Diversion of the Brahmaputra's waters is another – and much more portentous – potential use. Planned diversion of this river's waters from India's water-surplus northeast to drought-stricken western and southern states, though at least temporarily on hold, is the key to India's long-delayed River Linking Project (RLP). China's diversion plans, on the other hand, are lodged in the mammoth and already underway South-North Water Diversion Project (SNWDP). Thus far, the SNWDP has been confined to entirely indigenous rivers. If currently discussed proposals to include the Brahmaputra in an extended version of the still pending Western Route of the SNWDP were implemented, the consequences for downstream India and, even more so Bangladesh, might be disastrous.

River diversion on the drawing board China's southern belt has historically been a water surplus region while its north and northwest have been increasingly water scarce. China's north, with 42 percent of the country's population in 2003, had only 14 percent of available fresh water supplies; while its south, with 58 percent of population, held 86 percent of fresh water supplies. While China ranks sixth in the world in total naturally available fresh water flows from all surface and underground sources, its per capita ranking is one of the lowest in the world for a populous country.

A similar (but geographically reversed) pattern of spatial variability in water supply also exists in India, whose north and northeast regions have been water surplus while large portions of its west and south are water scarce. About 61.6 percent (1,202 km^3) of annual fresh water availability in India is found in the river basins of India's north, which cover only about 33 percent of the country's geographical area, leaving about 67 percent of the country – mainly its west and south – with water availability of about 38 percent (742.14 km^3).

Driven by this disturbing irregularity in nature's design, Chinese and Indian hydrologists have naturally been giving attention to the prospects for water diversion – for transferring major quantities of river water from south to north in China, from north to south in India. China launched the massive SNWDP in 2001; India gave official sanction to its equally massive RLP in 2002.

It is of course where Indian water diversion plans meet up with China's that trans- boundary concerns emerge; and it is the distinct possibility that they may meet up on the Brahmaputra that is currently exercising the imaginations of the region's strategic analysts.

A convergence of divergence?

Unknown presently is whether India's RLP will ever get off the ground. Also unknown is whether the RLP, if fully implemented, will include the Brahmaputra in its Himalayan component. Clearly, however, India's future diversion of the Brahmaputra's waters remains a live possibility – even a probability should the more threatening projections of the country's coming water scarcity prove correct. Moreover, should China move towards the Brahmaputra in coming years with an eye not just on hydro-power but also on diversion, pressure on New Delhi to match Beijing's with an aggressive plan of its own would likely become irresistible.

As for Beijing's plans in this regard, we are confronted with towering uncertainty. Official denials of any Chinese plans to divert the Brahmaputra's waters are common. Of late, however, there have been a number of to China's arid northeast from the Brahmaputra's middle reaches. This alternative route would allegedly transport over 200 billion cubic meters of water extracted annually from the Brahmaputra River at a point just to the southeast of Lhasa along a route moving north/northeast towards the headwaters of the Yellow River.

It would be premature to declare that the Chinese are without fail going to undertake a mammoth water diversion project anywhere on the Brahmaputra. However, it seems fairly certain that the Chinese are currently weighing various diversion proposals in terms of engineering feasibility and costs, and the possibility cannot be dismissed that they may at some point give one of them the go-ahead.

Brahma Chellaney, one of India's foremost strategic thinkers, has argued that it is not a question of if but when China will go ahead with the proposed diversion of Brahmaputra waters to its parched north. And such a diversion, he warns, "would constitute the declaration of a water war on lower-riparian India and Bangladesh".

The relations between India and China are driven, of course, by much more than water; and even water cannot be confidently said to be driving things relentlessly and unalterably in the direction of violent conflict between them. Still, China's dire water circumstances, combined with its impressive economic strength, military power, and uniquely advantageous upper riparian position, give us little reason for optimism when it comes to the offer of generous river sharing agreements with lower riparian countries. There are today no formal agreements at all between China and India in regard to water sharing of the transboundary Brahmaputra; and if the reasoning of many observers in regard to China's plans on the Brahmaputra is accurate, one should not expect any grand cooperative interstate scheme to develop any time soon in regard to that river. On the contrary, mounting tensions and at least verbal skirmishing between China and India over the

Brahmaputra's contested waters seem more likely. There will surely be water woes impacting their relationship, in other words, even if water wars never materialize.

GEOPOLITICAL RISKS: TRANSBOUNDARY RIVERS

The Qinghai-Tibetan Plateau, extends an impressive 2.5 million km^2 constituting what is euphemistically known as the roof of the world. Often referred to as the Third Pole, the Plateau is home to the largest freshwater reserves outside the north and south poles. It is also the source of some of Asia's main river arteries, which from west to east include the Indus, Ganges, Brahmaputra, Irrawaddy, Salween, Mekong, Yellow and Yangtze.

With the exception of the Yellow and Yangtse, these rivers are transboundary, in some instances, such as the Mekong, crossing several countries as they descend from the Plateau eventually discharging into the Bay of Bengal, Andaman and South China Seas. In combination, they are a major source of fresh water for the following countries: Pakistan, India, Nepal, Bangladesh, Burma, Laos, Thailand, Cambodia and Vietnam.

SETTING THE SCENE: THE SECURITY LANDSCAPE

Water scarcity in many countries has raised the thorny issue of water security. In Asia, Pakistan has been identified as at extreme water security risk, while China, India, Bangladesh, Thailand and Cambodia are considered as high risk, according to a 2010 index by Maplecroft. The Index identifies risks across supply chains, operations and investments of multinational companies and is calculated by measuring the four key areas : i)access to improved drinking water and sanitation; ii)the availability of renewable water and the reliance on external supplies; iii) the relationship between available water and supply demands; and iv) the water dependency of each country's economy.

This should come as no surprise. Put simply, the global population is projected to increase by nearly 50% in just 40 years, a sobering thought as water crises emerge globally, and inequitable access to water causes disease and death of millions every year. There is after all no substitute for water and by 2025 water scarcity is expected to affect more than 1.8 billion people, millions across the Asia region.

Renowned water experts such as Peter Gleick talk of reaching "Peak Water" or more accurately "Peak Ecological Water", a worrying concept that Gleick suggests signals an end to any cheap and easy access to this essential resource.

Considering that ten of Asia's key rivers are sourced in Chinese Territory, without equitable agreements on managing these strained water resources, conflict is perhaps inevitable. On the topic of water conflict, a brief internet search quickly yields a world of discussion highlighting the growing concern over potential water wars, pointing to where security risk is deemed highest; China and India appear frequently.

According to the United Nations, an estimated 40 percent of intrastate conflicts over the past 60 years are associated with natural resources, and since 1990 at least 18 violent conflicts have been fuelled by the exploitation of natural resources and other environmental factors.

According to Peter Gleick's water chronology, since 1947 water has been associated with conflict in over 150 instances, more frequently than not involving some form of violence. Water conflicts can take several forms such as water being a military target, a military tool, a political weapon and as the focus in development disputes.

About 45 percent of these conflicts have included some form of developmental dispute and nearly a third have been in Asia, two thirds of which have involved India, China or Pakistan. Most water conflicts to date however appear to be intrastate, relatively few involving more than one country. In China's case, conflict usually involves citizen on citizen clashes or citizen versus government clashes. Of the two bilateral conflicts identified involving China, other parties have been Tibet and India respectively.

As the United Nations Environment Program points out, however, some of the world's greatest potential tensions over water resources, for example over the Indus River system, have been addressed through cooperation rather than violent conflict,. Thus, integrating environmental management and natural resources into peace building is today considered a security imperative.

In some instances, even before water crises were apparent, efforts have been made to manage transboundary rivers such as the lower reaches of the Mekong. As far back as 1957, Cambodia, Laos, Thailand and the Republic of Vietnam established the joint Committee to supervise planning and investigation of water development projects in the lower Mekong basin. Later in 1995 the Mekong River Commission (MRC) was established with a vision to bring about an economically prosperous, socially just and environmentally sound Mekong River Basin, with regional cooperation and basin-wide planning at the heart of its operation.

The MRC, however, relies on consensus and today strains are showing as Laos plans to build the first dam on the Mekong outside of Chinese Territory.

TROUBLED WATERS – DAMS, DIVERSIONS AND GEOPOLITICS

The real crux of the matter as regards China and its management of transboundary waters, is concern over unilateral damming and diversion of upstream rivers that feed into Asia's main water arteries.

China has long recognized gaps in its water supply and demand, exacerbated by uneven distribution across the country. The ambitious south to north water diversion project has raised alarm bells among those concerned over China's potential to divert rivers that are transboundary in nature, with the Brahmaputra being of particular concern. As Isabel Hilton of China Dialogue points out in – "Diverting the Brahmaputra: Much Ado About Nothing?" Such a diversion would, however, be staggeringly expensive and complex to the point of being almost incalculable.

Hilton further clarifies that only 14 percent of the Brahmaputra's flow is in the river at the point at which it enters a huge high altitude gorge in the Himalaya, dropping 3,000m before re-emerging in Assam. The other 86 percent enters the river after it has entered India, thus the impact of a diversion, even if technically feasible would be unlikely to have the catastrophic impacts imagined.

Perhaps, what is more relevant in the geopolitical context, is China's intention to dam rivers that flow for hundreds of kilometres through its lands before entering neighboring countries downstream, notably the Mekong and Salween, as well as the Brahmaputra.

In line with its 12th Five Year Plan and a move to widen the contribution of non-fossil fuels to the nation's vast power generating capacity, dam building appears firmly on China's development agenda. Some analysts believe that the country will have installed about 348GW hydropower capacity by 2020 a rise of 37per cent from 2011.

Take the Mekong as an example. As Asia's longest river, the Mekong starts life in the Tibetan Plateau as the Dza-chu, from here it flows 500km through the Three Rivers Basin, running aside the Yangste and Salween. It descends across Yunnan Province in China where it's known as the Lancang, before continuing its descent, forming borders between Burma, Laos and Thailand. Finally, the river enters the South China Sea after flowing across Cambodia and Vietnam respectively.

China is already building eight dams along the Lancang section of the Mekong with little consultation with its downstream neighbours. Several are operational, reportedly influencing downstream hydrology and leading to a range of impacts such as sedimentation, erosion of riverbanks and changing nutrient profiles. Local fishermen in Thailand hold the dams responsible for the depletion of what was once a plentiful fish supply. The Mekong's flow is also reported to be unpredictable since China started damming the Lancang and is blamed for both uncharacteristic droughts and floods downstream.

While China's thirst for water is worrying its neighbours, it seems that it's is not alone in dam building, with downstream countries also engaged in controversial projects. Twelve dams, estimated at over 14.5 MW installed capacity are currently in the offing with regard to the lower Mekong, amongst claims that altered flood hydrology immediately downstream of the Lancang dams makes the economics of dam building more favourable than previously.

The first, the controversial Xayaburi dam being proposed by Laos, is in limbo, with further studies needed given scientific consensus that not enough is understood about the potential impacts of this and other dams proposed. Laos has already built several dams on tributaries of the Mekong.

The Lao government is treading murky waters; it seems Vietnam and Cambodia are against the Xayaburi Dam, while not only are Thai banks set to provide the capital with a Thai company leading construction, but most of the power generated would be for Thai consumers. All four countries are part of the Mekong Rivers Commission.

As if transboundary water management and geopolitical implications were not complicated enough, the Economist reported earlier this year of US concerns, that if the Xayaburi dam goes ahead, this would make way for Chinese companies to strengthen their lead in constructing additional dams, thereby providing China a greater foot hold in the region.

While the Mekong serves to illustrate the rising tensions and geopolitical machinations, similar tales are unfolding as a result of potential dam developments in relation to the Salween, the Irrawaddy and the Bramaputra.

The Salween (the Nu River in China, and the Thanlwin River in Burma) has the added complication of flowing through an environmentally rich United Nations World Heritage site. Currently, it faces 13 dams planned in Chinese territory with a total generating capacity of 21.3GW, similar to that of the Three Gorges Dam, and a further cascade of dams planned along the river in Burma and Thailand.

Some of these dams are located in highly sensitive areas environmentally and according to WWF, China's Yunnan Provincial Government appears to proposing one of the highest dams in the world without consulting either Burma or Thailand.

Turning to the Irrawaddy, political maneuvering is evident with China lobbying the Burmese Government to build the Myitsome Mega Dam Project, despite President Theon Sein's suspension of the damin September last year; a surprising move apparently in response to significant protests over environmental and also safety issues as a result of the dam being located in an area of seismic activity. The dam, it is estimated, would have an installed capacity of up to 6,000MW, supply 90% of its electricity to China and would be the 15th largest hydropower station worldwide.

This upsurge in Chinese pressure coincidentally comes at a time when the US and Europe are making diplomatic gestures to Burma's military Junta. Adding to tension over shared water resources is lack of transparency. Information needed to assess the potential impacts of dams, such as hydrological data, is seemingly less than forthcoming in many cases. Such claims have been made against both China and India.

Given the scramble for dams along these transboundary rivers, the protocols of operating dams upstream and how this affects downstream operators remains an interesting question and one that China Water Risk will explore further in coming months. The purpose of the dams is inevitably important, those designed for power generation will wish to maintain water flow, whereas should flood control be an objective, then a different protocol would be employed. Without cooperation, communication and agreement, the potential for conflict between upstream and downstream dam operators seems likely.

Out of Sight out of Mind – transboundary aquifers

The question of shared aquifers, while not widely discussed in the geopolitical context, is also a potential cause for concern given increasing depletion and or pollution of these resources. Peter Gleick points to some facts we shouldn't forget. That, 99 percent of the Earth's accessible freshwater can be found in aquifers and 2 billion people rely on them for their sole source of water. There are in fact more shared aquifers than river basins, yet aquifers are typically excluded from transboundary water agreements and are rarely discussed in relation to water conflicts. Over a quarter of the world's transboundary aquifers are in Asia.

GEOPOLITICAL RISK IS HERE TO STAY

Rising tensions and political maneuvering in Asian countries whose main water arteries stem from the Tibetan plateau are a result of a unique combination of factors: a densely populated area with increasing water scarcity exacerbated by climate change and pollution; significant dependence on water intensive agriculture and; an unrivaled appetite for rapid economic growth and development led by China. As a result of these factors, the water and closely related food security landscape is changing.

The region's rivers are essential to economic development and to sustaining millions Asia-wide through the provision of food, water and livelihoods. Yet the transboundary nature of many of these water resources and China's ownership of the upper reaches of key rivers provides an ideal environment for political jockeying and conflict.

In particular, China has the political clout and access to capital if it should choose to manage water reserves in a manner that may not be in the interests of neighboring countries.

Tensions are increasingly evident between China and its neighbours over lack of transparency and consultation in relation to its dam-building activities in its own territory. Strains are appearing among downstream neighbours as countries plan dams and align themselves with selected parties, and tensions are rising as China pursues its dam interests beyond its own borders.

Looking forward, the geopolitics associated with transboundary waters in this region are only likely to intensify as the impacts of glacial retreat and the cumulative effects of escalating dam development over finite water resources become clear. Geopolitical risks are therefore here to stay and are a worthy consideration for investors and businesses operating in the region.

The issue of risk associated with shared water resources and particularly dams is as broad as it is complex. This article serves only to provide an introduction to geopolitical risk and does not detail the myriad social and environmental risks associated with the enormous programme of dam development in the region. Such issues will be addressed by China Water Risk in future.

CHINESE BIGGEST HYDRO-ELECTRIC PROJECT IN BRAHMAPUTRA RIVER AT TIBET

Chinese hydropower lobbyists are calling for construction of the world's biggest hydro-electric project on the upper reaches of the Brahmaputra river as part of a huge expansion of renewable power in the Himalayas. Zhang Boting, the deputy general secretary of the China Society for Hydropower Engineering, told the Guardian that a massive dam on the great bend of the Yarlung Tsangpo - the Tibetan name for the river - would benefit the world, despite the likely concerns of downstream nations, India and Bangladesh, which access water and power from the river.

Zhang said research had been carried out on the project, but no plan has been drawn up. But documents on the website of a government agency suggest a 38 gigawatt hydropower plant is under consideration that would be more than half as big again as the Three Gorges dam, with a capacity nearly half as large as the UK's national grid. "This dam could save 200m tonnes of carbon each year. We should not waste the opportunity of the biggest carbon emission reduction project. For the sake of the entire world, all the water resources than can be developed should be developed." That CO_2 saving would be over a third of the UK's entire emissions.

The mega-facility is among more than 28 dams on the river that are either planned, completed or under discussion by China, according to Tashi Tsering, a Tibetan scholar of environmental policy at the University of British Columbia. Tsering publishes a map today of all of the projects that have been reported by Chinese newspapers and hydro-engineering websites.

From this, he concludes that the Tsangpo-Brahmaputra – until recently considered the last great undammed river in Tibet – will be the next focus of government efforts to increase the nation's power supply. One of them is a map of planned dams showing a 38-gigawatt hydro-plant at Motuo on the website of Hydro China, an influential government enterprise responsible for dam construction. A separate State Grid map of future transmission lines indicates the remote area will soon be connected to the rest of China's power supply. Hydro China and State Grid declined requests for clarification.

The government has not confirmed the existence of the scheme, but Tsering cites several newspaper reports of survey teams exploring the area and provides links to other online documents that indicate preparations for large-scale hydro-development of the area.

Given the huge expense, technical difficulties and political sensitivities of the scheme, it is far from certain of final approval by the government. But several Chinese hydroengineers see it as the ultimate goal in an accelerating race with India to develop water resources in one of the planet's last remote regions.

Tapping the power of the river as it bends and plunges from the Himalayan roof of the world down towards the Indian and Bangladeshi flood plains has long been a dream of the world's hydro-engineers. Along with the Congo river at the Inga falls, this is considered one of the two greatest concentrations of river energy on earth, but it was long thought impossible to access because of the rugged, high-altitude terrain and the risk of water-related conflict with neighbouring countries.

But China has overcome many engineering obstacles with the construction of the railway to Tibet, and its growing energy demands are spurring exploration of ever more remote areas. "Tibet's resources will be converted into economic advantage," Yan Zhiyong, the general manager of China Hydropower Engineering Consulting Group, told ChinaEnergy News earlier this year. "The major technical constraints on damming the Yarlung Tsampo have been overcome." He declined the Guardian's request for an interview, saying the subject was too sensitive.

The exploitation of the Brahmaputra is already under way. China recently announced plans to build five dams further upstream, including a 500MW hydroplant at Zangmu, which is under construction by the power utility Huaneng. According to Tsering, the biggest of them will be a huge plant at the great bend – either at Metog, known as Motuo in Chinese, or at Daduqia. The former would involve the construction of a series of tunnels, pipes, reservoirs and turbines to exploit the spectacular 2,000-metre fall of the river as it curls down towards India.

Although there has been no official confirmation of plans for a dam, the discussion is far from secret. On a prominent Chinese science forum, Zhang said a dam on the great bend was the ultimate hope for water resource exploitation because it could generate energy equivalent to 100m tonnes of crude coal, or all the oil and gas in the South China sea. He warned that a delay would allow India to tap these resources and prompt "major conflict" in a region where the two nations have sporadically clashed over disputed territory.

"We should build a hydropower plant in Motuo... as soon as possible because it is a great policy to protect our territory from Indian invasion and to increase China's capacity for carbon reduction," he wrote last year Any step forward is likely to be controversial. Tibetans consider Metog a sacred region, and environmental activists warn against building such a huge project in a seismically active and ecologically fragile area.

"A large dam on the Tibetan plateau would amount to a major, irreversible experiment with geo-engineering," said Peter Bosshard of International Rivers. "Blocking the Yarlung Tsangpo could devastate the fragile ecosystem of the Tibetan plateau, and would withhold the river's sediments from the fertile floodplains of Assam in northeast India, and Bangladesh." China's construction of dams also raises the prospect of a race with India to develop hydropower along south Asia's most important river.

"India needs to be more aggressive in pushing ahead hydro projects (on the Brahmaputra)," Jairam Ramesh, the Indian environment minister, told the Guardian during a recent visit to Beijing. "That would put us in better negotiating position (with China). To minimise the risk of water-related conflict, the two nations have agreed to share information about hydro-plans on the Tsangpo-Brahmaputra.

Indian media have raised concerns that Beijing may ultimately embark on a gigantic diversion scheme that would channel water away from India to the dry northern plains of China, but such fears are dismissed by Tsering, who says the dam at Metog would be for hydropower, not water diversion. "The laws of physics will not allow water diversion from the Great Bend."

CHINA AS HYDRO- HEGEMON : THE ONSET OF WATER WARS

The Chinese civilization is characterized by its ability to do long term perspective thinking of an unusual order. As far back as 1952, Chairman Mao Ze dong had articulated that Water Stress in the Northern and Western parts of China would be a very major challenge that would emerge a half century or so later. In fact this strategic long term thinking seems to have originated much earlier than 1952 and seems to have been instrumental in China's decision to invade and conquer Tibet – the Water Tower of Asia – in 1950 itself.

The following facts are pertinent:-

- The region South of the Yangtze River in China has 36% of Chinese territory and 81% of its water resources.
- The Northern Areas of China (that include the major metropolises of Beijing and Tianjin) have 64% of the nation's territory but only 19% of its water resources. These plains also have 47% of China's total population.
- Due to rapid industrialization, increasing urbanization and massive population pressure, by 2030 China is expected to face a severe supply gap in its projected water demand of over 25%. In fact by 2050 China's water deficit will be a staggering 400 Billion cubic meters. Two thirds of China's cities are already experiencing serious insecurities about water supply. In fact out of 640 Chinese cities, 300 are currently facing water shortages and 100 are faced with severe scarcities.
- The problems of water stress are being exacerbated by environmental pollution, highly uneven distribution of water within its territory leading to disproportionate levels of water availability.
- China's agriculture in fact is a miracle of 22% of the world's total population being fed as just 7% of its land area.

- Over-pumping of water has caused the water table to fall at an alarming rate. Over- pumping has depleted shallow aquifers. Due to overuse of fertilizers and chemicals each year China looses 180,000 hectares of farm land to salinity and 200,000 hectares become desert.
- Hence water stress is not a theoretical issue in China. It is a civilisational nightmare for a nation that tends to look far ahead into the future and do perspective thinking of an order that systematically spans the decades. These cold statistics bear testimony to the grave seriousness of the problem and the decision pressure they are bound to put on the Chinese decision makers and leadership.

THE ROOTS OF WATER HEGEMONY

The severe nature of the water stress in China needs to be seen in the light of another set of circumstances that make China a natural hydro (or water) hegemon. Consider the following:-

- China has 10 major rivers flowing out of its territory to 11 countries. No river flows into China from outside. This puts China in the unique position of being the Upper Riparian State to all its neighbours.
- China controls Tibet which is the water tower of Asia. 46% of the world's population depends on Tibetan rivers.
- China can control the flow of the Irrawady and Mekong which are the lifelines of South East Asia. China can also control the flow of the Indus, Satluj and Brahmaputra and hence hold South Asia to ransom. It equally dominates the flow of the Ili and Irtugush rivers that flow into Central Asia.
- Uttam Kumar Sinha, a scholar at the IDSA observes that this upper riparian status feeds China's hydro- arrogance, hydro-egoism and hydro-aggression. China is the Hydro Hegemon of Asia and shows scant regards for the sensitivities and needs of the lower riparian states.
- Legal Frame Work The fact is that there are some 260 river basins in the world that cater for nearly 40% of the world's population. Sharing of these river waters is covered by

some 145 sharing agreements/ treaties. China has not signed a single water sharing agreement with any of its neighbours. In fact China is one of the world's only three countries that voted against the 1997 UN Convention on non-navigational uses of international water courses. This international convention had sought to lay down norms and rules which China rejects. Its plan for the utilization, harnessing and diversion of its water resources are highly opaque and secretive and are increasingly becoming a cause for serious concern for all its Lower Riparian neighbours.

- Power Asymmetry The situation is further compounded by the huge power asymmetries that have arisen between China and each and every one of its neighbours in terms of economic and military power and in fact the entire gamut of Comprehensive National Power (CNP).
- All this provides the basis for the highly hegemonic behavior of China in terms of trans- boundary water relations. China is the natural hydro-hegemon of Asia. This is in stark contrast to the carefully cultivated image of China's peaceful rise

WATER WARS

Many strategic experts have been forecasting that the 21st Century will see the era of Water Wars as opposed to the earlier wars for the control of hydro carbon energy resources. However, acuteness of Water Stress was supposed to reach threshold levels of conflict only sometimes around the middle point of this century. Unfortunately, China's hydro-aggression is now threatening to usher in the start of water wars many decades in advance.

DIVERTING THE BRAHMAPUTRA

The Chinese leadership has always thought in hydrological terms. Hence its very early attempts to seize Tibet and assume control of the water tower of Asia. That is why the Chinese leadership invests such strategic significance in the TAR. Even today many top Chinese leaders are hydrological engineers. In fact Prime Minister Wen Jiabao is a Geological Engineer and

President Hu Jintao is a Hydraulic Engineer. The plan to divert the Brahmaputra (Yarling Tsangpo to the Chinese) was initially mooted by a Chinese Engineer called Liling in his book "Tibet Water will save China". He elaborated the idea of a massive Shuomatan Canal (stretching from Sumatan in Tibet to Tanjiang in North China). This canal would take off from the bend of the Yarlung Tsangpo and divert its water to the North of China. This grandiose plan was vociferously supported by Gen Gao Kai of the PLA. This was supposed to commence in 2002. This issue caused considerable concern in India. In 2006 when President Hu Jintao was visiting India, the Chinese Water Resources Minister Wang Shucheng tried to allay these fears. He deemed this grandiose project as "unnecessary, unfeasible and unscientific". The Chinese Foreign Ministry spokesperson (Lui Jian chao) confirmed that, "The Chinese government had no plans to build a dam on the Yarlung Tsangpo to divert its waters to the Yellow river". Liu Changming, a hydrologist at the Chinese Academy of Sciences stated that the proposal to tap the Brahmaputra would be "far too expensive, technologically unfeasible and controversial" (in terms of international reaction)

Medong Project Despite these denials China commenced a $ 60 Billion plan in March 2009 to construct a series of dams on the Yarlung Tsangpo bend. A 141 km long road has been constructed in the Nymchang area and a Tunnel in the Galuglya Mountain. Zongmi is the first dam in a series of dams that will be built at Jicho, Zagola, Leyla and Medong. When quizzed about these dams, the Chinese replied that these were run of the river hydro power projects and would not affect the down stream flow to India's North Eastern States or to Bangladesh. India's Foreign Ministry tamely agreed. To prepare our people for a virtual fait accompli, a canard was spread that the bulk of the water in the Brahmaputra came from South of the Himalayan water shed and hence diversion of the Yarlung Tsangpo waters would not affect us adversely. This anxiety to avoid conflict with China on such an ultra sensitive issue is baffling. As per the tenets of International law, *an act of diverting water away from reaching towards India is tantamount to an act of war.* However, with Armed Forces that have most deliberately been under funded and under resourced for the last two decades,

India today is hardly in any position to wage war against China (It has shied away so far from even taking Pakistan to task on the issue of terrorism).

We have therefore chosen to put blind faith in China's pronouncements that these are just run of the river projects. Claude Arpi writes that after five years, Prof Wang Guang Quian of the Chinese Academy of Science has clearly said that China has no choice but to divert the waters of the Yarlung Tsangpo. He, in fact, speaks of a new proposed route "The Brahmaputra waters are expected to be routed to Xinjiang along the Quinghai – Tibet railway line alignment and the Hexi corridor part of the Silk Route located on the Gansu Corridor". Wang conceded "We thought this would be a plan 50 years later". He added that "Chinese experts and government officials are still studying the feasibility and impact of these new proposals".

The entire problem is the speed of Chinese decision making on subjects of such great enormity. The Three Gorges Dams were pushed through without a thought for their adverse ecological and Seismic consequences. These are now coming to the fore and causing serious disquiet.

The water stress factor weighs heavily on the Chinese leadership. It is now compounded with great fears regarding food security for the huge Chinese population. Over farming in China is leading to desertification. Over use of chemicals and fertilizers is leading to soil salinity. Add water scarcity to this and the mix is explosive. Gen Ma Xiiaotian, China's former Defense Minister, had in a series of startling speeches highlighted a Chinese concept of Lebensaraum or the need for living space for the Chinese masses in neghbouring countries. Water-hegemony is the thin edge of that wedge. Water shortage is becoming a major impediment to China's goal of food security. Therefore the quest for water is an unyielding imperative for China. Chinese needs seemingly override the needs of all other countries in the region. The Chinese have shown scant regard for the sensitivities of the lower Riparian States of the Mekong and the Brahamaputra Rivers. The Medong Project on the Yarlung Tsangpo bend will be completed by 2015.

What can India do? It can at the very least strongly articulate its concerns. We cannot feed the paranoia in the North Eastern States by signaling that for Delhi they could not matter less. It will only strengthen the narrative of callous neglect and unconcern in the North East. India therefore urgently needs to: -

- Draw China into a dialogue on Water Issues and raise hydrological concerns at all bilateral meetings.
- Advocate the principles of International Water Law and make common cause with other lower riparian States in South, South East and Central Asia. It must commence a concerted Information campaign on this theme. Global pressure must be mounted on China to accede to the UN Convention on the use of international water courses and sign bilateral treaties with all its lower riparian states.
- Shed its perplexing diffidence and assert its legitimate national interests through firm dialogue.
- Should dialogue fail, be prepared to exert leverages by playing, if necessary, the Tibet Card.
- In all eventualities prepare for the contingency of military conflict. This implies an urgent speeding up of our military equipment modernization and force expansion programs. We urgently need to raise 6 to 8 additional Mountain Divisions for the Chinese front.
- It would be essential to deter the Chinese from such a disastrous course which could cause ecological and seismic catastrophes in the North Eastern States and in Bangladesh. Chinese companies are also proposing to construct a series of dams on the Indus in POK, another seismically ultra sensitive zone.
- It would be essential to put in place an alliance architecture of concerned lower Riparian States as also bring in extra-regional balancers like the USA and Japan into this equation.
- Above all we must rapidly develop the means to safeguard our own vital national interests. Deliberately underfunding of our armed forces makes us weak. Such self-induced weakness forces us to compromise on our vital national interests. We must break this vicious cycle.

2

India-China: A Water War over the Brahmaputra

WATER CONFLICT?

Discourses over the waters of the Brahmaputra River have been doing the rounds ever since China's announcement about the construction of three dams on the river last year. Despite diplomatic talks, China is keen to divert the waters from the Brahmaputra. In the past, China did not have a strong raison d'être to divert the flow of the river. China's Vice Minister of Water Resources, Jiao Yong, stated in 2011 that the Chinese government was not planning to conduct any diversion projects along the Brahmaputra River given that there wasn't a pressing need.

However, at present, China's per capita water reserve is approximately 2300 cubic metres – one-fourth of the world's average. China is, therefore, considered as the 13th most 'water-poor' country in the world with 80 per cent of its cities severely water stressed. More so, China's northern region possesses only 14.5 per cent of the entire country's water resources. As water supplies tighten, the water quality is degrading, ecology is suffering, and lands are becoming barren. This threatens the country's economic growth. Thus, the ever-increasing gap in the demand and supply chain in China's northern region has now pushed the country to move forward with its many dam projects.

China is keen to divert 150 billion cubic meters (BCM) of water and 'push' the waters to irrigate northern China. Of this, 50

BCM would be diverted from the Brahmaputra. In October 2013, India asserted the need for a water sharing treaty with China. This came about, following the paranoia generated after the announcement of the 510-MW Zangmu project along the course of the river.

However, although Indian Prime Minister Manmohan Singh returned with an agreement on sharing water-related information during the monsoon months, there was no mention of the planned diversion of the Brahmaputra. So far, India has been incapable in convincing China into building bilateral cooperation over the Brahmaputra River. The previous government in New Delhi did not want to antagonise bilateral relations with Beijing, and it is possible that the new government will follow suit.

India recognises that it is not in a position to wage a war with China. However, despite tensions and disagreements over common rivers, India has maintained relatively peaceful hydrological relations with its neighbours – with the Indus, Teesta, and Ganga Rivers being cases in point. On no occasion, did India seek to wage war as a means to resolve its water woes. In this light, India may not enter into a conflict with China over the Brahmaputra, but tensions seem probable.

ROLE OF THE NEW GOVERNMENT

The next government in New Delhi needs to assess the interventions made by Beijing. With the mounting demand for water and the absence of a comprehensive water-sharing policy between India, China and Bangladesh, it is certain that the vast water resources of Tibet and the Eastern Himalayas will be debated, continually. Irrespective of whether a significant diversion in the flows takes place or not, a water sharing agreement between the upper and lower riparian states will ensure that any violation of international norms of water-sharing is avoided.

At present, the northern regions of both China and Bangladesh face an acute water shortage. India, being a middle riparian state, too may have to bear the brunt in an event of diversion of the Brahmaputra waters; and it will directly impact the Northeastern region. The Indian government lags far behind China in terms of tapping the Brahmaputra's water. India's hydro-power potential is 84,044 megawatts (MW). Approximately 31,857 MW can be accessed by the northeastern part of the country. However, only three per cent of it is presently being utilised. The government recently sanctioned an 800 MW hydro-electric project on the Brahmaputra in Arunachal Pradesh, and there are more plans to generate 55,000 MW of hydro-power by constructing mega dams.

With both India and China making large scale interventions along the Brahmaputra, they are ignoring the possible implications on the ecology. The next government in New Delhi needs to cater to these concerns and push for a comprehensive tripartite water sharing treaty with all three riparian states.

BRAHMAPUTRA RIVER

The Brahmaputra , also called Tsangpo-Brahmaputra, is a trans-boundary river and one of the major rivers of Asia. Majuli is the riverine island formed by River Brahmaputra in Assam in India.

With its origin in the Angsi Glacier, located on the northern side of the Himalayas in Burang County of Tibet as the Yarlung Tsangpo River, it flows across southern Tibet to break through the Himalayas in great gorges (including the Yarlung Tsangpo Grand Canyon) and into Arunachal Pradesh (India), where it is known as Dihang or Siang. It flows southwest through the Assam Valley as Brahmaputra and south through Bangladesh as the Jamuna (not to be mistaken with Yamuna of India). In the vast Ganges Delta, it merges with the Padma, the main distributary of the Ganges, then the Meghna, before emptying into the Bay of Bengal.

About 1,800 mi (2,900 km) long, the Brahmaputra is an important river for irrigation and transportation. The average depth of the river is 124 ft (38 m) and maximum depth is 380 ft (120 m). The river is prone to catastrophic flooding in spring when the Himalayan snows melt. The average discharge of the river is about 19,300 m^3/s (680,000 cu ft/s), and floods can reach over 100,000 m^3/s (3,500,000 cu ft/s). It is a classic example of a braided river and is highly susceptible to channel migration and avulsion. It is also one of the few rivers in the world that exhibit a tidal bore. It is navigable for most of its length. The river drains the Himalaya east of the Indo-Nepal border, south-central portion of the Tibetan plateau above the Ganges basin, southeastern portion of Tibet, the Patkai-Bum hills, the northern slopes of the Meghalaya hills, the Assam plains, and the northern portion of Bangladesh. The basin, especially south of Tibet, is characterized by high levels of rainfall. Kangchenjunga (8,586 m) is the only peak above 8,000 m, hence is the highest point within the Brahmaputra basin.

The Brahmaputra's upper course was long unknown, and its identity with the Yarlung Tsangpo was only established by exploration in 1884–86. This river is often called Tsangpo-Brahmaputra river.

The lower reaches are sacred to Hindus. While most rivers on the Indian subcontinent have female names, this river has a rare male name, as it means "son of Brahma" in Sanskrit (*putra* means "son").

COURSE

Tibet

The Brahmaputra River, called Yarlung Tsangpo in Tibetan language, originates on the Angsi Glacier located on the northern side of the Himalayas in Burang County of Tibet and not Chema-Yungdung glacier, which was previously identified by geographer Swami Pranavananda in the 1930s. The river is 3,848 km (2,391 mi) long, and its drainage area is 712,035 km^2 (274,918 sq mi) according to the new findings, while previous documents showed its length varied from 2,900 to 3,350 km and its drainage area between 520,000 and 1.73 million km^2. This finding has been given by Mr. Liu Shaochuang, a researcher with the Institute of Remote Sensing Applications under the analysis using expeditions and satellite imagery from the Chinese Academy of Sciences (CAS).

From its source, the river runs for nearly 700 mi (1,100 km) in a generally easterly direction between the main range of the Himalayas to the south and the Kailas Range to the north. Throughout its upper course, the river is generally known as the Tsangpo ("Purifier"); it is also known by its Chinese name (Yarlung

Zangbo) and by other local Tibetan names. In Tibet, the Tsangpo receives a number of tributaries. The most important left-bank tributaries are the Raka Zangbo (Raka Tsangpo), which joins the river west of Xigazê (Shigatse), and the Lhasa (Kyi), which flows past the Tibetan capital of Lhasa and joins the Tsangpo at Qüxü. The Nyang Qu (Gyamda) River joins the river from the north at Zela (Tsela Dzong). On the right bank, a second river called the Nyang Qu (Nyang Chu) meets the Tsangpo at Xigazê.

After passing Pi (Pe) in Tibet, the river turns suddenly to the north and northeast and cuts a course through a succession of great narrow gorges between the mountainous massifs of Gyala Peri and Namjagbarwa (Namcha Barwa) in a series of rapids and cascades. Thereafter, the river turns south and southwest and flows through a deep gorge (the "Grand Canyon" of the Tsangpo) across the eastern extremity of the Himalayas with canyon walls that extend upward for 16,500 ft (5,000 m) and more on each side. During that stretch, the river enters northern Arunachal Pradesh state in northeastern India, where it is known as the Dihang (or Siang) River, and turns more southerly.

Assam and adjoining region

The Brahmaputra enters India in the state of Arunachal Pradesh, where it is called Siang. It makes a very rapid descent from its original height in Tibet, and finally appears in the plains, where it is called Dihang. It flows for about 35 km (22 mi) and is joined by the Dibang Riverand the Lohit River at the head of the Assam Valley. Below the Lohit, the river is called Brahmaputra, enters the state of Assam, and becomes very wide--as wide as 10 km (6 mi) in parts of Assam. It is joined in Sonitpur by the Kameng River (or Jia Bhoreli).

The Dihang, winding out of the mountains, turns toward the southeast and descends into a low-lying basin as it enters northeastern Assam state. Just west of the town of Sadiya, the river again turns to the southwest and is joined by two mountain streams, the Lohit and the Dibang. Below that confluence, about 900 mi (1,450 km) from the Bay of Bengal, the river becomes known conventionally as the Brahmaputra ("Son of Brahma"). In Assam, the river is mighty, even in the dry season, and during the rains, its banks are more than 5 mi (8 km) apart. As the river follows its braided 450-mi (700-km) course through the valley, it receives several rapidly rushing Himalayan streams, including the Subansiri, Kameng, Bhareli, Dhanṣiri, Manas, Champamati, Saralbhanga, and Sankosh Rivers. The main tributaries from the hills and from the plateau to the south are the Burhi Dihing, the Disang, the Dikhu, and the Kopili.

Between Dibrugarh and Lakhimpur Districts, the river divides into two channels—the northern Kherkutia channel and the southern Brahmaputra channel. The two channels join again about 100 km (62 mi) downstream, forming the Majuli island, which was, until some time back, the largest river island in the world. At Guwahati, near the ancient pilgrimage centre ofHajo, the Brahmaputra cuts through the rocks of the Shillong Plateau, and is at its narrowest at 1 km (1,100 yd) bank-to-bank. Due to the river's narrow width, the Battle of Saraighat was fought here in March 1671. The first combined rail/road bridge across the Brahmaputra was opened to traffic in April 1962 at Saraighat.

The environment of the Brahmaputra floodplains in Assam have been described as the Brahmaputra Valley semi-evergreen forests ecoregion.

Bangladesh

In Bangladesh, the Brahmaputra is joined by the Teesta River (or Tista), one of its largest tributaries. Below the Tista, the Brahmaputra splits into two distributary branches. The western branch, which contains the majority of the river's flow, continues due south as the Jamuna (Jomuna) to merge with the lower Ganges, called the Padma River (Pôdda). The eastern branch, formerly the larger, but now much smaller, is called the lower or old Brahmaputra (Bromhoputro). It curves southeast to join the Meghna River near Dhaka. The Padma and Meghna converge near Chandpur and flow out into the Bay of Bengal. This final part of the river is called Meghna.

The Brahmaputra enters the plains of Bangladesh after turning south around the Garo Hills below Dhuburi, India. After flowing past Chilmari, Bangladesh, it is joined on its right bank by the Tista River and then follows a 150-mi (240-km) course due south as the Jamuna River. (South of Gaibanda, the Old Brahmaputra leaves the left bank of the main stream and flows past Jamalpur and Mymensingh to join the Meghna River at Bhairab Bazar.) Before its confluence with the Ganges, the Jamuna receives the combined waters of the Baral, Atrai, and Hurasagar Rivers on its right bank and becomes the point of departure of the large Dhaleswari River on its left bank. A tributary of the Dhaleswari, the Buriganga ("Old Ganges"), flows past Dhaka, the capital of Bangladesh, and joins the Meghna River above Munshiganj.

The Jamuna joins with the Ganges north of Goalundo Ghat, below which, as the Padma, their combined waters flow to the southeast for a distance of about 75 mi (120 km). After several smaller channels branch off to feed the Ganges-Brahmaputra delta to the south, the main body of the Padma reaches its confluence with the Meghna River near Chandpur and then enters the Bay of Bengal through the Meghna estuary and lesser channels flowing through the delta. The growth of the Ganges-Brahmaputra Delta is dominated by tidal processes. The Ganges Delta, fed by the waters of numerous rivers, including the Ganges and Brahmaputra, is 59,570 square kilometres (23,000 sq mi) the largest river deltas in the world. The Ganges-Brahmaputra system has the third-greatest average discharge of the world's rivers—roughly 1,086,500 ft^3(30,770 m^3) per second; about 700,000 ft^3 (19,800 m^3) per second of the total is supplied by the Brahmaputra alone. The rivers' combined suspended sediment load of about 1.84 billion tons per year is the world's highest. In the past, the course of the lower Brahmaputra was different and passed through the Jamalpur and Mymensingh districts. In a 7.5 magnitude earthquake on 2 April 1762, the main channel of the Brahmaputra at Bhahadurabad point was switched southwards and opened as Jamuna due to the result of tectonic uplift of the Madhupur tract.

FLOODING

During the spring season (June–October), floods are a very common occurrence. Deforestation in the Brahmaputra watershed has resulted in increased siltation levels, flash floods, and soil erosion in critical downstream habitat, such as the Kaziranga National Park in middle Assam. Occasionally, massive flooding causes huge losses to crops, life, and property. Periodic flooding is a natural phenomenon which is ecologically important because it helps maintain the lowland grasslands and associated wildlife. Periodic floods also deposit fresh alluvium, replenishing the fertile soil of the Brahmaputra River Valley. Thus flooding, agriculture, and agricultural practices are closely connected. Flood-control measures are taken by water resource department and the Brahmaputra Board, but until now the flood problem remains unsolved. At least a third of the land of Majuli island has been eroded by the river. Recently, it is suggested that a highway protected by concrete mat along the river and excavation of the river bed can curb this menace. This project, named the Brahmaputra River Restoration Project, is yet to be implemented by the government.

International cooperation

The waters of the River Brahmaputra are shared by China, India, and Bangladesh. In the 1990s and 2000s, repeated speculation was mentioned about China building a dam at the Great Bend, with a view to divert the waters to the north of the country. This was denied by the Chinese government for many years. At the Kathmandu Workshop of Strategic Foresight Group in August 2009 on Water Security in the Himalayan Region, which on a rare occasion brought together leading hydrologists from the basin countries, the Chinese scientists argued that it was not feasible for China to undertake such a diversion. However, on 22 April 2010, China confirmed that it was indeed building the Zangmu Dam on the Brahmaputra in Tibet, but assured India that the project would not have any significant effect on the downstream flow to India.

In a meeting of scientists at Dhaka at 2010, 25 leading experts from the basin countries issued a Dhaka Declaration on Water Security calling for exchange of information in low-flow periods, and other means of collaboration. Even though the UN Convention on Trans-boundary Water of 1997 does not prevent any of the basin countries from building a dam, customary law offers relief to the lower riparian countries. Also, potential exists for China,

India, and Bangladesh to develop hydroelectricity projects and transboundary water navigation.

HISTORY

Early accounts give its name as Dyardanes. In the past, the course of the lower Brahmaputra was different and passed through the Jamalpur andMymensingh districts. Some water still flows through that course, now called the Old Brahmaputra, as a distributary of the main channel.

A question about the river system in Bangladesh] is when and why the Brahmaputra changed its main course, at the site of the Jamuna and the "Old Brahmaputra" fork that can be seen by comparing modern maps to historic maps before the 1800s. The Brahmaputra likely flowed directly south along its present main channel for much of the time since the last glacial maximum, switching back and forth between the two courses several times throughout the Holocene.

One idea about the most recent avulsion is that the change in the course of the main waters of the Brahmaputra took place suddenly in 1787, the year of the heavy flooding of the river Tista. It is, however, well known that the Tista has always been a wandering river, sometimes joining the Ganges, sometimes being shifted westwards by the superior strength of that river and forced to join the Brahmaputra.

In the middle of the 18th century, at least three fair-sized streams flowed between the Rajshahi and Dhaka Divisions, viz., the Daokoba, a branch of the Tista, the Monash or Konai, and the Salangi. The Lahajang and the Elengjany were also important rivers. In Renault's time, the Brahmaputra as a first step towards securing a more direct course to the sea by leaving the Mahdupur Jungle to the east began to send a considerable volume of water down the Jinai or Jabuna from Jamalpur into the Monash and Salangi. These rivers gradually coalesced and kept shifting to the west till they met the Daokoba, which was showing an equally rapid tendency to cut towards the east. The junction of these rivers gave the Brahmaputra a course worthy of her immense power, and the rivers to right and left silted up. In

Renault's Altas they very much resemble the rivers of Jessore, which dried up after the hundred-mouthed Ganges had cut her new channel to join the Meghna at the south of the Munshiganj subdivision.

In 1809, Buchanan Hamilton wrote that the new channel between Bhawanipur and Dewanranj "was scarcely inferior to the mighty river, and threatens to sweep away the intermediate country". By 1830, the old channel had been reduced to its present insignificance. It was navigable by country boats throughout the year and by launches only during rains, but at the point as low as Jamalpur it was formidable throughout the cold weather. Similar was the position for two or three months just below Mymensingh also.

As early as in 1830, there were resumption proceedings for chars which had formed in the new bed. Enquiries showed that many of the new formations were on the site of permanently settled villages which had been washed away by the changes in the course of the Jamuna and the Daokoba.

The process has gone on ever since, and Buchanan Hamilton's remarks on the villages of Bengal are specially applicable to this area. He says that "a change in the site of a village 4 or 5 miles causes little inconvenience and is considered no more than a usual casualty, which produces on the people no effect of consequence. Even the rich never put up buildings of a durable nature.

Other Usage

The BrahMos missile, which is a short range ramjet supersonic cruise missile that can be launched from submarines, ships, aircraft or land, is named after a portmanteau formed from the names of two rivers, the Brahmaputra of India and theMoskva of Russia. It is a joint venture between the Russian Federation's NPO Mashinostroeyenia and India's Defence Research and Development Organisation (DRDO) who have together formed BrahMos Aerospace Private Limited.

It is based on the Russian P-800 Oniks cruise missile and other similar sea-skimming Russian cruise missile technologies.

CHINESE DAM ON BRAHMAPUTRA MEANS TO INDIA

China's official Xinhua news agency said the first section of the $1.5 billion dam went into operation on Sunday afternoon. Five other sections will be completed next year. The dam will generate 2.5 billion kilowatt hours of electricity every year, reported the agency.

The implications of construction of the dam for India are on several fronts. It reduces water flow in the river. This is not so serious if the dams are RoR (run of river) hydro stations. But if reservoirs are built, or waters diverted, it could affect the river's ecosystem in the upper stretches.

Second, it gives China a stronger say in water sharing discussions because it has established claim of use of these waters. India will have to move quickly to establish its own user rights quickly.

Also, rapid development of infrastructure in the N-E could create social tensions with local tribes. That must be avoided to prevent China instigating Arunachal Pradesh locals to agitate against India.

The Zangmu dam construction began in 2010. It sparked off panic among China's southern neighbours, including India. The fear was that China may actually drain this river of water, just as it had done with the Mekong river.

The 4,350 km long Mekong is the 12th largest river in the world, the 7th largest in Asia. It originates from Tibet (China) and flows through Myanmar, Laos, Thailand, Cambodia and Vietnam. Today, all the downstream countries of the Mekong river accuse China of starving them of water.

Could this become the fate of India's North-East and Bangladesh as well? This is because out of the Brahmaputra's total length of 2,880km, 1,625km is in Tibet (or China), 918km in India, and 337km in Bangladesh.

But, on the other hand, the average annual rainfall is just 400mm in Tibet, but 3,000mm on the Indian side. This is in spite of the fact that (according to data provided by the Central Water

Commission), of the total catchment area of 580,000 sq km, 50% lies in Tibet, 34% in India, and the balance in Bangladesh and Bhutan. Significantly, only 40% of the water comes from the Chinese catchment area.

Some policymakers in Delhi believe that the precipitation in China contributes only 7% to the flow. It is the Brahmaputra's tributaries in Arunachal Pradesh, along with the rains in India, that contribute to the rest of the river's water supply.

That could explain the absence of any shrill reaction from New Delhi. But there is tremendous cause for concern.

First, many experts believe that the 7% precipitation theory is all hogwash. You cannot compartmentalise any river, they say. Brahma Chellaney, a noted China and water expert, warns that any diversion of water from the upper reaches of the Brahmaputra could have devastating consequences for the way the river flows for downstream areas. He believes that all sorts of data is being fed to journalists, and that the only reliable data is from the United Nations.

According to the United Nations, the cross border annual aggregate flow of Brahmaputra river system is around 165.4 billion cubic metres (bcm). That, add experts, is greater than the combined trans-boundary flow of the three key Asian rivers—Mekong, Salween and Irrawady—that run from the Tibetian plateau to South East Asia.

Second, reservoirs along the river could staunch the flow of water into India. True, most of the hydro-projects China is building are of the run-of-the-river (RoR) type, generating electricity from the flow of the river and not trapping any of the water in dams. However, reservoirs are also being built, and it is only a matter of time that much of the water originating and collected in China could get trapped in reservoirs for diversion to the northern parts of China.

But, most critically, almost every policymaker in New Delhi is painfully aware that under international law, a country's right over natural resources it shares with other nations becomes stronger if is already putting these resources to use. China has already begun first use of the Brahmaputra waters.

If India does not move fast and establish its own claims over water use, it could lose out in subsequent water sharing discussions under international law.

That partly explains the Modi government's urgency in building projects and linking Arunachal Pradesh to the rest of India. It also throws light on why Indian strategists are suspicious of any moves by environmental groups protesting against the setting up of such projects along the Brahmaputra.

INDIA AND CHINA SHOULD LEAVE THE BRAHMAPUTRA ALONE

In October 2012, Indians learned that China had begun to construct a 700 megawatt (MW) capacity dam on the Brahmaputra river (Yarlung Tsangpo). The news aroused fears that China intended not only to generate power from the river but also divert some of its waters to the arid northern regions of the country.

This possibility was first mentioned at the international conference of the Global Infrastructure Fund in Anchorage, Alaska, in 1986. Although Chinese officials rubbished the idea as being impossibly expensive to implement, they did not rule out the possibility of constructing dams on the river to generate power. This ambivalence raised understandable alarm in Bangladesh and India, but Beijing sought to allay their fears by assuring them that it intends to build run-of-the-river dams that will redirect, but not stop, the flow of its waters into India and Bangladesh.

These reassurances have not, however, prevented China and India from entering into an undeclared race to capture the hydroelectric potential of the Brahmaputra river basin. Chinese writers began to air plans for harnessing the Brahmaputra in 2005, but it is possible that the Indian government had already begun to formulate its plans after the publication of a book by Li Ling in 2003 entitled *Tibet's waters will save China.*

As the downstream riparian, India is hoping to establish first user rights to stake its claim to an uninterrupted flow of the Brahmaptura's waters. In international law, first user rights start upon the completion of a project, so the number of projects that India has signalled it will take up in the Brahmaputra basin has risen rapidly – from 146 announced in a 10-year hydroelectricity plan unveiled by India's Central Electricity Authority in 2007, to about 200 today. What is more, a scramble has developed to start as many of these as soon as possible.

The pace of planning and implementation has also picked up in China. Citing the need to cut down carbon dioxide emissions, the 12th Five Year energy plan, shifted its emphasis back onto giant hydroelectric projects once more. One of its most important goals is to harness the hydropower potential of the Brahmaputra basin.

In all, China intends to build 40 dams on the river and its tributaries. Of these, 20 dams on the Brahmaputra will generate 60,000 MW of power, while 20 smaller dams upon its tributaries are expected to generate another 5,000 MW. Eleven of the 20 projects on the Brahmaputra will be located between its source and the Great Bend where the Brahmaputra turns northwards, executes a huge 'U' turn and falls from 3,500 metres on the Tibetan plateau to 700 metres in the undulating hills of Arunachal Pradesh in India. These will generate 20,000 MW of power, while the balance of 40,000 MW will be generated at the Great Bend itself.

The plan for doing this has been put forward by ex-premier Li Peng's family-dominated corporation, the Three Gorges Dam Company. It envisages building a vast tunnel under the ridge that separates the two arms of the Great Bend to divert 50 billion cubic metres of water a year from the northwestern flowing arm of the river to the southeastern arm over a succession of nine cascading hydropower dams that will generate 40,000 MW of power. India, for its part, plans to generate 22,000 MW from two large dams on the Brahmaputra in Arunachal Pradesh and 10,000 MW from dams on its tributaries. In all, therefore, the two countries plan to generate 97,000 MW of power from this tiny region of their respective countries.

Such ambitious but conflicting plans were bound to have political repercussions. The first was a statement by the Chinese ambassador in New Delhi that China considered the whole of the northeastern state of Arunachal Pradesh to be a part of Tibet. This was a reversal of its earlier position, developed in a succession of bilateral negotiations since 1994, that China was prepared to settle for a substantial modification of some parts of the existing temporary boundary, called the Line of Actual Control.

The announcement took the Indian government by surprise and was followed by three years of rising tension along the border. China began to refer to Arunachal as "South Tibet", and to its principal monastery at Tawang as Tibet's second most important monastery after Lhasa. It also began to deny visas to Indian officials who were serving in Arunachal Pradesh. The tension was not defused until there was a meeting between then premier Wen Jiabao and prime minister Manmohan Singh, at Hua Hin, Thailand, in October 2009, designed specifically to prevent its spilling over into military conflict.

CALAMITY WAITING TO HAPPEN

These plans are engineers' dreams run amok. If they have their way, up to 360 dams will be built on slopes with a gradient of as much as 60 degrees, at the meeting point of three of the youngest and most unstable mountain ranges in the world. But neither the Chinese nor the Indian government have made even a rudimentary assessment of the impact that gouging out billions of cubic metres of rock and earth to build dams, tunnels and roads, and store millions, in some cases billions, of cubic metres of water, will have on the stability of the earth's crust in this region.

Both governments know that the Himalayas have experienced the most powerful earthquakes on land in recorded history. Four of these, measuring 7.8 to 8.9 on the Richter scale, occurred within a span of 53 years between 1897 and 1950. The first and last occurred in the region immediately south and west of the Great Bend in the Brahmaputra.

The 1897 earthquake measured 7.8 on the Richter scale (equivalent to the explosion of 7.6 million tonnes of dynamite, or a medium sized hydrogen bomb) and caused widespread damage and loss of life in what was then called Upper Assam. It was caused by the build up of pressure as the Indian (tectonic) plate pressed against the Shillong Plate, a part of the far older Eurasian Plate.

The 1950 earthquake was the strongest ever recorded in the Himalayas. It occurred at Rima, in Tibet, not far from the site of the 1897 quake. Measuring 8.7 on the Richter scale, it is one of the 10 most severe earthquakes in recorded history. Its epicentre also lay on the fault line where the Indian continental plate smashes into the Eurasian plate. Survivors from the region reported mudslides damming rivers and causing giant floods that brought down sand, mud, trees, giant boulders and all kinds of debris.

These were neither isolated nor exceptional events. Earthquakes in the Himalayas regularly cause landslides that block rivers, causing them to rise until the pressure of the stored water breaks through. The result is a flash flood downstream that brings havoc to the villages and towns that lie in its path. The avalanches caused by the 1950 earthquake blocked several of the tributaries of the Brahmaputra. One such dyke in the Dibang valley broke quickly and caused relatively little damage. But another, at Subansiri, broke only after water had collected behind it for eight days and unleashed a seven-metre-high wave that submerged several villages and killed 532 people.

Geological studies, including the radio carbon dating of sand found on the surface, have uncovered at least one other giant earthquake in the same area in 1548, and two others in the central region of the Himalayas that were severe enough to rupture the earth's surface. The first of these occurred in 1255. The second was the devastating Bihar earthquake of 1934.

The 1934 earthquake, which measured 8.1 on the Richter scale had its epicentre about 10 kilometres south of Mount Everest. It devastated the northern part of the Indian state of Bihar and large parts of eastern Nepal, and killed at least 30,000 people. This was the death toll when there were no dams in the mountains. The dykes that the landslides created were made of mud and boulders, and they broke in a matter of days. But earthquakes of this magnitude will almost certainly crack concrete dams as well.

India and Bangladesh at highest risk

The Richter scale is a logarithmic scale, which means that an 8.1 magnitude earthquake releases three times as much energy as a 7.8 magnitude quake. For an 8.7 magnitude quake, it's 23 times as much. Should any of the giant dams contemplated by the two countries crack during an earthquake, the colossal wave of water, mud and boulders released would kill millions of human beings and devastate tens of thousands of square miles of the downstream areas of Tibet, India and Bangladesh. The overwhelming majority of deaths would take place in India and Bangladesh.

India got a taste of what a flash-flood upriver in the Brahmaputra basin could do when one wiped out an entire island in the Brahmaputra in 2000, killing nearly all who lived on it, and another in June 2013, when a landslide caused by three days of incessant rain blocked a tributary of the Bhagirathi river, one of the two main tributaries of the Ganges. When the dyke it had created broke on the third day, the resulting flash-flood destroyed the entire pilgrimage town of Kedarnath and killed between 5,000 and 10,000 pilgrims in a matter of hours. Had the hillsides overlooking the Bhagirathi not been ravaged by the construction of dams and tunnels for the Tehri hydroelectric project, this catastrophe might not have happened.

The Tehri project is a pygmy compared with the nine-cascade project proposed for the Great Bend, as its generating capacity is only 1,000 MW. The death toll from the fracture of even one of these dams would, therefore, run into millions. If the two governments go through with their plans for the Brahmaputra–Yarlung Tsangpo basin, the entire region will become a calamity waiting to happen.

3

Water Wars: China, India and the Great Dam Rush

China's grand plans to harness the waters of the Brahmaputra River have set off ripples of anxiety in the two lower riparian states: India and Bangladesh. China's construction of dams and the proposed diversion of the Brahmaputra's waters is not only expected to have repercussions for water flow, agriculture, ecology, and lives and livelihoods downstream; it could also become another contentious issue undermining Sino-Indian relations.

The 2,880 km-long Brahmaputra originates in Tibet, where it is known as the Yarlung Tsangpo. It flows eastwards through southern Tibet for a distance of 1,625 kilometers and at its easternmost point it swings around to make a spectacular U-turn at the Shuomatan Point or Great Bend before it enters India's easternmost state, Arunachal Pradesh. Here it is known as the Siang River. After gathering the waters of several rivers it announces itself as the Brahmaputra in the state of Assam. The river snakes lazily through Assam to then enter Bangladesh, where it is known as the Jamuna. In Bangladesh it is joined by the Ganges (known as the Padma in Bangladesh) and Meghna and together these rivers form the world's largest delta before emptying their waters into the Bay of Bengal.

As with other rivers originating in the icy Tibetan plateau, Beijing's plans for the Brahmaputra include two kinds of projects. The first involves the construction of hydro-electric power projects on the river and the other, more ambitious project, envisages the diversion of its waters to the arid north. In November last year, China's plans for the Brahmaputra took a leap forward when the first unit of the $1.5 billion Zangmu Hydropower Station project, which is located in the middle reaches of the river, became operational. Once completed – five other generating units of this project are due for completion this year – the project is designed to generate 2.5 billion kilowatt hours of electricity annually.

Besides the Zangmu power station, the Chinese government has approved other hydropower projects along the Brahmaputra. It maintains that all these are run-of-the-river projects that involve no storage or diversion and that they will not affect the river's downstream flow into northeast India. Still, its plans have generated apprehensions in India's Northeast and in Bangladesh, where the Brahmaputra is a veritable lifeline and a core part of the cultural life here.

Fuelling anxiety over the Chinese dams on the Brahmaputra is the impact that a reduction of the flow of the Ganges has had on millions in the region. India's damming of the Ganges has reduced the water flow into Bangladesh. The increased salinity of soil has adversely impacted agriculture and over the last several decades millions of Bangladeshis have been forced to relocate, many migrating to India's northeast. This migration changed the demographic composition of vast tracts of Northeast India (especially in Assam) and triggeredserious ethnic conflicts and insurgencies there. Will a reduction in the flow of the Brahmaputra add fuel to the conflicts already raging in the region?

"India has nothing to be worried about," Romesh Bhattacharji, a former Indian bureaucrat who has travelled along much of the India-China border, told *The Diplomat.* The Zangmu hydropower station being a run-of-the-river project, "the Brahmaputra's waters will continue to flow to India as before, after their brief storage period is over." As for the other dams that China proposes to build on the river, "they are on tributaries like the Nyingchi further to the east from Zangmu and none of these are large storage dams," he pointed out, reiterating that "there is no need for India to panic." Others are less optimistic. China's dams on the Brahmaputra may be run-of-the-river projects but they are "a matter of utmost concern to lower riparian countries," argues Ramaswamy Iyer, former secretary of Water Resources with the Government of India and currently an honorary research professor at the New Delhi-based Centre for Policy Research. A "break in the river between the point of diversion to the turbines and the point of return of the waters to the river ... can be very long, upwards of 10 km in many cases, even 100 km in some cases; and there would be a series of such breaks in the river in the event of a cascade of projects," he points out. Besides, "far from being environmentally benign, as often claimed," a run-of-the-river hydroelectric project "spells death for the river." Turbines operate intermittently in these projects, "which means that the waters are held back in pondage and released when the turbines need to operate, resulting in huge diurnal variations – from 0 percent to 400 percent in a day – in downstream flows. No aquatic life or riparian population can cope with that order of diurnal variation."

NORTHWARD REROUTING

More worrying than China's construction of hydropower dams on the Brahmaputra is the proposed northward rerouting of its waters at the Great Bend. This diversion would result in a significant drop in the river's water level as it enters India. It will have a serious impact on agriculture and fishing in the downstream areas as the salinity of water will increase.

Bhattacharji dismisses these fears. Drawing attention to the enormous technological and other challenges posed by the difficult terrain through which the Brahmaputra runs in Tibet – it flows here at an altitude of around 3500 meters above sea level – he points out that if the Chinese have to divert its waters to the north, they will have to haul the water up over an altitude of another thousand meters at least. "It's impossible to even think of such a diversion," he observes. Besides the technological challenges, there are financial and environmental costs that stand in the way of implementing the water diversion plan.

Even if the diversion project goes ahead, its impact on India will not be severe, Bhattacharji argues, as the "Brahmaputra gets most of its waters after entering India." It is the Brahmaputra's tributaries in India and the heavy rainfall here that provides roughly 70 percent of the water volume of the Brahmaputra River, points out Jabin Jacob, Assistant Director at the Delhi-based Institute of Chinese Studies.

Even though the Brahmaputra gathers the bulk of its volume in India, Iyer warns against "complacency." The 30:70 ratio applies to the rainy season only. Besides, "30 percent of the flows is not an insignificant figure, and even a 10 percent diversion could have serious consequences," for downstream areas.

Analysts predict that "water wars" could break out between India and China. "Upstream dams, barrages, canals, and irrigation systems can help fashion water into a political weapon that can be wielded overtly in a war, or subtly in peacetime to signal dissatisfaction with a co-riparian state. Even denial of hydrological data in a critically important season can amount to the use of water as a political tool," warns strategic affairs expert Brahma Chellaney.

Other experts reject predictions of a Sino-Indian war over the Brahmaputra.

"China and India see themselves as responsible regional and global powers and a war of any kind between them will not only set back bilateral relations but also damage their reputations internationally. At the moment, this is not a cost that either side is willing to pay," Jacob argues.

However, the lack of communication on the issue is deepening suspicion and tension. This underscores the need for dialogue that includes all the riparian countries. China must share data with India and Bangladesh on its dam construction and other plans for the Brahmaputra.

Meanwhile in a bid to exploit the immense hydropower potential of the Brahmaputra and importantly, to establish prior use rights, the Indian government is on a massive dam building spree – including mega dams as well micro-hydel projects – in Arunachal Pradesh. Environmental and other norms are being flouted in the construction of these projects. These could worsen the water flow for the people further downstream in Assam and Bangladesh, deepening existing problems and triggering new conflicts.

Some have suggested that a joint India-Bangladesh effort on the question of China's damming of the Brahmaputra may be effective. This is unlikely given China's preference for bilateral approaches to dispute resolution.

And importantly, there is little difference between the strategies of India and China on dam building or water diversion. India may worry about Chinese plans for diverting the Brahmaputra's waters but the present Indian government too is keen on diverting India's northern rivers. While such plans are still on the drawing board, it has not consulted its neighbours, the lower riparian countries, on this project or on hundreds of others in the past.

CLIMATE CHANGE WILL DEVASTATE

South Asia

A final draft of a report leaked from the Intergovernmental Panel on Climate Change (IPCC) to the authors lays out shocking scenarios for India and the rest of South Asia. The summary for policy makers that was released by the IPCC on Friday is a call for urgent action globally. While shocking, the fuller final draft version of the Second Working Group of the IPCC's Fourth Assessment Report, which may be watered down before final publication, makes for even more sobering reading: It lays out in explicit detail what lies ahead for India and the rest of Asia. It also presents an opportunity for the country to take the lead in defining a more secure and sustainable future for itself.

Here are some of the devastating consequences detailed in the provisional February 16, 2007, IPCC report on Asia: Sea levels will rise by at least 40 cm by 2100, inundating vast areas on the coastline, including some of the most densely populated cities whose populations will be forced to migrate inland or build dykes — both requiring a financial and logistical challenge that will be unprecedented. In the South Asian region as a whole, millions of people will find their lands and homes inundated. Up to 88 per cent of all of Asia's coral reefs, termed the "rainforests of the ocean" because of the critical habitat they provide to sea creatures, may be lost as a result of warming ocean temperatures.

The Ganga, Brahmaputra, and Indus will become seasonal rivers, dry between monsoon rains as Himalayan glaciers will continue their retreat, vanishing entirely by 2035, if not sooner. Water tables will continue to fall and the gross per capita water availability in India will decline by over one-third by 2050 as rivers dry up, water tables fall or grow more saline. Water scarcity will in turn affect the health of vast populations, with a rise in water-borne diseases such as cholera. Other diseases such as dengue fever and malaria are also expected to rise.

Crop productivity will fall, especially in non-irrigated land, as temperatures rise for all of South Asia by as much as 1.2 degrees C on average by 2040, and even greater crop loss — of over 25 per cent — as temperatures rise to up to 5.4 degrees C by the end of the century. This means an even lower caloric intake for India's vast rural population, already pushed to the limit, with the possibility of starvation in many rural areas dependent on rainfall for their crops. Even those areas that rely on irrigation will find a growing crisis in adequate water availability.

Mortality due to heat-related deaths will climb, with the poor, the elderly and daily wage earners and agricultural workers suffering a rise in heat-related deaths. This grim future awaits India in the coming century. The irony is that much of this damage will be self-inflicted, unless the country is prepared to make a radical, enlightened change in its energy and transportation strategies.

We are truly at a crossroads: Either we can be complacent or wait for leadership from a reluctant United States, the largest greenhouse gas emitter in the world, or begin to take action now, regardless of what other countries do.

The path that India has taken thus far, of waiting until wealthy countries take action on global warming, is understandable if viewed in isolation. The U.S., the U.K., and other countries in the wealthy North, have developed their economies largely thanks to fossil fuels. It is only fair that India be allowed to attain the same standard of living before curbing its emissions.

But as the IPCC report makes clear, while it may be "fair" to do so, it is also suicidal for India to pursue any strategy but the least carbon-intensive path toward its own development. Wealthy, less populous countries in the North are very likely — and very unfairly — going to suffer fewer devastating blows to their economies, and may actually benefit with extended growing seasons, while India and other South Asian nations will dramatically and painfully suffer if action is not taken now.

Today, much of India's energy comes from coal, most of it mined in the rural areas of Orissa, Jharkhand, and Bihar with devastating consequences. Tribals and small and marginal peasants are being forced to resettle as these mines grow wider by the day. Inadequate resettlement plans mean more migration of landless populations to urban slums. The environment is being destroyed by these mines and their waste products — among them fly ash laced with heavy metals and other toxic materials. But the biggest irony of this boom in coal-fired power is that much of the power is going to export-oriented, energy-intensive industry. Look at Orissa's coal belt and you will find a plethora of foreign-owned and Indian aluminium smelters, steel mills, and sponge iron factories — all burning India's coal, at a heavy cost to local populations — then exporting a good share of the final product to the China, the U.S. or other foreign markets.

Volatile Mix

Add to the problem of export-oriented, energy-intensive industry the problem of carbon trades, and you have a volatile mix. India is one of the top destinations globally in the growing carbon market. In exchange for carbon trade projects in India, wealthy polluters in the North are able to avoid restrictions on their own emissions. Rather than financing "clean development" projects as promised, many of these trades are cheap, dirty, and harmful to the rural poor. Fast-growing eucalyptus plantations are displacing farmers from their land and tribals from their forests. Sponge-iron factories are garnering more money from carbon trades earned by capturing "waste heat" than from the production of the raw material itself. Toxic fly ash from coal-fired power plants is being turned into bricks, and the carbon that would have been released from traditional clay-fired brick kilns, is now an invisible commodity that can be sold as carbon credits. These carbon trades are not helping finance clean energy and development for India's rural poor.

Add to this the special economic zones or SEZs — forcing people off their land, where blood, often of the most vulnerable, is shed at the altar of development.

Global warming will tighten this growing squeeze to a noose, as huge areas of Bangladesh go underwater and environmental refugees flood across India's borders. The leaked final draft of the IPCC report shows that Bangladesh is slated to lose the largest amount of land globally — approximately 1000 square km of cultivated land — due to sea level rise. Where will all of those hungry, thirsty, landless millions go? Most will flock to the border looking for avenues to enter, exacerbating an already tense situation not only in the States contiguous to Bangladesh but in cities as far off as Mumbai and Delhi.

Undoubtedly, global warming is not fair. It is exacting the highest price on those least responsible for the problem. But India can show the world that there is another way forward: A self-interested, self-preserving way, focused on clean energy such as solar and wind; on energy efficiency; on providing for its own population's energy needs ahead of foreign corporations; on public transportation plans that strengthen India's vast network of rail and bus transportation routes, rather than weakening it with public subsidies to massive highways and to automakers. The IPCC final draft report urges India and other Asian countries to prepare for the coming climate apocalypse with crop varieties that can withstand higher temperatures, salinated aquifers, and an increase in pests. It also advises better water resource management and better disease monitoring and control. While important, prevention is always the best medicine.

The IPCC final draft report should be seen as a conservative assessment of what lies in store. It clearly implies that incremental or palliative responses to reduce vulnerability are not the answer. India and the other countries of the region need to take a preventative approach by moving their economies away from fossil fuels and toward clean, renewable forms of energy. This is the only way of preserving a sustainable way of life that could be a model for the world. If it pursues what is "fair" in a warming world by continuing to argue that industrialised nation are to blame and need to take urgent action, it will be placing the noose around its own neck while the hangman looks on.

WATER WARS: CHINA'S NEW 'POLITICAL WEAPON'

The wall of water raced through narrow Himalayan gorges in northeast India, gathering speed as it raked the banks of towering trees and boulders. When the torrent struck their island in the Brahmaputra river, the villagers remember, it took only moments to obliterate their houses, possessions and livestock.

No one knows exactly how the disaster happened, but everyone knows whom to blame: neighboring China.

"We don't trust the Chinese," says fisherman Akshay Sarkar at the resettlement site where he has lived since the 2000 flood. "They gave us no warning. They may do it again."

About 800 kilometers (500 miles) east, in northern Thailand, Chamlong Saengphet stands in the Mekong river, in water that comes only up to her shins. She is collecting edible river weeds from dwindling beds. A neighbor has hung up his fishing nets, his catches now too meager.

Using words bordering on curses, they point upstream, toward China. The blame game, voiced in vulnerable river towns and Asian capitals from Pakistan to Vietnam, is rooted in fear that China's accelerating program of damming every major river flowing from the Tibetan plateau will trigger natural disasters, degrade fragile ecologies, divert vital water supplies.

A few analysts and environmental advocates even speak of water as a future trigger for war or diplomatic strong-arming, though others strongly doubt it will come to that. Still, the remapping of the water flow in the world's most heavily populated and thirstiest region is happening on a gigantic scale, with potentially strategic implications.

On the eight great Tibetan rivers alone, almost 20 dams have been built or are under construction while some 40 more are planned or proposed.

China is hardly alone in disrupting the region's water flows. Others are doing it with potentially even worse consequences. But China's vast thirst for power and water, its control over the sources of the rivers and its ever-growing political clout make it a singular target of criticism and suspicion. "Whether China intends to use water as a political weapon or not, it is acquiring the capability to turn off the tap if it wants to – a leverage it can use to keep any riparian neighbours on good behavior," says Brahma Chellaney, an analyst at New Delhi's Center for Policy Research and author of the forthcoming "Water: Asia's New Battlefield."

Analyst Neil Padukone calls it "the biggest potential point of contention between the two Asian giants," China and India. But the stakes may be even higher since those eight Tibetan rivers serve a vast west-east arc of 1.8 billion people stretching from Pakistan to Vietnam's Mekong river delta.

Suspicions are heightened by Beijing's lack of transparency and refusal to share most hydrological and other data. Only China, along with Turkey, has refused to sign a key 1997 U.N. convention on transnational rivers. Beijing gave no notice when it began building three dams on the Mekong – the first completed in 1993 – or the $1.2 billion Zangmu dam, the first on the mainstream of the 2,880-kilometer (1,790-mile) Brahmaputra which was started last November and hailed in official media as "a landmark priority project."

The 2000 flood that hit Sarkar's village, is widely believed to have been caused by the burst of an earthen dam wall on a Brahmaputra tributary. But China has kept silent.

"Until today, the Indian government has no clue about what happened," says Ravindranath, who heads the Rural Volunteer Center. He uses only one name.

Tibet's spiritual leader, the Dalai Lama, has also warned of looming dangers stemming from the Tibetan plateau.

"It's something very, very essential. So, since millions of Indians use water coming from the Himalayan glaciers... I think you (India) should express more serious concern. This is nothing to do with politics, just everybody's interests, including Chinese people," he said in New Delhi last month.

Beijing normally counters such censure by pointing out that the bulk of water from the Tibetan rivers springs from downstream tributaries, with only 13-16 percent originating in China.

Officials also say that the dams can benefit their neighbours, easing droughts and floods by regulating flow, and that hydroelectric power reduces China's carbon footprint.

China "will fully consider impacts to downstream countries," Chinese Foreign Ministry spokeswoman Jiang Yu recently told The Associated Press. "We have clarified several times that the dam being built on the Brahmaputra River has a small storage capacity. It will not have large impact on water flow or the ecological environment of downstream."

For some of China's neighbours, the problem is that they too are building controversial dams and may look hypocritical if they criticize China too loudly.

The four-nation Mekong River Commission has expressed concerns not just about the Chinese dams but about a host of others built or planned in downstream countries. In northeast India, a broad-based movement is fighting central government plans to erect more than 160 dams in the region, and Laos and Cambodia have proposed plans for 11 Mekong dams, sparking environmental protest.

Indian and other governments play down any threats from the Asian colossus. "I was reassured that (the Zangmu dam) was not a project designed to divert water and affect the welfare and availability of water to countries in the lower reaches," India's Foreign Secretary Nirupama Rao said after talks with her Chinese counterpart late last year.

But at the grass roots, and among activists and even some government technocrats, criticism is expressed more readily. "Everyone knows what China is doing, but won't talk about it. China has real power now. If it says something, everyone follows," says Somkiat Khuengchiangsa, a Thai environmental advocate.

Neither the Indian nor Chinese government responded to specific questions from the AP about the dams, but Beijing is signaling that it will relaunch mega-projects after a break of several years in efforts to meet skyrocketing demands for energy and water, reduce dependence on coal and lift some 300 million people out of poverty.

Official media recently said China was poised to put up dams on the still pristine Nu River, known as the Salween downstream. Seven years ago as many as 13 dams were set to go up until Chinese Premier Wen Jiabao ordered a moratorium.

That ban is regarded as the first and perhaps biggest victory of China's nascent green movement. "An improper exploitation of water resources by countries on the upper reaches is going to bring about environmental, social and geological risks," Yu Xiaogang, director of the Yunnan Green Watershed, told The Associated Press. "Countries along the rivers have already formed their own way of using water resources. Water shortages could easily ignite extreme nationalist sentiment and escalate into a regional war."

But there is little chance the activists will prevail. "There is no alternative to dams in sight in China," says Ed Grumbine, an American author on Chinese dams. Grumbine, currently with the Chinese Academy of Sciences in Yunnan province, notes that under its last five-year state plan, China failed to meet its hydroelectric targets and is now playing catch-up in its 2011-2015 plan as it strives to derive 15 percent of energy needs from non-fossil sources, mainly hydroelectric and nuclear.

The arithmetic pointing to more dam-building is clear: China would need 140 gigawatts of extra hydroelectric power to meet its goal. Even if all the dams on the Nu go up, they would provide only 21 gigawatts.

The demand for water region-wide will also escalate, sparking perhaps that greatest anxieties – that China will divert large quantities from the Tibetan plateau for domestic use.

Noting that Himalayan glaciers which feed the rivers are melting due to global warming, India's Strategic Foresight Group last year estimated that in the coming 20 years India, China, Nepal and Bangladesh will face a depletion of almost 275 billion cubic meters (360 billion cubic yards) of annual renewable water.

Padukone expects China will have to divert water from Tibet to its dry eastern provinces. One plan for rerouting the Brahmaputra was outlined in an officially sanctioned 2005 book by a Chinese former army officer, Li Ling. Its title: "Tibet's Waters Will Save China," Analyst Chellaney believes "the issue is not whether China will reroute the Brahmaputra, but when." He cites Chinese researchers and officials as saying that after 2014 work will begin on tapping rivers flowing from the Tibetan plateau to neighboring countries Such a move, he says, would be tantamount to a declaration of war on India.

Others are skeptical. Tashi Tsering, a Tibetan environmentalist at the University of British Columbia who is otherwise critical of China's policies, calls a Brahmaputra diversion "a pipe dream of some Chinese planners."

Grumbine shares the skepticism. "The situation would have to be very dire for China to turn off the taps because the consequences would be huge," he said. "China would alienate every one of its neighbours and historically the Chinese have been very sensitive about maintaining secure borders."

Whatever else may happen, riverside inhabitants along the Mekong and Brahmaputra say the future shock is now. A fisherman from his youth, Boonrian Chinnarat says the Mekong giant catfish, the world's largest freshwater fish, has all but vanished from the vicinity of Thailand's Had Krai village, other once bountiful species have been depleted, and he and fellow fishermen have sold their nets. He blames the Chinese dams.

Phumee Boontom, headman of nearby Pak Ing village, warns that "If the Chinese keep the water and continue to build more dams, life along the Mekong will change forever." Already, he says, he has seen drastic variations in water levels following dam constructions, "like the tides of the ocean — low and high in one day."

Jeremy Bird, who heads the Mekong commission, an intergovernmental body of Laos, Cambodia, Thailand and Laos, sees a tendency to blame China for water-related troubles even when they are purely the result of nature. He says diplomacy is needed, and believes "engagement with China is improving."

Grumbine agrees. "Given the enormous demand for water in China, India and Southeast Asia, if you maintain the attitude of sovereign state, we are lost," he says. "Scarcity in a zero sum situation can lead to conflict but it can also goad countries into more cooperative behavior. It's a bleak picture, but I'm not without hope."

WATER: THE NEW DIMENSION IN INDIA-CHINA RELATIONS

India-China Ties: Will the Use of Water Resources or the securitization of water lead to a 'water war' between the two neighbours, overshadow the border dispute and make relations more strained and complex? The paper dwells on this question and more.

GLOBAL WATER CRISIS

Water Wars are becoming inevitable today as the progressive rate of population expansion, along with rapid urbanization and climate change, has created a situation where the ratio of fresh-water to human population is immensely unproportionate. Though the issue of depleting fresh-water resources does not get the attention as oil does, in a world where a third of the population suffers from water shortage, water can be seen as the new oil. The geopolitical implication of water shortages is often not recognised. A study conducted by the *Strategic Foresight Group (SFG)*, Mumbai titled

'The Himalayan Challenge' alarmingly predicts that *"in the next 20 years, the four countries in the Himalayan sub-region (India, Nepal, China, Bangladesh) will face the depletion of almost 275 billion cubic metres of annual renewable water. For comparison, this is more than the total amount of water available in...Nepal at present."*

Developing countries face the biggest threat of potential water conflict as they often lag behind in effective management of water resources. The South and Southeast Asians regions have tried to limit the possibility of conflict over common water resources by drawing up numerous treaties which include the Mekong River Commission, the treaties of Sarada (1920), Kosi (1954), and Gandak

(1959) between India and Nepal, the Indus Water Treaty between India and Pakistan (1960), the Ganges Waters Treaty between India and Bangladesh (1977), and the Agreement on the Use of Water and Energy Resources of the Syr Darya Basin between Kazakhstan and Uzbekistan in 1998.

Recently, the issue of water war has cropped up in South Asia, home to about half of the world's population, especially between India and China over the river Brahmaputra, large parts of which flows through the northeastern Indian states of Arunachal Pradesh and Assam. Statistics show that from 1999 to 2008, the volume of internal renewable water resources decreased from 2,220 to 2,092 cubic meters per capita in China and from 1,762 to 1,631 cubic meters per capita in India, placing them amongst the countries with the lowest per capita reserve base4. Environmentalist Lester Brown insists that water shortages in the two countries present the largest threat to food security humanity has ever faced.

A large population, need for national water resources, and ineffective water-sharing policies might lead to potential armed conflict between China and India. Moreover, climate change could actually trigger a real water war with India sucked into the vortex of this possible conflict. Melting glaciers would badly affect rivers originating in the Tibetan Plateau and this may force nations in the sub-region to protect its water resources. In fact, these nations might look even beyond their borders and if this happens, tension is bound to mount. Such a situation would force India and China to securitize water sources, leading to real tension. Top leaders of both the countries have already recognised the significance of water security. In 1998, then Chinese vice prime minister Wen Jiabao stated that the "survival of the Chinese nation" was threatened by the country's shortage of water.

In 2007, Prime Minister Manmohan Singh remarked, "Dry land agriculture, changing climate and water scarcity are the new challenges we are facing... given the threat of climate change and global warming, we face the real prospect of reduced supply of water. This threat is of particular concern to us in India as we have, since times immemorial, depended on glaciers for our water supply in this part of our sub-continent."

The cause for conflict not only lies in the fact that both India and China face acute water crisis but also because the Tibetan plateau serves as the common source of water resources for the major South Asian actors- India, Pakistan, Bangladesh, Nepal and China. For China, the Tibetan plateau is a whole new untapped resource, which, if exploited, would help China meet its growing water demands, whereas it is the starting point for the major rivers so crucial for India and Pakistan- the Indus, the Brahmaputra and the Ganges.

WATER CRISIS IN CHINA

China, as the next emerging superpower, is faced with diminishing access to fresh water resources. This increasing water crisis, affecting more than half of the country's 660 cities, is largely due to the uneven distribution of water resources. The arid north and northwest, home to 35 per cent of the population, has only 7 per cent of the country's water resources.

China has three main sources of water: glaciers, surface water and ground water. As of now, China's most pressing problem is not the volume of fresh water available but over-utilisation of water resources by industries, its huge population and mismanagement of resources.

Glaciers

About 49,873 square kilometres of the Tibetan Plateau covering most of the Tibet Autonomous Region and Qinghai province is the most important source of water in China, giving rise to China's two main rivers- the Yellow River and the Yangtze River. Moreover, the Indus, Ganges and Brahmaputra rivers, crucial for China's neighbours—Pakistan, India and Bangladesh—originate from the Tibetan plateau.

Surface Water

China's surface water bears the biggest impact of the water shortage. Though the main source of China's surface water - its rivers and lakes - are replenished by melting glaciers and rainfall,

China over-exploits these resources towards more industrialisation, generating hydroelectric power and for transportation. This over-exploitation of lakes and rivers could cause them to dry up and leave the population in a drought-like situation without any access to fresh water.

Ground Water

Over-extraction of groundwater and falling water tables are big problems in China, particularly in the north. China gets about 70 per cent of its drinking water and about 40 per cent of its agricultural irrigation waters from its ground-water sources.

However, these reserves are fast getting dried-up due to over-utilisation and pollution.

Faced with acute water shortage, China responded by proposing two major water diversion projects to transfer water from one region to the other: the *South-North Water Diversion Project* and the *Great Western Route Diversion Project*. The idea of a South- North water diversion was first introduced by Mao Zedong in 1952 and is estimated to be completed by 205013. This project is supposed to transfer nearly 44.8 million cubic meters of Southern waters from the Yangtze River to Beijing and Tianjin in the dry North. The issue of controversy, however, surrounds the Great Western Route Diversion Project which will have huge ramifications for the lower riparian states of India and Bangladesh. It involves building a dam on the 'Great Bend' of the Brahmaputra, known as the *Shuomatan Point* —where the river does a u-turn and starts flowing east to India-- into Arunachal Pradesh and then crossing the plains of Assam, eventually flowing into Bangladesh.

SINO-INDIAN HISTORICAL RELATIONS

The Sino-Indian War of 1962 over a disputed Himalayan border left a legacy of suspicion and tense relations between the two countries. The border dispute remains unsolved even today with China claiming India's northeastern state of Arunachal Pradesh bordering southern Tibet. India, too, claims that China is occupying about 15,000 square miles of the Himalayan plateau- Aksai Chin. Even after a series of bi-lateral dialogues, the border issue has not been resolved. Now, in the light of China's race towards superpower status, Beijing appears more determined than ever to ward off competition from other emerging Asian countries, particularly India. This is a reason why China has adopted a hard- line strategy towards India, including a heavy presence of People's Liberation Army in the disputed Himalayan border, many incidents of violation of the McMohan line-of-control, increased aggressiveness in claiming Arunachal Pradesh and offensive attacks on India in the state- controlled Chinese media.

India and China has had a series of bilateral dialogues but the issue of water never came up until recently. Now, the issues causing tension between China and India extend beyond border disputes. Water is becoming a key security issue in India-China relations, paving the way for a new era of hostility.

The Zangmu Dam and Diversion issue

Both India and China's economic growth and development depends on the availability of water. Both the Indian and Chinese economies continue to grow at a frantic pace and both countries face acute water shortage which soon can be comparable to the kind of water scarcity prevalent in the Middle East in terms of per capita availability. The expansion of irrigated farming, growing industries and rising demands of the middle class calls for both countries to ensure a stable source of water supply. As such, China has been engaged in major inter-river water transfer projects on the Tibetan plateau, the world's largest freshwater repository after the polar ice-caps. However, these activities are of great concern to India and other lower riparian states such as Bangladesh and Pakistan. Tibet is the source of major Indian rivers and any water transfer or diversion projects on the Tibetan plateau would reduce international river flows into the lower riparian countries. India depends on rivers that originate in China for one third of its renewable water supplies.

China is expected to face 25 per cent water shortfall by 2030[18]. With rising power shortage and international pressure to reduce carbon emission, China is now focusing on generating hydro power that requires building dams. As such Brahmaputra and other rivers originating in its territory could become pawns in the political game. So far China's hydropower focus was on Yangtze River –

across which the Three Gorges Dam was built – and the Yellow River. Now China is eyeing the Yarlung Tsangpo (in Tibet), known as Brahmaputra in India and Yaluzangbu in China.

It is the world's highest river, and also one of the fastest-flowing. China's plans for the Yarlung Tsangpo has two components- one focusing on generating hydropower, and the other, which China restrains from talking about in public, is the northward re-routing of the Brahmaputra's water to the dry Yellow river in the northwestern provinces of Xinjiang and Gansu.

There is concern in India over China's plans to dam the Yarlung Tsangpo (Brahmaputra). The Zangmu Dam that China is building is just the first of 28 dams that Beijing plans to build on the Yarlung Tsangpo in Tibet, including a hydel power generation plant at Zangmu on the middle reaches of the Brahmaputra, less than 200 kilometres from the Indian border. China had initially denied that they were constructing a dam on the Brahmaputra river, even after the contract was awarded. It was only in April 2010 that Yang Jiechi, Chinese Foreign Minister, officially revealed that they were constructing the Zangmu Dam. The Zangmu dam is part of the Zangmu Hydropower Project and is estimated to support a 510 MW power station. It is being built at Gyaca County in the Shannan Prefecture of Tibet Autonomous Region. Construction on the dam began in 2009 and is expected to be completed by 2015. Specifications for the dam are uncertain as China has not shared much information.

The issue of more serious concern to India is China's plans of diverting the Brahmaputra. The Brahmaputra originates in southwestern Tibet as the Yarlung Tsangpo River. In India, it is called Dihang (Arunachal Pradesh) and Brahmaputra (Assam) and in Bangladesh is called Jamuna. This 2900 km long river lies partly in India – 918 km, China – 1625 km and Bangladesh – 337 km. The Brahmaputra emerges from the Khanglung glacier at an altitude of 5,300 metres in Southern Tibet and flows in an easterly direction parallel to the Himalayas for 1,100 kilometres. The average discharge of the river is about 19,300 cubic metres per second (cusecs) and floods can reach over 1,00,000 cubic metres per second (cusec). The Brahmaputra Basin accounts for 573 billion cubic meters of surface water resource in the Northeast. It was declared National Waterway No. 2 of India in 1988.

The real worry for India, however, is not whether China will divert the Brahmaputra but when, as China has already identified the point of diversion- the U-bend where the Brahmaputra forms the world's longest and deepest canyon just before entering India. It is at this Great Bend that China plans to divert water, and also build hydroelectric power projects that could generate 40,000 megawatts of power. The diversion of the water is part of a larger hydro- engineering project, the South-North water diversion scheme, which involves three man-made rivers carrying water to its arid North region. With 56.5 per cent of Brahmaputra River's length and 50.5 per cent of the area of the drainage basin lying within Tibet, China naturally has a claim to at least a share of Brahmaputra's water. Moreover, with weak international laws and no candid water-sharing arrangements between the two countries, China has all the leverage in the issue. Beijing gave no notice when it started building the $1.2 billion Zangmu dam on the Brahmaputra. Also, China still chooses to remain secretive about the diversion issue as it "implies environmental devastation of India's northeastern plains and eastern Bangladesh and would thus be akin to a declaration of water war...".

More dams on the Brahmaputra: China's Plan for Energy Development 2011-15

China has approved construction of three more dams on the Brahmaputra in Tibet in addition to the Zangmu dam. A document titled 'Plan for Energy Development during the Period of the Twelfth Five-year Plan', which has been posted in China's State Council website, mentions three dams to be built at Dagu, Jiacha and Jiexu over the river Brahmaputra. The document, listing projects to be completed in China's 12th five year plan (2011-15), made a passing reference to the three dams without any details. The new projects were reportedly approved by China at the State Council or Cabinet meeting on January 23, 2013.

During an informal discussion between Indian and Chinese officials on February 5, 2013, the latter claimed that the new dams would not have any impact on the flow of water to downstream areas in India. Beijing also reassured that the run-of-the-river hydropower projects on the river would not come in the way of the flood control and disaster reduction efforts in the lower reaches and would not disturb the ecological balance.

But this news led to a wave of protests in India. The head of the main opposition Bharatiya Janata Party (BJP) Rajnath Singh said February 13, 2013 India should register its strong protest and also take up at international forums the issue of China's plan to build dams on the Brahmaputra as it would harm downstream interests, particularly that of Northeast India. Chief Minister of Arunachal Pradesh, the state closest to China, Nabam Tuki said February 16, 2013: "China building the three dams will affect the interest of people in the downstream areas. We will soon move New Delhi to take up this issue with China in the interest of the people." Assam Chief Minister Tarun Gogoi also wrote to Prime Minister Manmohan Singh requesting him to take up the matter regarding the construction of the three dams on the Brahmaputra with Beijing.

If China continues with its plan to build more dams on the upper reaches of the Brahmaputra, it would surely affect the downstream areas in Northeast India. As this region is primarily dependent on agriculture, such depletion in water resources due to dam building would have an adverse impact on the economy of the region. On February 3, 2013, an NGO in Guwahati alleged that China is building 26 hydropower dams on the upper reaches of the Brahmaputra in Tibet. They further said that once China completes these projects, India will receive 64 per cent less water during the monsoon and 85 per cent less in the non-monsoon season. If these claims turn out to be true, it could seriously harm India's interests.

IMPLICATIONS OF CHINA'S HYDRO PROJECTS

Building of mega dams on the Brahmaputra is opposed by certain political parties and organizations in the Northeast. Rising protests against building dams in Arunachal Pradesh could make the Indian government decide to stop construction of dams there.

But what about the dams China is likely to build on the Yarlung Tsangpo in Tibet? Even if construction of dams in Arunachal Pradesh stops, the existence of similar dams would still be a threat and would nullify any security acquired from preventing mega dams in Arunachal Pradesh. In such a case, what would be the stand of the anti-dam protestors? China would surely not be bothered even if there are protests against it in India.

India's Lower Subansiri Dam is the biggest hydroelectric project undertaken in India so far and is a run- of-the- river scheme on the river Subansiri. The project is facing stiff protests from political parties like Asom Gana Parishad, Bhartiya Janata Party and organizations like the Krishak Mukti Sangram Samity (KMSS), All Assam Students Union (AASU) etc. arguing that the project would affect the downstream riverine environment and could have an devastating effect in case of a major earthquake in the region. The Lower Subansiri dam is at an altitude of about 150 metres, 116 metres high and where the river perhaps flows at a gradient of not more than 30 cm/km. In contrast, the Zangmu dam has been constructed at an altitude of 3,200m where the river flows over a much steeper gradient. As such, the Zangmu dam is far more vulnerable to a dam break caused by an earthquake. Even if the dam doesn't collapse in an earthquake, damages to the sluices through which the water flows and to the spillways used to get rid of excess water could create havoc downstream. The Indian government and political parties should look into the Zangmu Dam issue first before worrying over the Subansiri project.

Moreover, diversion of the Brahmaputra, the lifeline of India's Northeast, would wreak havoc in the region. With the water being diverted, the amount of water in the Brahmaputra will fall significantly, affecting the region. Environmental experts report that roughly 60 per cent of the total water flow will fall drastically if China is successful in diverting the Brahmaputra. India has raised concerns about the project on the grounds that it could pose a grave threat to the farmers and environment in northeast India. It will severely impact agriculture and fishing as the salinity of water will increase, as will silting in the downstream area. Moreover, India being a lower riparian state would be at the mercy of upper riparian China in matters of releasing pre-regulated water flows back into the river whenever needed.

The threat to Bangladesh is even greater as Bangladesh is the lowest riparian state of the Brahmaputra and the river is more vital to it than even India. Bangladesh is very much concerned over water diversion of the Brahmaputra by China as well as on the building of dams by China and India on the Brahmaputra. It fears the quantity of water reaching Bangladesh would reduce drastically leading to lowering in agricultural production and aggravate environmental problems.

China's dam projects on the Mekong have already caused tension with its neighbours- Vietnam, Laos, Cambodia and Thailand. China's Minister for Water Resources, Wang Shucheng, said that this project is "unnecessary, unfeasible and unscientific. But no matter what China's real plans may be, if Beijing goes ahead with its plans on the Yarlung Tsangpo without any sort if international agreement, it would affect not only China's nuclear neighbours, India and Pakistan, both facing water crisis, but could also lead to regional instability in an already volatile South Asia.

Solutions

Experts like Brahma Chellaney insists that, "*interstate conflict will surface only when an idea is translated into action to benefit one country at the expense of a neighbouring one.*" In this context, South Asia will not have a real water war unless China goes ahead with its proposed plans of diverting the Brahmaputra at the expense of its neighbours India and Bangladesh.

As such, international water sharing treaties will play a key role in addressing the threat of a water war. India is an upper riparian state with respect to Pakistan and Bangladesh and a lower riparian to China, Nepal and Bhutan. Therefore, India needs to recognise its geo-strategic location and aim to effectively pursue new trans- boundary riparian treaties while reworking on the existing treaties.

India has water treaties with Bangladesh and Pakistan (both downstream) and with Bhutan and Nepal (both upstream) but it doesn't have any water treaty with China. China has about 10 major rivers - Yangtze, Yarlung Tsangpo, Yellow, Heilongjiang, Songhuajiang, Zhujiang, Lancang, Nujiang, Hanjiang and Liaohe flowing out of its territory to 11 countries - India, Bangladesh, Vietnam, Russia, Kazakhstan, North Korea, Myanmar, Mongolia, Laos, Thailand and Cambodia and none flow in from outside. This puts it in the unique position of controlling international rivers and India urgently needs to pursue a regional water treaty with China. The Indus Water Treaty (1960) which demarcated the Indus river waters between India and Pakistan shows that despite historical conflicts, water sharing treaties could prove to be quite successful.

Also, even though China has leverage over rivers flowing out from its territories, the Berlin Rules on Water Resources, 2004 states that nations sharing water should make reasonable efforts not to cause harm to one another by the ways in which the water is used. The document states the requirement of transparency of information related to water resources and their usage to the international community, particularly in those cases where nations share a water resource. It asks for equitable and reasonable utilization of the water resources by the water sharing nations. China cannot unilaterally start massive hydro-engineering projects without formal river-basin arrangements with downstream states. It would have been wise on the part of India and China to have signed the UN convention on non-navigational uses of international water courses, 1997, which provides a mechanism to deal with trans-border waters. Only 17 nations signed this convention which doesn't include the major South Asian actors— India, Nepal, Bangladesh and China. Also, building up on the issue of transparency, China has always been opaque on its hydro-engineering plans, refusing to share information or permitting on-site visits. India should keep track of what China is doing with the Brahmaputra. Talks with China should be held at regular intervals so that India remains apprised of the situation.

The Brahmaputra River has not been properly utilized in India. Out of the total of 84,044 MW hydropower potential of the country, the Northeast carries a potential of 31,857 MW (37 per cent of the country), of which only 3 per cent has so far been tapped (Brahmaputra Board, 2005). Enough projects are needed on the Brahmaputra if India wants to have a stake on the river.

Retired Colonel P K Gautam, research fellow at the Institute for Defence Studies and Analyses, adds that *"if China builds a dam on the Brahmaputra now, and we complain about lesser water flows later, it could say that India doesn't have any projects in the northeast."*

The Brahmaputra was declared National Waterway No. 2 of India and though the river is navigable most time of the year, it has not been fully utilised. Water transport services are used for the transportation of passengers and goods alike across the state and to neighbouring West Bengal but the infrastructure is not good. Water transport service should be modernized on the Brahmaputra so that it can also become a major mode of transport for passengers and cargo. There is urgent need for utilising the water of the Brahmaputra in an effective way through multi-purpose big dams on the river, with provisions for irrigation and flood control besides generation of electricity. However, environmental norms should not be flouted for this.

In an interview with Tariq Ahmed Karim, Bangladesh's High Commissioner to India on this important issue, the need for better monitoring and regulating fresh water sources in South Asia was highlighted. He stated, "...In such a diminishing fresh-water world, water may have to be declared as a scare and fungible resource whose management and administration needs to be reposed with an authority that is larger than the present geo-political configurations of states-provinces and national governments. Citizenry of such a hard-pressed fresh-water world must adopt rules analogous to the rights of citizenry in today's nation-states, the fundamental underpinnings of which are two, namely: rights go hand in hand with responsibilities (to the state and fellow citizens): and no one citizen's rights can be at the expense of the rights of another fellow citizen..."

What Karim suggests is a South Asian water regulatory and monitoring body, something that is in India's interest like a Himalayan Rivers Commission to better manage water issues in the sub-region. He goes on: "... In this context, we in South Asia must, sooner rather than later, politically evolve to a regime of water governance, in which the member states will have, by mutual consensus and consent, set up a South Asian Water Resources Management Authority (which will have real authority and powers vested in it, as opposed to the present configuration of a 'South Asian Association for Regional Cooperation'). This supra- national authority will measure, monitor and keep track of all available water resources (whether ground or surface), set strict uses, conservation and management regulations, and oversee adherence to and enforcement of these regulations, to ensure the rights equally for all its denizens."

Another option that China and India could explore is constructing shared dams that would mutually benefit each other. The concept of having shared dams has worked out for Brazil and Paraguay with the Itaipu Dam, located on the border of Brazil and Paraguay. It is the world's largest operating hydroelectric project. The electricity generated from Itaipu Dam is estimated to be greater than the electricity generated by China's Three Gorges Dam. The dam supplies Paraguay with more than 90 per cent of its electrical needs.

The government should hold awareness camps, conduct seminars, prepare documentaries to make the general public aware about the requirement of building dams across the Brahmaputra so that people stop protesting over projects like the Subansiri Dam and instead focus on the broader picture.

Conclusion

Water is becoming the source of a potential conflict between India and China. Lack of transparency from the Chinese side is further aggravating the situation. Lack of a water sharing treaty and bare minimum data sharing on water flow is causing India to look at China's intentions on use of the Brahmaputra waters with suspicion. Adding to it, the potentially devastating effect that Chinese dams may have on the downstream reaches is a major cause of concern for India.

There are two components to the threat of a water war between India and China. First is the problem of water shortage in both the countries which would seriously hinder development if not fulfilled. Second, this problem of water shortage would thereby force both countries to securitize water resources which means China may unilaterally carry out diversion projects if need be. If Beijing goes ahead with its plans on the Yarlung Tsangpo without any international agreements with the lower riparian states of India and Bangladesh, it may lead to a major conflict over water.

The silent 'water war' is now finally becoming a reality and India should be ready to face it. The water conflict is also slowly adding a deeper layer of intricacy to the border dispute. In order to prevent the conflict from escalating, the Indian government needs to diplomatically take up the issue with the Chinese government and push for a water sharing treaty. Also India needs to work on a rapid pace so that the Brahmaputra river can be optimally utilized, both for navigable and non-navigable purposes. The concept of shared dams need to thought of and discussed at diplomatic levels between the two countries. Efforts to douse the conflict before it takes a greater form need to be made in earnest. That alone may reduce the threat of a full blown conflict between the two Asian giants over water. And how could the longstanding border dispute unfold in the days ahead? Market forces, in fact, may come to dictate terms and trade could well keep the Chinese, or the Indians for that matter, away from taking recourse to any military adventure or misadventure.

4

South Asia's Water: Unquenchable Thirst and Politics

Compared with much of South Asia, Kashmir, a disputed territory in northern India, has many rivers and relatively few people. But even here fresh water is running short. To see how contentious this can be, drive half a day south to where the Baglihar dam (shown above) is rising up. An enormous wall bisects the valley, dressing it in white spray, and three huge jets of water blast from its sluices.

Half complete, the dam is already a local wonder that tourists gape at. It generates 450MW for the starved energy grid of Jammu and Kashmir. Once the scheme fully tames the water, by steering it through a tunnel blasted into the mountain, the grid will gain another 450MW.

The river swirls away, white-crested and silt-laden, racing to the nearby border with Pakistan. But there Baglihar is a source of bitterness. Pakistanis cite it as typical of an intensifying Indian threat to their existence, a conspiracy to divert, withhold or misuse precious water that is rightfully theirs. Officials in Islamabad and diplomats abroad are primed to grumble about it. Pakistan's most powerful man, the head of the armed forces, General Ashfaq Kayani, cites water to justify his "India-centric" military stance.

Others take it further. "Water is the latest battle cry for *jihadis,*" says B.G. Verghese, an Indian writer. "They shout that water must flow, or blood must flow." Lashkar-e-Taiba, a Pakistani terror group, likes to threaten to blow up India's dams. Last year a Pakistani extremist, Abdur Rehman Makki, told a rally that if India were to "block Pakistan's waters, we will let loose a river of blood."

Assorted hardliners cheer them on. A blood-curdling editorial in *Nawa-i-Waqt*, a Pakistani newspaper, warned in April that "Pakistan should convey to India that a war is possible on the issue of water and this time war will be a nuclear one."

Upstream such outbursts are usually dismissed as proof that troubled Pakistan is, as ever, spoiling for a fight. Water is merely the latest excuse. India is not misbehaving, says Mr Verghese placidly. It fails to take all it is entitled to from cross-border rivers in Kashmir. Run-of-the-river dams like Baglihar consume nothing, since water must flow to run turbines. Such a dam, he says, merely briefly delays a river.

Indians point out, too, that Pakistan enjoys a rare guarantee: the Indus Water Treaty, struck in 1960 by far-sighted engineers and diplomats who saw that after the partition of land, water had to be shared out too. The treaty, which has survived three wars, details exactly how each side must use cross-border rivers. Mostly this applies to the tributaries that flow from Kashmir to form the massive Indus river, Pakistan's lifeblood.

If Indians abide by the treaty, then in theory at least they cannot be misbehaving. They see Baglihar as proof of co-operation, not a threat. When Pakistan objected to the dam's design, India accepted international arbitration, the first case in the treaty's history. Outside experts studied the dam and ordered small changes. But in effect they said it posed no threat to Pakistan. And last year the dispute was officially ended by the two governments.

Downstream, however, few sound satisfied. "The Baglihar decision...allowed a reservoir on a river coming into Pakistan, and now a precedent is set," laments John Briscoe, a water expert formerly of the World Bank who advises Pakistan. The Pakistanis fear Indian control over the headwaters of the Indus. And Indian bureaucrats fuel these fears with obsessive secrecy about all water data.

Bashir Ahmad, a geologist in Srinagar, Kashmir who studied the Baglihar dam, gives grim warning about the Indians' future intentions: "They will switch the Indus off to make Pakistan solely dependent on India. It's going to be a water bomb." A less excitable report in February by America's Senate offered a similar assessment: "The cumulative effect of [many dam] projects could give India the ability to store enough water to limit the supply to Pakistan at crucial moments in the growing season." Dams are a source of "significant bilateral tension", the report concludes.

More dams are to come, as India's need to power its economy means it is quietly spending billions on hydropower in Kashmir. The Senate report totted up 33 hydro projects in the border area. The state's chief minister, Omar Abdullah, says dams will add an extra 3,000MW to the grid in the next eight years alone. Some analysts in Srinagar talk of over 60 dam projects, large and small, now on the books.

Any of these could spark a new confrontation. The latest row is over the Kishanganga river (called the Neelum in Pakistan) as each country races to build a hydropower dam either side of Kashmir's line of control. India's dam will divert some of the river down a 22km (14-mile) mountain tunnel to turbines. To Pakistani fury, that will lessen the water flow to the downstream dam, so its capacity will fall short of a planned 960MW.

Pakistan also claims (though the evidence is shaky) that 600,000 people will suffer by getting less water for irrigation. Again it insisted on international arbitration at The Hague. In September, to Pakistani delight, India was ordered to suspend some of its building for further assessments to be made. But India still looks likelier to come away happy in the end, as the treaty foresaw and permitted the Indian design, and India is likely to finish its dam ahead of Pakistan in any case, by 2016 rather than 2018.

WHEN CHINA'S UPSTREAM

Countries downstream have genuine reasons to fret. Pakistan is exposed. Like Egypt it exists around a single great river, though the Indus is nearly twice the Nile's size when it reaches the sea. It waters over 80% of Pakistan's 22m hectares (54m acres) of irrigated land, using canals built by the British. In turn that farming provides 21% of the country's GDP, as well as livelihoods for a big proportion of its 180m people. Many of them are already thirsty.

On average each Indian gets just 1,730 cubic metres of fresh water a year, less than a quarter of the global average of 8,209 cubic metres. Yet that looks bountiful compared with each Pakistani's share: a mere 1,000 cubic metres. Worse yet, South Asia's fresh water mostly falls in a few monsoon months. The dreadful floods this year and last showed that untamed and unpredictable rivers can be both resource and threat.

More rows between India and Pakistan are certain. India may keep on dismissing them as Pakistani bluster, an easy thing to do if you are upstream. But India is downstream in another highly tricky area: its border with China.

Tension already exists over the status of India's Arunachal Pradesh state, which China refuses to recognise. A quarrel over rivers in the region could serve as a focus for wider disputes about territory. A measure of the recent slump in relations came when, to the fury of India's authorities, China blocked an attempt by the Asian Development Bank to prepare for a dam project in Arunachal Pradesh. And one of India's largest rivers, the Brahmaputra (Tsangpo in China), flows south from the Tibetan plateau and into Assam not far from the disputed land.

Angry Indian politicians, activists, bloggers and journalists claim that water-starved China (with 8% of the world's fresh water but 20% of its population) has plans to divert the Tsangpo/Brahmaputra to farmers in its central and eastern regions. Feelings are running so high that India's prime minister, Manmohan Singh, felt obliged to issue a statement on August 4th saying that China's leaders had assured him there were no such plans afoot. And though a few run-of-the-river hydroelectric schemes are being built upstream on the Tsangpo, none of these could change the river's course. Cool heads point out that speculation about China channelling the torrent from near the border, at a spot known as the Great Bend, looks fantastical, at least at present.

Chinese engineers would need to use nuclear explosions to have a chance of making tunnels through a series of ridged mountains to get water east from the Great Bend. Although plans have existed since the fourth century to take water from China's west to the east, and the scheme was pushed by Mao Zedong, the engineering, at least for now, appears to be technically impossible. Yet broader Indian strategic fears—the fact that the Chinese control the Tibetan plateau, which is the source of water for parts of densely populated northern India—will evaporate no more easily than Pakistani fears of India.

An ever-thirstier region

The scarcity of water in South Asia will become harder to manage as demand rises. South Asia's population of 1.5 billion is growing by 1.7% a year, says the World Bank, which means an extra 25m or so mouths to water and feed: imagine dropping North Korea's entire population on the region each year. Greater wealth in South Asia brings with it a soaring demand for food, especially for water-intensive meat and other protein. Industry and energy-producers also use water, though unlike farms they return it, eventually, to the rivers.

Worse, overall supply will not only fail to keep up with rising demand but is likely to fall (unless a cheap way is found to turn sea water fresh). The Himalayan glaciers are melting. A Dutch study last year of the western Himalayas reckoned that shrunken glaciers will cut the flow of the Indus by some 8% by mid-century. Flows may also get less regular, especially if glacial dams form, withholding water, and then collapse, causing floods.

Others give even scarier predictions. Sundeep Waslekar, who heads a Mumbai think-tank, the Strategic Foresight Group, which has picked water as a long-term threat to Asian stability, sees a "mega-arc of hydro insecurity" emerging from western China along the Himalayas to the Middle East and farther west. The strain of bigger populations, diminishing water tables and a changing climate could all conspire to produce a storm of troubles. South Asia is especially vulnerable: Mr Waslekar sees a cut of 20% in total available fresh water over the next two decades.

The greatest threat of all would be from any change to the monsoon, which delivers most of the region's fresh water each summer. Here, again, worries arise. Indian meteorologists who have studied rainfall data from 1901 to 2004 have noted signs in recent decades of more dry spells within the peak monsoon months. If these lead to weaker, or less predictable, monsoons in future (though this year's was about normal) the consequences for farmers could be dire. In any case, the cost of running short of water is already becoming clearer. The*Lancet*, a British medical journal, reported last year that up to 77m Bangladeshis had been poisoned by arsenic—the largest mass-poisoning in history. It was the result of villagers pumping up groundwater from ever deeper aquifers. The same poison is now entering crops and more of the food chain. Filthy water and bad sanitation spread diseases, such as diarrhoea and cholera, which kill hundreds of thousands of Indian children every year, says Unicef, the UN's children's agency. Several South Asian rivers, suffering from weaker flows, have become a sludge of human and animal waste, dangerous to drink and wash in and unsafe even for watering crops.

All over the region water tables are dropping as bore holes drive deeper. In the dry season even some of the larger rivers slow to a trickle. Knut Oberhagemann, a water expert in Dhaka, Bangladesh, says that the flow of the mighty Ganges where it enters Bangladesh is at times a pitiful few hundred cubic metres a second, so low that "you can walk across the river". When the same river, at this point called the Padma, reaches the coast, it is often so feeble that the sea intrudes, poisoning the land with salt.

The same problem curses the delta of the Indus in Pakistan. There a semi-desert was turned into some of the most fertile land on earth by British-built irrigation canals. But as the sea encroaches on low, flat land, rivers at times are flowing backwards, laments a local environmental activist. Take away the fresh water—around 60% of which is now lost to seepage and evaporation because of the bad management of those canals—and the desert will eventually come back.

Save or snatch

Governments in South Asia can respond to growing scarcity in one of two ways. The first is to improve the way they use the water they have, both by managing it better and by co-operating with one another. The second is to try to grab as much water as they can from their neighbours.

Better management of irrigation canals and better farming techniques would help hugely to cut waste. In Pakistan bitter rows between provinces have long scotched coherent planning. Wealthy Punjab, a big farming province, is routinely accused by downstream Sindh (and by others too) of taking an unfair share of the water.

And Pakistan badly needs more dams to control floods, store monsoon water and make electricity (China is said to have offered to help Pakistan build a series of big dams, and has already sent engineers to help speed along the new one on the Neelum/ Kishanganga). Only about 10% of the potential hydropower of the Indus has been tapped so far, and only 30 days' average river flow can be stored (by contrast, the Colorado in America has dams to store 1,000 days'-worth).

Many governments are at least thinking in terms of dams and co-operation. Mr Waslekar reckons that 60-80 big dams (mostly for energy) will be built in South Asia in the next two or three decades, at a cost of hundreds of billions of dollars. In many cases—as for example in mountainous Bhutan, where the economy gets a huge boost from selling hydropower to India—this can foster economic and diplomatic co-operation. India has visions of one day persuading unstable but immensely water-rich Nepal to follow suit. The country is the source of more than 40% of the Ganges's water, and Indian analysts talk dreamily of 40GW of hydropower potential waiting to be used.

Other cross-border water deals are pending. Cosy ties with Bangladesh's government mean that India can more easily build dams on some of the several dozen rivers that cross their shared frontier. In September Mr Singh visited Dhaka to sign a deal with Bangladesh to allow the latest hydro dam to go up on the Teesta river. Though the deal was postponed at the last minute by a row with a regional Indian leader, it now looks set to go ahead. However there are bitter memories in Bangladesh of an earlier deal, on the Ganges, which allowed India to put up a barrage to block the river's flow in the dry season.

Tentative signs of wider co-operation exist. China issues twice-daily reports on the Tsangpo river flow in the flood season, separately to India and to Bangladesh. This could be seen as encouraging, if the two giants of the region wished to consider getting together over water. Indeed if full-scale friendliness were ever sought, an immense opportunity awaits.

Mr Verghese points out that the Tsangpo/Brahmaputra falls 2,450 metres (8,000 feet) over a few kilometres in China just before it reaches the Indian border. Send it through a 100km tunnel from the Tibetan plateau down to Assam and an enormous 54,000MW could be generated. One day its power could light not only much of northeast India and Bangladesh, but nearby Myanmar and beyond. Such a mega-structure would become a keystone for regional co-operation.

It will almost certainly never be built. Analysts have suggested that, given the generally dire relations between South Asian countries, water will provoke clashes rather than co-operation. A 2009 report for the CIA concluded that "the likelihood of conflict between India and Pakistan over shared river resources is expected to increase", though it added that elsewhere in the region "the risk of armed interstate conflict is minor". And a Bangladeshi security expert, Major-General Muniruzzaman, predicts that India's "coercive diplomacy", its refusal to negotiate multilaterally on such issues as river-sharing, means that "if ever there were a localised conflict in South Asia, it will be over water."

WATER SHORTAGES, MEGA-PROJECTS AND ENVIRONMENTAL POLITICS IN CHINA, INDIA, AND SOUTHEAST ASIA

Since we tend to take water for granted, it is almost a bad sign when it is in the news; and lately there have been plenty of water-related stories from South, East, and Southeast Asia. They have ranged from the distressingly familiar — suicides of North Indian farmers who can no longer get enough water – to stories most people find surprising (evidence that pressure from water in the reservoir behind the new Zipingpu dam may have triggered the massive Sichuan earthquake last May). Meanwhile, glaciers, which almost never made news, are now generating plenty of worrisome headlines.

Conflicts over water are found in every era and region: the English word "rivalry" comes from a Latin term for "one who uses the same stream as another." And more recently, questions about who gets to exploit water have become intertwined with questions about where the technological and ecological limits of our ability to do so lie – or should lie.

Nowhere are the stakes higher than in the Himalayas and on the Tibetan plateau: here the water-related dreams and fears of half the human race come together. Other regions have their own conflicts: the Jordan, the Tigris, the Colorado, and the Parana are just a few of the better-known cases where multiple states make societies make claims on over-stressed rivers. But no other region combines comparable numbers of people, scarcity of rainfall, dependence on agriculture, tempting sites for mega-projects, and vulnerability to climate change. Glaciers and annual snowfalls in this area feed rivers serving 47% of the world's people; and the unequalled heights from which those waters descend could provide staggering amounts of hydropower. Meanwhile, both India and China face the grim reality that their economic and social achievements — both during their "planned" and "market" phases – have depended on unsustainable rates of groundwater extraction. As hundreds of millions face devastating shortages and the technical and financial power of these states (and of some of their smaller neighbours) increase, plans are moving forward for harnessing Himalayan waters through the largest construction projects in history. Even when looked at individually, some of the projects carry enormous risks; and even if they work as planned, they will hurt large numbers of people as they help others. (Nor is it at all clear that many of them will help as much as spending comparable sums on less heroic measures, such as fixing leaky pipes or tightening enforcement of wastewater treatment standards, would do.) Looked at collectively – as overlapping, sometimes contradictory demands on environments that will also feel some of the sharpest effects of global warming over the next several decades – their possible implications are staggering.

The projects to manipulate Himalayan water now completed, planned or underway are numerous, and their possible interactions are complex. And since many of the agencies responsible for them are far from transparent, the possible scenarios quickly multiply to a point where they are almost impossible to keep track of. But some basic – and frightening – outlines do emerge if we start from China – which is, for various reasons, the most dynamic actor in the story — and then move across the lands that border it to the Southwest, South, and Southeast.

CHINA'S WATER WOES AND THE PUSH TO THE SOUTHWEST

Water has always been a problem in China, and effective control of it has been associated with both personal heroism and legitimate sovereignty for as far back as our records go – or perhaps even further, since the mythological sage ruler Yu proved his right to rule by controlling floods. But water scarcity has probably been an even greater problem than excesses, especially in the modern period. Surface and near-surface water per capita in China today is roughly ¼ of the global average, and worse yet, it is distributed very unevenly. The North and Northwest, with about 380 million people (almost 30% of the national population) and over half the country's arable land, have about 7% of its surface water, so that its per capita resources are roughly 20-25% of the average for China as a whole, or 5-6% of the global average; a more narrowly defined North China plain may have only 10-15% of the per capita supply for the country as a whole, or less than 4% of the global average. Northern waters also carry far heavier sediment loads than southern ones – most readings on Southern rivers fall within EU maxima for drinking water, while some readings on the middle and lower Yellow River, and the Wei and Yongding Rivers are 25 -50% of that level; water shortages are such that Northern rivers also carry far more industrial pollutants per cubic meter, even though the South has far more industry. Northern China also has unusually violent seasonal fluctuations in water supply; both rainfall and river levels change much more over the course of the year than in either Europe or the Americas. North China's year to year rainfall fluctuations are also well above average (though not as severe as those in North and Northwest India). While the most famous of China's roughly 90,000 large (over 15 meters high) and medium-sized dams are associated with hydro-power — about which more below — a great many exist mostly to store water during the peak flow of rivers for use at other times.

The People's Republic has made enormous efforts to address these problems – and achieved impressive short-term successes that are now extremely vulnerable. Irrigated acreage has more than tripled since 1950 (mostly during the Maoist period), with the vast majority of those gains coming in the North and Northwest. It was this, more than anything else, that turned the notorious "land of famine" of the 1850-1950 period into a crucial grain surplus area, and contributed mightily to improving per capita food supplies for a national population that has more than doubled since 1949. Plentiful water supplies made it possible for much of northern China to grow two crops a year for the first time in history (often by adding winter wheat, which needs a lot of water); and plentiful, reliable supplies of water were necessary to allow the use of new seed varieties and plenty of chemical fertilizer (which can otherwise burn the soil). And, of course, irrigation greatly reduced the problem of rain coming at the wrong time of year, or not coming at all some years. During the previous two centuries farming in northern China had become steadily more precarious in part because population growth had lowered the water table – early 20th century maps show much smaller lakes than 150 years earlier, and there are many reports of wells needing to be re-drilled at great expense – and in part because the safety net the Qing had once provided fell apart. But beginning in the 1950s, and especially in the 1960s (after the setbacks of the Great Leap Forward) things turned around very impressively.

Much of that turnaround, however, relied on very widespread use of deep wells, using gasoline or electrical power to bring up underground water from unprecedented depths. Large-scale exploitation of North China groundwater began in the 1960s, peaked in the 1970s at roughly 10 times the annual extraction rates that prevailed during 1949 -1961, and has remained level since about 1980 at roughly 4 times the 1949-1961 level. But this amount of water withdrawal is unsustainable. The North China water table has been dropping by roughly 4-6 feet per year for quite some time now, and by over 10 feet per year in many places; some people estimate that if this rate of extraction is maintained, the aquifers beneath the plain will be completely gone in 30-40 years. This is by no means a unique situation; in the United States, for instance, the Ogallala Aquifer — which lies beneath portions of western South Dakota, Nebraska, Kansas, Oklahoma, and Texas, and eastern Wyoming, Colorado, and New Mexico — is being depleted at roughly the same rate. (Serious excess withdrawals began there in the 1950s, and as in China, turned areas previously marginal for farming — the land of the 1930s Dust Bowl – into a breadbasket.) But consider the following: while the 175,000 square miles served by the Ogallala Aquifer are home to less than 2 million people, the 125,000 square miles of the North China plain were home to 214,000,000 people in 2000 (80% of them rural). The 2008 North China drought – the worst since the late 1950s drought that exacerbated the Great Leap famines – focused global attention on the problem for a brief moment, but chronic water shortages – both in cities and in the countryside – have been a fact of life for years, and conflicts over scarce and/or polluted water have become common events. So what is to be done?

One hears periodically about various ways water is used inefficiently by urbanites; the Chinese steel industry, for instance, uses about twice as much water per ton produced as steel-makers in the most technologically advanced countries (though the Indian steel industry, for instance, is considerably worse than China's on this score). Leaky pipes and other fairly straightforward infrastructure problems create considerable waste. But relatively speaking, industrial and urban residential losses are small potatoes; agriculture still uses at least 65% of all water in China (though less, even in absolute terms, than 20 years ago) and has by far the lowest efficiency rates. Moreover, urbanites are sufficiently prosperous that price increases – unless they are very large – are unlikely to cause them to cut back on use very much. Certainly this is not where the most water waste is in commercial terms. According to some estimates, a marginal gallon of water sent from the countryside to Tianjin produces as much as 60 times as much income in its new urban locale as it did in the countryside. The best hope in terms of moderating China's overall water demand pressure is probably to keep per capita urban use from growing very much while water use efficiency and living standards there continue improving, and urban population grows sharply. Any significant *reductions* will have to come from the countryside. That process has begun, but it is unclear how far it can go without devastating social consequences.

A great deal of water is wasted in agriculture, in part because costs to farmers are kept artificially low; and since many rural communities have no way to transfer water to those who would pay more for it, anyway, "waste" has very little short-run opportunity cost for them. But it is worth noting here that "waste" has different meanings depending on what time frame one adopts. Irrigation water that never reaches the plants' roots and seeps back into the soil is wasted in the short term – it can't be used for anything else that year. But in the long term, it can help recharge the local aquifer. On the other hand, polluted water that could be re-used if treated properly but instead flows out to sea untreated is wasted in both senses, and thus represents a bigger problem. Chinese agriculture is not necessarily more wasteful in this regard than agriculture in many other places – and the deviations from market prices are no worse than in much of the supposedly market-driven United States – but its limited supplies make waste a much more pressing problem.

Various technologies that would reduce water waste exist, but many are sufficiently costly that farmers are unlikely to adopt them unless they are donated. Center-pivot irrigation systems, for instance, can save a lot of water, but at roughly $35,000 each – almost 60 years' worth of an average North China farmer's income — they make sense only for China's largest farms; they are also poorly suited to the geometry of existing fields, and to the particular requirements of rice and some other crops. Drip-irrigation (sometimes called micro-irrigation) is another technological fix, which has been greeted enthusiastically by many analysts despite being relatively expensive. The idea is that water is moved through small plastic tubes directly to the roots of the plants so that much less of it is wasted; it has been a huge success in Israel (where it was first developed) and in various other water-scarce environments. More recently, however, doubts have been raised about its benefits, in large part because of precisely the ambiguity in defining "waste" mentioned above. Since drip irrigation makes sure that a higher percentage of the water used gets to the roots of the plants, it will enable a fixed, visible water source – for instance, an above-ground tank that catches winter rains for use in the spring – to irrigate more crops than if the water was distributed through traditional ditches or less-precisely targeted (and timed) sprinklers. Alternatively, one could irrigate the same amount of crops, and have some water to sell to other users. But if the water source is an underground aquifer, which can be depleted (in contrast to a system of stored rainfall, where you can't over-withdraw in the same way, because next year's rain isn't yet available), the benefits become less clear. In that situation, much of the water that seeps away through the bottom of ditches and so forth helps recharge the aquifer, so that it isn't necessarily "wasted" from a long-run perspective. On the other hand, precisely because drip irrigation means that almost every gallon of water a farmer buys helps that farmer's crops in the current year, that water is a better buy for the farmer than water run through a less "efficient" system; the farmer is thus tempted to buy more of it. Thus, drip irrigation may be good for maximizing *current*food output while actually exacerbating longer-run water shortages in situations like those in northern China (or, as we shall see, much of northern India and Pakistan) where over-use of ground-water is a big problem. This possibility is not merely a theoretical one; a recent study of drip irrigation in the Upper Rio Grande Valley (on both sides of the US-Mexican border) came to the conclusion that water use increased in precisely this way. In short, selectively implemented high-tech solutions may help in some ways, but they cannot provide a total answer — even if, miraculously, all the funding for them could be found.

Ironically, low-tech solutions may actually have greater potential. It is almost impossible to get a clear sense of how much could be saved by technologically simple measures that can be implemented on either a large or a small scale – re-lining and/or covering irrigation ditches, fixing leaky pipes, and so on. The amounts are probably very big, given the low quality of much of the water infrastructure in China (and elsewhere). But these measures also cost money, and many farmers, or even whole rural communities, are unlikely to invest in them without subsidies and/or greater incentives. More effective pollution control – some, though not all, of which is perfectly possible with fairly simple and relatively inexpensive technologies — could also help enormously, but here, too, there are serious incentive problems. Local officials generally have more to gain by protecting local factories and jobs than by conserving water (especially, of course, the water of people downstream).

More commercially realistic pricing of irrigation water would help provide such incentives – but here there are serious social and political constraints. More expensive water would almost certainly mean decreased agricultural output – and though China certainly has enough foreign exchange to buy more food abroad, the government is quite reluctant to become much more dependent on imports. More expensive water might be particularly bad for the many farmers who have been switching from grain production to fruits and vegetables – crops that it otherwise makes sense for China to produce more of, since they demand much more labor per acre than grain, and can produce relatively high incomes for people with small plots. And even if China – and the world – were content to see Chinese demand for imported food rise significantly, there is the question of what would become of the farmers themselves in such a scenario. With farmers' incomes already lagging far behind those of other Chinese, any significant rise in water prices would probably drive millions of marginal farmers to the wall, and greatly accelerate the already rapid rush of people to the cities. Consequently, further water savings in agriculture, though vital, potentially huge, and far less environmentally risky than large water-moving projects, are likely to come slowly and painfully.

Under the circumstances, many officials see no alternative to technologically ambitious mega-projects: above all, the South-

North water diversion scheme. The idea behind this $65 billion plan – which had been tossed around for decades, and was officially green-lighted in 2001 – is simple: to take water from the Yangzi and its tributaries and move it to North China, where water is much more scarce. But implementing the scheme is extraordinarily difficult, and the consequences of any one of several possible failures could be enormous.

If completed, the Diversion will be the largest construction project in history. It would carry almost 45 billion cubic meters of water per year – roughly the average annual flow of the Yellow River. It has three parts:

1) an Eastern route, which would take water from the Lower Yangzi in Jiangsu province up to Tianjin (roughly following the route of the Ming-Qing Grand Canal) and, via a branch line, to the Shandong peninsula. This is the technologically simplest part of the project – though it still raises plenty of questions. Parts of it began operation in 2008; it is scheduled to be complete in 2010.
2) a Central route, running from near the Three Gorges Dam in Sichuan to Beijing. Work on this route was recently suspended – in response to environmental problems that have proved to be more complicated than was originally foreseen, and to problems with the relocation of people in the path of the project. (There were large protests in March near Danjiangkou in Hubei, where over 300,000 people are supposed to be moved.) Still, the official projection is that water will be reaching Beijing through this route by 2014.
3) a Western route that is really two routes, taking water from the Yarlong-Tsangpo, Dadu, Tongtian and Jinsha Rivers (all of which flow into the Yangzi) across mountains and the Tibet-Qinghai plateau, directing it into the Yellow River, which would then carry it across North China. This is by far the most complex part of the project; work is currently scheduled to begin in 2010, but it would not be completed until 2050.

The project carries uncertainties commensurate with its size and cost. Among other things, there is considerable uncertainty about how dirty southern waters will be by the time they arrive in the north; diversions on this scale change flow speeds, sedimentation rates, and other important rates in unpredictable ways, and the original plans have already been modified to add more treatment facilities than were originally thought necessary. (Changes in water volume will also affect the ability of other rivers to scour their own beds – effects on the Han River, one of the Yangzi's largest tributaries, are a particular concern.) Conveyance canals passing through poorly drained areas may also raise the water table and add excess salts to the soil – already a common problem in irrigated areas of North China – and salt water intrusion rates in the Yangzi Delta. For better or worse, we will begin learning about the effects of the Eastern line soon, and probably about the Central line in just a few years.

But despite its long time horizon, it is the Western line – along with other projects in China's far west — which is the big story. First of all, it offers the most dramatic potential rewards. The idea is that it will tap the enormous water resources of China's far Southwest – Tibet alone has over 30% of China's fresh water supply, most of it coming from the annual snow melt and the annual partial melting around the edges of some Himalayan glaciers. These water resources are an aspect of the Tibet question one rarely hears about, but the many engineers in China's leadership, including Hu Jintao and Wen Jiabao, are very much aware of it. (And ordinary Chinese are increasingly aware of it too – advertisements for bottled Tibetan water now adorn the backs of passenger train seats and other common locations, offering an icon of primitive purity of a type long familiar to Western consumers.) And hydro projects in this very mountainous region offer enormous potential rewards in electricity as well as in water supply. How much electricity water can generate is directly proportional to how far it falls into the turbines: the Yangzi completes 90% of its drop to the sea before it even leaves Tibet to enter China proper, and the Yellow River 80% of its decline before it leaves Inner Mongolia. On April 21, the Chinese government announced plans for 20 additional hydro projects on the upper Yangzi and its tributaries; if they are all completed, they would theoretically add 66% to the already existing hydropower capacity on the river (which includes Three Gorges).

But secondly, the western route also poses by far the biggest complications. It is here that the engineering challenges are most complex and the solutions most untested. It is here (and in nearby Yunnan) that the needs of agrarian and industrial China collide most directly with the lives of Tibetans, Yi, Miao, and other minority groups. It is here that the environmental risks of dam building become major *international* issues, with enormous implications for the Mekong, Salween, Brahmaputra and other rivers relied on by hundreds of millions of South and Southeast Asians. And it is here that major water projects – which always include many uncertainties – collide with what has always been an extraordinarily fragile environment, and one which now faces far more than the average amount of extra uncertainty from climate change: Tibet, home to by far the largest glaciers outside the two polar regions, is expected to warm at twice the average global rate during the 21st century.

STATE-BUILDING AND DAM-BUILDING IN THE HIMALAYAS

From the 1950s to the mid-1980s, China built plenty of dams, but relatively few of them were in the far west. This may seem surprising, given the concentration of hydro potential in that region, but makes perfect sense in other terms. The need to maximize energy production was less urgently felt before the boom of the 1990s, and there was much less concern about relying on coal (which still provides 80% of China's electricity). Many of the dams that were built were constructed by mobilizing large amounts of labor (especially off-season peasant labor) in place of scarce capital, and it was a lot easier to use that labor close to home than to send it far away. The supporting infrastructure (e.g. roads) and technology for dam building in remote mountain locations was not available; the far reaches of the upper Yangzi were not even surveyed until the late 1970s. And the government was much more ambivalent about rapid development in the far west than it is today, with some leaders prioritizing more paternalistic policies that would avoid radical cultural change as the best formula for assuring political stability in the region.

But in the last two decades, all of this has changed, leading to a sharp shift towards the building of huge dam projects in Yunnan and Tibet above all. The technical capacities and supporting infrastructure needed for capital-intensive projects in these areas are now available; the pressure to increase domestic supplies of energy (and other resources, including of course water) has become intense; and the regime has clearly decided that raising incomes in the far west is the best way to keep control and make use of those territories – even if the wrenching cultural changes, massive Han immigration, and severe inequalities accompanying this development increase conflict in the short to medium term. For better or worse, a kind of paternalism in western frontier policy dating back to at least the Qing (albeit one that has long been gradually weakening) is now being discarded quite decisively. Meanwhile, changes in the relationships among the central government, provincial governments, and private investors have helped create enormous opportunities to gain both power and profit through accelerated dam building.

Plans to "send western electricity east," with a particular focus on developing Yunnan hydropower for booming Guangdong, date back to the 1980s; seasonal deliveries of power began in 1993. Beginning in 2001, Guangdong officials began concluding deals for regular annual power purchases with Yunnan officials – and at the same time, officials in Beijing began vetoing plans for additional coal-fired power plant construction in Guangdong, which made reliance on hydropower an absolute necessity for the rapidly growing Pearl River Delta. It is not clear, at least to me, exactly what the relationship between provincial and central government power is in this story. One can see wealthy Guangdong reaching out to secure its own energy supplies here; but complaints from Guangdong about Beijing preventing the construction of power plants in the province, and about power shortages emerging when sufficient hydropower failed to come online on time, suggest that new inter-provincial agreements may often be shotgun weddings imposed by the center: a center for which creating these configurations is both a means of maintaining leverage over coastal boom areas and of integrating peripheral regions more deeply into Beijing's vision of a national political economy.

More generally, the "corporatizing" of the electrical power industry has created complex webs of public and private actors with strong interests in Southwestern hydro development. In 2002, the government-owned State Power Corporation of China was broken into 5 corporations, each of which was given exclusive development rights in particular watersheds. (There is also a sixth, connected to Three Gorges, which is directly under the State Council.) These companies were 100% state-owned, but have created partially-owned subsidiaries which sell shares to private parties (on the Shanghai, Hong Kong and New York stock exchanges), thus raising capital while retaining control. (For investors, meanwhile, power generation stocks provide a way to bet on the growth of the Chinese economy in general without needing lots of reliable information on the factors that might cause a particular manufacturer to succeed or fail.) And these subsidiaries, in turn, have combined with other subsidiaries of the big 5 and/ or companies established by provincial governments to establish still other companies that undertake particular projects.

While this organization allows dam-builders to take advantage of private capital markets and corporate organization, their links to the state remain crucial. Huaneng Power Group, which holds development rights for the Lancang (Upper Mekong), was until recently headed by Li Xiaopeng, son of former Premier (and chief advocate of the Three Gorges project) Li Peng. (The younger Li, who like so many other Chinese leaders has a background in engineering, has since moved on to become deputy governor of Shanxi, with responsibility for industry and coal mining.) His sister, Li Xiaolin, is the CEO of Huaneng's most important subsidiary, China Power International Development Ltd. (a Hong Kong corporation). The transactions which create subsidiaries often involve the parent company giving the subsidiary some important asset (such as generators, transmission lines, or development rights) in return for a large stake in the new company; since there are rarely well-developed markets for these assets and the state-owned parent company does not face the same pressures to be profitable as the subsidiary, the prices at which these assets are transferred can be easily manipulated to artificially lower the costs (and increase the profits) of the subsidiary and its investors. And since all of these companies continue to do business with each other (sending power over somebody else's lines, for instance), there are many opportunities to transfer costs back and forth between entities that need to show a profit and others that do not (or that are less favored by powerful actors).

Powerful government connections also make it all the more likely that these companies will be able to avoid acknowledging (much less bearing) the full social and environmental costs of their work. Last but not least, the large and sometimes unpredictable fluctuations in water volumes far upstream mean that the turbines will not always be fully utilized, so that the actual amount of power generated may be much less impressive than is suggested by the enormous figures for "installed capacity" that are listed for these projects: uncertainties which holders of development rights seeking either investment partners or permission to build have no incentive to highlight. This does not mean, of course, that dams – including large dams – may not make economic and even environmental sense in many cases, given China's limited options. It does mean, however, that both political motives and profit seeking by politically-connected people are almost certainly causing dams to be built in a number of additional cases, where even a narrowly economic analysis would not justify them.

Implications for Tibet and Tibetans

Even many projects that will genuinely help millions in northern and eastern China – and perhaps others that will curb China's carbon emissions and its future food imports — have serious implications for people who live near the projects. Tibetans and other ethnic minorities in the far Southwest are likely to be the most affected. An unconfirmed report by the Tibetan government-in-exile says that at least 6 Tibetan women were recently shot by security forces as they protested a hydro project on the Tibet/Sichuan border.

First, there is the question of human tampering with sacred lakes and rivers. A good deal of this has already happened in Tibet (as with the large dam at Yamdrok Tso). A massive dam proposed at the great bend in the Yalong Zangbo (Yarlong Tsangpo) – 40,000 megawatts, or almost twice the capacity of Three Gorges — would again dramatically change a sacred site, to create power and water supplies that would mostly go to Han Chinese very far away. Meanwhile, the project poses serious risks for the traditional livelihoods of many people. Road-building and railway-building – particularly the Qinghai-Tibet highway and the railroad that runs near it, completed in 2006 – seem to have substantially damaged the permafrost layer in adjacent areas; the permafrost, in turn, protects a series of underground lakes, so that damaging it is likely to exacerbate an already worrisome drying trend in the region. (A Chinese surveying team recently reported that some of the sources of the Yangzi itself are drying up, and the area turning to desert.) Wetlands and grasslands that are important to the large numbers of livestock herders in Tibet have already shrunk quite significantly; this is likely to make them shrink faster. (A video on the Asia Society website covers some of these issues very well.) Dams in Yunnan appear to be interfering with local fisheries, and new ones pose significant threats to China's greatest concentration of biodiversity. And since much of this region is seismically quite active, the risk of an earthquake precipitating a catastrophic dam failure and sudden floods cannot be dismissed.

The Other Side(s) of the Mountains: Pakistan, India, Nepal, Burma, Vietnam

Of course, people and governments further downstream also use rivers that start in the Himalayas – and many have plans to do so much more intensively. Many of them are very worried about Chinese initiatives that may preempt their own current or future water usage.

On December 9, 2008, *Asia Times Online* reported that China was planning to go ahead with a major hydroelectric dam and water diversion scheme on the great bend of the Yalong Zangbo River in Tibet. The 40,000 megawatt hydro project itself raises huge issues for Tibetans and for China. But what matters most for people outside China is that the plan not only calls for impounding huge amounts of water behind a dam, but also for changing the direction that the water flows beyond the dam – so that it would eventually feed into the South-North diversion project. The water that would be diverted currently flows south into Assam to help form the Brahmaputra, which in turn joins the Ganges to form the world's largest river delta, supplying much of the water to a basin with over 300 million inhabitants. While South Asians have worried for some time that China might divert this river, the Chinese government had denied any such intentions, reportedly doing so again when Hu Jintao visited New Delhi in 2006. However, rumors that China was indeed planning to begin such a project soon continued to circulate. (As we will see later, some Indian essays published in 2007 already assumed that China would make a major diversion from the Brahmaputra, citing this as a reason for India not to proceed with its own plan to transfer water from the Brahmaputra to other river basins south and west of it.) Indian Prime Minister Singh reportedly raised the issue during his January 2008 visit to Beijing, but a December, 2008 report from *Asia Times Online* said that China provided no assurances this time, and is in fact planning to divert the river. (No public statement was made at that time, but fewer official denials have been issued; the latest came former water minister Wang Shucheng on May 26, 2009.) Chinese Prime Minister Wen Jiabao has said that water scarcity is a threat to the "very survival of the Chinese nation." Interestingly, unconfirmed reports back in 2000 had suggested that Beijing had already decided to go ahead; but not until 2009, when the Three Gorges would be completely finished.

Water is indeed a matter of survival – not only for China, but for its neighbours. Most of Asia's major rivers – the Yellow, the Yangzi, the Mekong, Salween, Irrawaddy, Brahmaputra, Ganges, Sutlej, and Indus – draw on the glaciers and snowmelt of the Himalayas, and all of these except the Ganges have their source on the Chinese side of the border in Tibet. In many of these cases, no international agreements exist for sharing the waters of those rivers that cross borders, or even sharing data about them.

There are water problems throughout South and Southeast Asia, but not the same ones in all places. Very crudely, the nature of the most pressing current problems varies with longitude. Pakistan and much of India (especially in the North and West) face very serious shortages of water for agriculture and for daily domestic use, as well as serious rural power shortages. The latter problem intensifies the former for many people, as it makes the operation of deep wells increasingly impractical; but in the longer run easing the power shortage without solving the water supply crisis will just intensify future shortages. In most of Southeast Asia, by contrast, there is plenty of water for now, but electricity is in short supply, and plans to alleviate that problem through hydropower threaten delicate riverine ecosystems.

Starting in the West, Pakistan may depend more on irrigation than any other large country on earth. Over half of the country receives less than 8 inches of rainfall per year; by way of comparison, Phoenix averages 8.4 inches. Only 8% of the country gets over 20 inches per year – the amount that falls in Tel Aviv. Yet the country is predominantly agricultural, and almost 80% of farming requires irrigation. As recently as 1990, irrigation accounted for a stunning 96% of water use. Meanwhile, much of the groundwater is brackish and/or badly polluted – partly due to current pollution, but also in part a legacy of past irrigation projects; some of the brackishness results from salination and waterlogging that goes back to colonial era projects. Consequently, people often rely on diversions from irrigation canals to get water for their daily needs. (Since increased use of drip irrigation would reduce the availability of water in surface canals, this may be another way in which more "efficient" technologies, though very helpful in some ways, could intensify the problems of certain people — in this case, some particularly vulnerable ones.) Agriculture remains central to the economy, and there are even plans, backed by foreign investors, to sharply increase grain exports (mostly to the Middle East). Efforts to increase irrigation efficiency are underway, but the government is also looking for ways to engineer large increases in supply.

Northern and Northwestern India are not quite as dry as Pakistan, but nonetheless have millions of farmers, several arid regions, and highly irregular, often inadequate rains elsewhere. For India as a whole, the per capita water supply is about ¼ of the global average – as it is for China. Moreover, half the annual rainfall comes in 15 days, and 90% of total river flow comes during 4 months. Yet India has built only 1/5 as much water storage capacity per capita as China (and about 1/25 as much as the US or Australia). Canals for surface irrigation were built on a large scale in some areas under the British, and on a considerably larger scale after Independence; but many have been poorly maintained and/or not run to serve those who lack political influence. So in north and northwest India (and some other regions), probably even more than in northern China, well-digging has been essential to enabling farmers to survive, and to a "green revolution" that raised agricultural yields enough to keep up with the enormous population growth of the last half century. (As in many other cases, the high-yielding hybrid wheat, rice, and cotton seeds all required more water than older varieties.) Groundwater now provides 70% of India's irrigation water, and close to 80% of water for domestic use.

This extremely aggressive exploitation of groundwater is unsustainable. Well water is free to any farmer who can reach it by drilling down from his land, and the electricity to run the pumps is heavily subsidized, greatly straining the budgets of many Indian states. Even at heavily subsidized prices, however, energy costs have become a huge burden for many small farmers as water levels drop and pumps must work harder; moreover, the irregular way electricity is provided, with frequent spikes and interruptions, often ruins pumps, wreaking sudden devastation on unfortunate farmers. The large inequalities in landholding within many Indian villages are a further complication which is much more pronounced than in any part of rural China. Richer farmers have every reason to drill deeper wells, take more water from aquifers, and re-sell whatever they don't use themselves at high mark-ups to people without wells for their domestic use; indeed, this is often more profitable than using the water to raise crops. Other people then also need to drill deeper in response; a sort of tube well race has developed, depleting aquifers ever faster. Suicides of farmers who cannot get enough water to continue planting have become common events in recent years, including instances of protest by mass suicide. (Some of these protests are aimed at state governments which have been raising electricity prices to farmers; these rates are still far below those charged to urbanites but too high for many farmers nonetheless. Some protests are also aimed at corporate users and polluters of water; Coca Cola has been a particularly popular target.) Meanwhile, there is increasing concern that water scarcity and pollution could create dangerous shortfalls of agricultural output, especially in Punjab – which produces India's largest agricultural surpluses, including roughly half the wheat and rice procured by the central government pool that aims to stabilize supplies and prices – and in neighboring Pakistan. The pollution in question, which is bad enough to cause large increases in birth defects and cancer, has many sources, including the legacy of years of intensive irrigation, fertilization, and use of pesticides; salination and water-logging (with the latter problem also increasing the incidence of malaria) have in fact been mounting problems in the Punjab since the introduction of year-round irrigation by the British at the end of the 19th century. It is estimated that in East Punjab today, 50% of groundwater is recycled water from irrigation canals; in West Punjab, 80%. Near Karachi, where it reaches the sea, the Indus now often fills only a small fraction of its bed; fishing has disappeared, an invasion of seawater is harming agriculture, and water for domestic use is desperately short.

In this crisis, plans for new water projects have sprouted in large numbers. Though people are well aware that past projects often had unexpected effects that have led to current difficulties, the prospect of losing the agricultural output gains achieved through irrigation is terrifying, and possibilities for alleviating serious electricity shortages (which, among other things, inhibit manufacturing growth that could reduce reliance on agriculture) seem very tempting. And, ironically, the loss of water storage capacity that has occurred as some old dams have silted up has become an argument for more dam building.

While many of these plans are driven by very real needs, China is hardly the only country where political and economic interests create incentives to build some mega-projects that are incomprehensible in terms of overall costs and benefits. In India, for instance, the central government's inability to enforce water-sharing agreements among the states has led some upstream states to build extra water storage in order to keep for themselves water that is at least as badly needed downstream; meanwhile, some downstream states, despite desperate shortages, have balked at implementing water-saving measures that might weaken their claims to need a larger allocation from rivers flowing through multiple states. And since only direct human uses of water count as "needs" in these allocations, any other uses – e.g. releasing water to help maintain estuarial eco-systems – count as "waste" that might weaken future claims, and are thus discouraged. (Somewhat surprisingly, water-sharing agreements between India and Pakistan have thus far been more consistently observed than have those among Indian states, despite decades of hostility between these countries.)

The most ambitious new plans are, not surprisingly, found amidst the highest mountains. Pakistan, India, Bhutan, and Nepal all have plans for huge dams in the Himalayas. Planned construction over the next decade totals 80,000 megawatts (versus 60-64,000 in all of Latin America); India alone plans to add a further 67,000 MW in the following decade. India, like China, exploited the hydropower in its less mountainous areas first, and has only 11,000 MW of non-Himalayan potential left; potential Himalayan capacity (not counting China) is a staggering 192,000 MW, almost half of it in India. (The entire world currently has about 675,000 megawatts of installed hydroelectric capacity.) Meanwhile, India's 2001 census reported that 44% of households had no access to electricity; the figure is about the same in Bhutan and closer to 60% in Nepal. Interest in dam building is just as intense in Pakistan, though there irrigation is a higher priority than electricity. However, the estimated cost of the projects planned for the next 10 years is roughly $90 billion, much of which remains unsecured. (India has financing for a bit over half of its planned dam construction through 2012, but much less for needs through 2017.) Pakistan has recently turned to Chinese financing and technical expertise for its Diamer Bhasha dam, a $12.6 billion project which was announced in 2006, but had trouble attracting capital. There has also been some financial support from Middle Eastern sources and various international development banks.

Meanwhile, other foreign-backed plans will place additional strains on Pakistan's water supply. Investors from various wealthy but arid Middle Eastern states have recently been making large purchases of farmland, both in Pakistan and elsewhere in Asia and Africa. (South Korea and China have also been doing this, though not, as far as I know, in Pakistan.) The Pakistani Minister of Investment, seeking to dispel any fear that local farmers will be displaced, has said that all of the 6 million acres (equal to roughly 10% of the country's current cultivated acreage) up for sale or lease to foreigners was currently unused. If true, this means that any water devoted to it will represent an addition to existing demand. Indeed, a recent story in The Economist noted that many of these land purchases seem to be aimed above all at the water rights that go with the land; it quotes the chairman of Nestlés referring to these purchases as "the great water grab."

India, like China, has both extremely dry areas and some with plenty of water; and, as we have seen, it is also like China in that it is currently mining groundwater to produce important grain surpluses in some of these dry areas. So it may be no surprise that, like China, it is also contemplating a major scheme for diverting water from some river basins to others. The most ambitious, Himalayan, part of its Interlinking of Rivers Project would move water from the upper parts of the Ganges, Yamuna (a major tributary of the Ganges) and Brahmaputra Rivers westward, ending in the Luni and Sabarmati Rivers in Rajahstan and Gujarat. (Other Northwestern areas that would receive water are in Haryana and Punjab; a second, Peninsular, part of the project would mostly direct water to dry parts of Orissa and Tamil Nadu.) And just as China seems to be retreating from its earlier representations to India that it had no plans to divert water from the Yalong Zangbo/ Brahmaputra, so this project suggests that India is hedging on its formal promises to Bangladesh (including a written understanding from 1996) that no water would be diverted away from the Ganges above the barrage at Farakka (a few kilometers from the India/ Bangladesh border).

Some of the intermediate links would create shipping channels, and the project also aims to reduce seasonal flooding problems on the Yamuna (especially near Delhi). The project is also supposed to generate 30,000 megawatts of net hydropower (i.e. power available for other uses after subtracting the energy it would use for moving water). The main purpose, however, would be to provide large amounts of additional irrigation water, mostly in Western India; official plans claim it could increase total irrigated area by as much as 35 million hectares. Official cost estimates for the total project, with 260 links between rivers, was estimated at $120 billion, which would make it larger than any construction project in history so far, and even bigger than China's planned river diversions; based on subsequent comments by members of the task force that drafted the plan, one study has suggested a revised price tag of $200 billion.

Plans for the project have been shrouded in a degree of secrecy unusual for India – even more so, it appears, than with China's river diversion projects; among other things it is hard to get an estimate of the number of people likely to be displaced, though two scholars put the number as high as 5.5 million. Many of the parts of the plan that have been revealed have been sharply criticized on a number of grounds, and it is unclear which parts will actually wind up being built. Aside from a number of technological and ecological questions about specific parts of the projects, both domestic critics and a World Bank study have noted that the transfers being contemplated are only politically feasible if enforceable legal agreements can be reached on allocating the waters and compensating the "givers," and such agreements have generally not fared well in India. There is also widespread agreement that Indian governments need to put more of their water conservancy money into improving maintenance and management of existing facilities (many of which are decaying quickly), rather than further construction. Indeed, even one scholar who is largely supportive of the project estimates that net water availability could be increased as much by improving the current efficiency of water utilization by 20% as by building this project (though he favors doing both, and points to hydropower and other benefits of the project besides increased water supply). Some opponents, on the other hand, have suggested that building this project would so deplete resources for other water works that the latter might have to be privatized to raise cash, at considerable risk to poorer customers.

We will turn momentarily to some of the environmental risks associated with these new and proposed water projects. First, though, it is worth noting that in the case of large dams, environmental uncertainties not only represent risks to others, but financial risks for the dam builders themselves. Big dams have huge construction costs, but very modest operational costs once they are finished; thus they can become big cash cows once they are generating power while incurring very low additional costs (especially if, as seems very likely in this part of the world, demand for electricity continues to rise). Profitability is therefore very much dependent on how long they continue producing after completion. That period can be cut short by many factors, of which sedimentation may be the most common. Sanmenxia dam on the middle Yellow River, completed in 1962, is a particularly notorious example — not only because it failed quickly and expensively, but because many of the problems were in fact predicted. (The project went ahead anyway, in part it seems because in the aftermath of the withdrawal of Soviet technical experts, China wanted to prove that it could build such a dam without outside help.) Because interest must be paid on the construction costs, profitability is also very much affected by how much time elapses between the beginning of the project and the beginning of this revenue stream; thus mega-projects that take a long time to complete are especially vulnerable, economically speaking, to any shortfall in power generation.

In the case of Himalayan dams, at least three factors could well make the lives of these projects shorter than anticipated. First, the Himalayas are relatively young mountains with relatively high rates of erosion, and their upper reaches have relatively little vegetation to hold soil in place. (There has also been a lot of deforestation in recent decades.) This tends to make for high sediment burdens in rivers descending from the Himalayas. In Tibet, for instance, a 1986 study found that almost 40 percent of the small hydrodams built since 1949 had become defunct or unusable by being silted up; similar problems have developed on a number of Pakistani dams (which have not only lost their utility for generating power but for seasonal water storage and irrigation). Second, any errors in predicting future river flow can also have dramatic effects on the durability of a dam, sharply reducing profitability. In many of the Himalayan cases, there is not a very long run of data available (particularly since the Chinese government has not been very forthcoming about sharing the data that it has assembled), and there are reasons (mostly connected with climate change) to think that the future may be drier than the last few decades, especially in the Western Himalayas (though there are also some reasons to believe the opposite). And, as hard as it is to model future river flows in any case, it becomes exponentially harder when a great many large projects are being planned on the same set of rivers and tributaries. Several analysts have questioned whether the Brahamaputra basin – a critical water source for this plan – can be meaningfully considered to have a water "surplus" even now; some add that the likelihood (in their view) of a major Chinese diversion upstream and of glacial retreat from global warming make the idea that any "surplus" is available to be transferred extremely dubious.

A World Bank study of India's water future argues that the Himalayas offer one of the world's "most benign environments" for dam building. The basis of this estimate is simple: a calculation of people to be displaced and acreage to be submerged per megawatt generated. Given the huge power potential in the denominators of these projects and the sparse population of many highland areas, these ratios are not surprising, and they deserve to be taken seriously. But they are by no means a complete measure of the costs and risks involved.

Like all dams, those planned for the Himalayas would submerge significant amounts of land – including forests and grazing lands important to a number of the remaining migratory people in the region. Several involve diverting parts of rivers through underground tunnels, creating large dry regions, with serious local impacts on fisheries and on farming. Moreover, the Himalayas – though we don't often think of them this way – are a major and fragile hotspot of biodiversity. Their rapid rise from 500 meters to over 8,000 meters creates a remarkable range of ecosystems within a relatively small space; Conservation International reports that of an estimated 10,000 plant species in one Himalayan sub-region, over 3,100 are found nowhere else. And here, too, as in Tibet and Yunnan, there are significant risks of major disasters from earthquakes and/or glacial lake outbreak floods.

Perhaps most surprising, it is no longer clear that large hydrodams are even a consistently climate-friendly source of energy. While hydro-electricity can clearly be a substitute for fossil fuel consumption that produces carbon dioxide, the reservoirs behind large dams often include large amounts of rotting vegetable matter, and thus are potent sources of methane – a much more potent greenhouse gas. (This is not an issue for "run of the river" dams, which have no reservoirs, but these make up a very small percentage of big projects.) These emissions are larger in tropical and sub-tropical climates, where vegetation both grows and decays faster. A 2007 study suggested that methane from dam reservoirs actually accounted for 19% of India's greenhouse gas emissions, while hydropower accounts for only 16% of the country's electricity (and thus a much smaller percentage of its total energy use). These figures are still preliminary estimates; moreover, methane emissions might well be lower than average for dams high in the Himalayas, which is not an area where plant matter grows and decays rapidly. And there may well be ways to mitigate these effects by capturing and burning the methane to generate more power. But they do raise questions about the common assumption that despite their environmental risks, large dams are a clearly "greener" energy source than the most common alternatives; the non-trivial greenhouse emissions involved in creating huge amounts of concrete and steel further complicate the picture.

Further east, the plans are not quite as ambitious, but they still portend dramatic changes for millions of people. The Salween (called the Nu River in Eastern Tibet and Yunnan) is shrouded in the most mystery, since for most of its length it is either in China or Burma (elsewhere it forms the Burmese-Thai border); neither regime welcomes publicity. Because the Salween still runs within steep mountain gorges for many miles after crossing into Burma (it drops quite suddenly just before reaching its delta), there is enormous hydro potential here, and much less domestic demand. To date, the Salween has not been tapped very much for human use; it remains one of the few large free-flowing rivers left in Asia. A major dam on the Chinese side of the border was stopped in 2004 for environmental reasons, and work has recently been suspended again. However there are now a number of dams planned and/or underway, in both China (where the maximal program calls for a staircase of 13 dams) and Burma, with the expectation that the power generated in Burma will be exported to Thailand, Vietnam, and perhaps China. A number of the Burmese projects are being built by Chinese companies (and will be operated by them for the first several years after completion). Many are located in highland areas of Burma's Shan state, where the government has been trying for many years to gain fuller control over ethnic minority populations; activists have charged that the regime is taking advantage of the relocation of people which dam building requires and of providing security to the builders to further its political and military aims in the area. Another planned dam would be built in what is essentially a war zone in the Karen minority area near the Burmese-Thai border; much of the area is theoretically a wildlife sanctuary, but it has been heavily logged in recent years (particularly after Thailand banned logging on its side of the border) and roads are now being built through it to facilitate dam construction (and control).

Given the difficulty of visiting these areas, and the absence of information on exactly what projects are at what stage, it is hard to even guess at the likely social and environmental impact of the projects. And since the Salween watershed, with 6-7 million people, is far less populated than the Mekong to its east (around 70 million people)—not to mention the Ganges/Brahmaputra to the west, or the major Chinese rivers to the north—it has not gotten as much attention as these other rivers. Nonetheless it raises the full range of complex issues and trade-offs, with fears about endangered species, fish and other resources that local people rely on, forced relocations (and according to some forced labor) on one side and pressures for development in an exceptionally poor country on the other.

The larger and more densely populated Mekong basin raises all these issues and more. Here both physical and political geography create an important divide more or less at the Chinese border. For one thing, the vast majority of the river's hydropower potential is on the Chinese side of the border. The river starts 5,500 meters up on the Tibet-Qinghai plateaus, and is down to 500 meters above sea level when it leaves China. Its hydro potential within Yunnan alone almost equals its potential in Burma, Laos, Thailand, Cambodia and Vietnam combined – though the latter is far from trivial – despite the fact that Yunnan accounts for just a bit over one-third of the river's descent within China. China has thus far completed three hydro dams on the Mekong, and has at least two more under construction; the complete plan appears to call for a cascade of at least eight and perhaps as many as fifteen large hydrodams.

Planning for the lower Mekong began under a U.S. and U.N.-backed Mekong River Committee in the 1950s; China and the Democratic Republic of (North) Vietnam were excluded, and Cambodian participation was also intermittent as its relations with the U.S. fluctuated. While Lyndon Johnson, among others, spoke frequently of a major Lower Mekong Project modeled on the U.S. Tennessee Valley Authority, no substantial work was done during the war years; what were apparently private U.S. promises to help build Mekong dams as part of postwar reconstruction aid for Vietnam were never implemented either. Only in the late 1980's did a new Mekong River Commission emerge, with Vietnam and Cambodia now full members. The Commission is relatively weak, however, and the riparian states are mostly developing their own projects, often in partnership with China, Japan (especially through the Asian Development Bank) or U.S. partners.

Moreover, China has remained largely outside even the limited coordination generated within the Commission framework. Today, it sometimes sends representatives to attend meetings, but neither it nor Burma is a member. So far China's main interest in the Lower Mekong has been in navigation. A series of projects have been carried out since 2000 to facilitate this, and traffic appears to have increased quite significantly in the last 3-5 years, along with quite a bit of road construction linking Yunnan province with Burma, Thailand and Laos. It is not clear just how important a shipping artery China hopes to develop along the Mekong; while one Chinese official spoke of Middle East oil shipments coming up the Mekong to China in case the U.S. Navy blocked the Straits of Malacca in some future conflict, it seems implausible that such shipments could ever be large enough to matter much. (Nonetheless, the idea of moving oil on the Mekong – with the possibility of toxic spills – is a matter of great concern to farmers and fisher-people who rely on the river.)

While the hydro potential of the Lower Mekong may not match that of the Upper Mekong, it remains large – and all the more tempting given the severe poverty of the Greater Mekong Sub-region, where per capita income is estimated at one U.S. dollar per day. At least 11 large hydropower dams are currently planned for the mainstream of the Mekong in Southeast Asia, mostly in Laos. While there are widespread concerns that these dams could harm agriculture and fishing in the Lower Mekong – both of which are absolutely essential to the lives of its almost 70 million residents – regimes thinking in terms of industry, cities, and "modern" development may give electricity a higher priority. Meanwhile, the rather weak coordination among lower Mekong states (despite the existence of the commission) and the absence of any real control on what China does may well create a "prisoner's dilemma" that encourages dam construction: if others may well take actions that will mess up the river's ecosystem anyway, why not at least get some electricity for oneself out of it?

An obvious but nonetheless important point here is that there is no such thing as the ideal state of a river divorced from any point of view or set of interests. For instance, if Chinese projections about the effects of the three existing dams and two further dams currently underway on the Lancang/Upper Mekong are correct, the results would be a much greater flow downstream in the dry season, and lesser flow in the wet season, with no change in overall annual flow. (The claim that these dams will have only limited effects is far from universally accepted – in fact many in Southeast Asia blame the Chinese dams already completed on the Lancang for the huge Mekong floods of 2008.) This would be good for navigation, for power generation, and perhaps for irrigation as well. Projects designed to aid navigation also generally aim to even out seasonal water flows. But even if this is true, dams on the Lancang could nonetheless have a serious impact on lower Mekong fisheries, for at least two reasons. First, dams inevitably trap some nutrient-rich sediment that would otherwise flow through to the Delta; this has been a problem with big dams elsewhere, appears to already be happening in parts of Yunnan affected by the first three Lancang dams, and is expected to happen on the lower Mekong as well. Second, many species of fish respond to subtle seasonal variations in water flow to know when to migrate and spawn; changes in the seasonal timing of peak flow after the completion of the Three Gorges Dam has, for instance, had a devastating effect on four species of Yangzi River carp. The United Nations estimates that 40 million people are active in Lower Mekong fisheries, and one report estimates that local fishing provides 80% of the protein for people living in the Lower Mekong region as well as significant export revenues. Thai and Lao fishermen claim that the Chinese dams already in existence on the Upper Mekong have begun affecting their catches, while spokesmen for the dam-builders claim these projects have had no significant impact on the Lower Mekong. There are also claims that reduced water flow at some times of year has led to greater invasion of the Delta by salt water, harming agriculture.

Dams on the Middle and Lower Mekong could have the same effects, and others as well. They will interfere with fish migration, which is concentrated on the lower and middle (especially lower) parts of the river. Mitigating technologies to allow for fish passage have proved only partially effective even on low dams in North America and Europe, and the Mekong poses a vastly more challenging problem: the amount of fish biomass is perhaps 100 times what it is on the Columbia (where fish ladders have achieved some positive results), and the number of species several times greater. (The more diverse the species, the more different times and places involved in migrations.) The territory that the Middle and Lower Mekong passes through is also much less steep and even more biodiverse than the Upper Mekong; and being lower and more tropical, would probably have higher methane emissions from any reservoirs. In various ways, then, downstream dams on the Mekong may be more dangerous than upstream ones, and they would be far more expensive per kilowatt generated. But their benefits would accrue mostly to people in the same countries that will suffer their probable harms – and that might be all that matters to planners thinking in terms of national interests.

But while everybody is looking to dam the rivers descending from the Himalayas, China's position is unique. It is not only that most of the rivers in question start on China's side of the border, so that their claims cannot be pre-empted by actions further upstream. A second crucial difference is that they alone, of the countries involved, can finance any project they choose without recourse to international lenders. And while the World Bank, Asian Development Bank and big private banks are not among the world's most ardent environmentalists, they have – either for their own reasons or because of pressures from third parties – refused to support some particularly controversial projects. China's domestic dam-building industry is also increasingly technically sophisticated, and is in fact now exporting its engineering know-how in this area. Thus, the only constraints Chinese dam-building faces are those generated within the country – and these are often (though not always) fairly weak.

Late in January, Jiang Gaoming of the Chinese Academy of Sciences released a sobering piece (China Dialogue, January 22, 2009, link) about how accelerating the construction of dams in China's Southwest – part of the P.R.C.'s ambitious stimulus package to fight the global recession – is worsening the already considerable environmental and social risks involved, with some projects beginning before any Environmental Impact Assessments have been completed. Protests against Three Gorges by some leading scientists and engineers did not stop that project; it remains to be seen whether they will have more effect in the future. Recent reports that some poorly built dams on the Yellow River in Gansu – and perhaps many others elsewhere in China – are in dire need of repair — may strengthen people, both within and outside the government, who are urging a more cautious approach to further mega-projects, but the outcome of such arguments remains unclear.

In short the possible damage to China's neighbours from this approach to its water and energy needs is staggeringly large – and the potential to raise political tensions is commensurate. Previous water diversion projects affecting the source of the Mekong have already drawn protests from Vietnam (and from environmental groups), and, as noted above, a project on the Nu River (which becomes the Salween in Thailand and Burma) which was suspended in the face of significant domestic and foreign opposition in 2004 and then re-started, has recently been halted again by order of Prime Minister Wen Jiabao. But some projects now underway or being contemplated have considerably larger implications, both for Chinese and for foreigners. The diversion of the Yalong Zangbo – if that is indeed on the agenda – would have the largest implications of all. If the waters could arrive in North China safely and relatively unpolluted – by no means sure things — and having generated considerable power along the way, the relief for China's seriously strained hydro-ecology would be considerable. On the other hand, the impact on Eastern India and Bangladesh, with a combined population even larger than North China's, could be devastating. The potential for such a project to create conflicts between China and India –and to exacerbate existing conflicts over shared waterways between India and Bangladesh – is gigantic.

CLIMATE CHANGE, DISAPPEARING GLACIERS, AND OTHER NIGHTMARES

Meanwhile, evidence is mounting that thanks to climate change, the water supplies all these projects seek to tap are much less dependable than planners have frequently projected. A report published in*Geophysical Research Letters* on November 22, 2008 noted that recent samples taken from Himalayan glaciers were missing two markers that are usually easy to find in ice cores: evidence of radiation from open air nuclear tests in 1951-2 and 1962-3. These markers are apparently absent because the glacier had lost all ice that had formed at any time since the mid-1940s, rather than just (as was previously known) some ice from its edges. And since the Inter-Governmental Panel on Climate Change estimates that the Himalayan highlands will warm at about twice the average global rate over the next century, there is every reason to think the situation will get worse. One estimate has 1/3 of the Himalayan glaciers disappearing by 2050, and 2/3 by 2100. (Models currently in use predict that this will happen much faster in the Western than the Eastern Himalayas; the situation for Pakistan and Northwest India is thus particularly grim, with an initial windfall period of increased flows to be followed by a devastating loss of water in the already-declining Indus, Sutlej, and other rivers.) If that scenario is right, then even if all the engineering challenges of South-North water diversion can be solved – and even if we ignore the costs to other users of these waters –the resulting benefits might prove short-lived.

Climate change poses other problems as well. Among the most serious are glacial lake outburst floods (GLOFs). As glaciers in high altitude regions melt, they can form large lakes behind natural dams of ice and rock. These are somewhat like the temporary lakes that formed behind dams of debris after the Sichuan earthquake last May, except that some of the "wall" is ice. And like those temporary lakes, such lakes are dangerous, because they can burst through their walls at any moment, creating devastating flash floods downstream. (Some readers may remember seeing Chinese soldiers dynamiting the walls of those lakes before they got any bigger, for just that reason.) Such floods could easily overwhelm man-made dams downstream, causing a chain reaction of disaster. Bhutan has identified 2,600 such lakes just within its borders, including 25 at high risk of bursting. Meanwhile, though projections of likely changes in the monsoon due to global warming vary significantly, most suggest that South Asia will see fewer days of rain per year but a larger number of extreme precipitation events – raising the need for water storage, but also increasing the risk of catastrophic failure should a large dam be built without sufficient allowances for these changes.

5

China's Dams: A Security Challenge for South Asia

China's proposed dams on the Yaluzangbu River in Dagu, Jiacha, Jiexu and Zangmu have added a new roadblock to improving Sino-Indian relations. What has aggravated tensions is China's reluctance to accede to India's call for a water commission or an inter-governmental dialogue or a treaty. Although Indian and Chinese officials have held talks and the latter have agreed to share hydrological information through a Memorandum of Understanding (MoU) on the Brahmaputra and the Sutlej in flood season, the absence of a bilateral treaty makes it next to impossible for India to verify China's claims as of now.

China's determination to implement the Great South-North Water Diversion (SNWD) Project could have serious environmental implications for China and its neighbouring countries by affecting the flow of rivers downstream. The project consists of three stages – eastern, central and western routes – out of which the first two stages involve diversion of waters from China's internal rivers while the third has transboundary ramifications, especially for South Asia.

The western route leg targets the Salween, the Mekong, the Brahmaputra and the Jinsha. Some reports even suggest that China is planning to build the world's largest dam and hydropower station on the Brahmaputra at the Great Bend (where the river takes a U-turn to enter the plains of Assam via Arunachal Pradesh). Approximately, 354 billion cubic metres (BCM) of water flows from Tibet to India out of which 131 BCM is accounted in the Brahmaputra River; on this river alone China is allegedly planning to build twenty-eight dams.

China's lack of transparency has left the governments in India and Bangladesh guessing about its future actions with respect to its diversion plans. One important point that needs to be taken into account while analysing these diversion projects from the point of view of the lower riparian countries is that the same river has an average run-off of 550 BCM of water when it reaches Bangladesh due to monsoonal waters and the water contributed by tributaries. Therefore, a dam intended for hydropower generation might not make any difference to the run-off. Water diversion during monsoons could be a blessing in disguise as the excess waters have been a cause for floods in both India (particularly Assam Valley) and Bangladesh.

However, if China diverts during the entire year, it could lead to damaging consequences for the two countries. Also, the possibility of contamination, sedimentation and flash floods is high. India has been arguing that since it has 58 percent of the total Brahmaputra drainage basin and is dependent on it for almost 30 percent of the country's water resources and 41 percent of its total hydropower resources while China controls only 20 percent of the basin, India has a greater right to the river's resources.

The Yangtze River on which the Three Gorges Dam has been built is the source of waters for the first two legs of this grand project. Brahmaputra River could be afflicted by the same problems that the Yangtze has been over the past few years. This would affect India and Bangladesh directly. Moreover, the areas where these dams are being proposed to be built are seismically unstable.

Accusations have also been levelled against China for flash floods inArunachal Pradesh in the past, which were supposedly caused by a breach in the upstream dam in Tibet that raised the level of the Brahmaputra by more than thirty metres. Similarly, Himachal Pradesh has also been affected allegedly by Chinese dam-building activities in the form of floods in 2000, 2001 and 2005. China's management of the Mekong River that originates in Tibet has faced criticism from Southeast Asia. Four countries of the lower Mekong basin – Laos, Cambodia, Thailand and Vietnam – that depend on this river for food, water and transportation have been heavily distressed by China's activities on the river. Dams on this river have been held responsible for drought in some of these countries.

In 2010, the river had acutely low water levels due to less monsoonal rainfall the previous year and light rainfall in the dry season. This is said to have been exacerbated by dams upstream in China. Itgenerated losses worth millions of dollars. In Thailand, fishing communities have been the most affected as they are forced to stop their fishery activities when the water levels go down significantly. The low-lying Mekong delta in Vietnam is home to more than 18 million people and contains vast farmlands from where nearly half of Vietnam's rice crop comes. It is already vulnerable to sea level rise. When the freshwater flow from Tibet decreases, seawater intrusion is expected to increase and reduce the agricultural yield further.

China has refused to be a full member of the Mekong River Commission, which was formed by the lower basin countries in 1995 to monitor hydropower development in the lower Mekong basin. Efforts by the four countries to urge China to assess downstream river changes caused by its dams and engaging in technical cooperation have not borne fruit. It has been a dialogue partner, a position that allows it to evade scrutiny of its dams and its rights to harness hydropower potential of the river of which 21 percent lies in China.

The fact that the environment is changing; and is now changing at an unprecedented pace due to both natural and human-induced causes could definitely culminate in conflicts between China and its neighbours. At the same time, China has always maintained 'strategic silence' on its water diversion proposals, which makes any form of cooperation between China and its neighbours a difficult proposition.

The spree of dams proposed by China would diminish India's manoeuvrability in the region in terms of its own plans of deploying hydroelectric projects in its territory to fulfil its energy requirements (particularly in the less developed regions in the Northeast) but also could spark political tensions with India's neighbours. Therefore it is time for India to galvanize the support of its neighbours such as Nepal, Bhutan and Bangladesh to prevent China from implementing large-scale diversion projects that could affect water security in the whole South Asian region.

The international community should put pressure on China to respect the 'commons' principle when it comes to transboundary waters. It would also be prudent for India to include the China factor in its water-sharing agreements with its own neighbours so that in the future, if contingency arises (such as flash floods or severely reduced water levels) the entire onus would not fall upon India's shoulders.

China needs to rexamine its dam policy to secure its own interests in the region. The zero-sum mentality towards its neighbours could lead to an 'insecure' regional environment. Far from serving as symbols of its engineering might, these dams could threaten the "Chinese dream" of achieving security, stability and sustainability.

IMPENDING WATER WARS IN SOUTH ASIA

Of the earth's total water availability, 97.5 per cent is saltwater, which leaves 2.5 per cent as freshwater available for consumption. But of this portion, 70 per cent is frozen in ice caps while 29 per cent lies underground as soil moisture. That leaves us with a miniscule one per cent freshwater available for human consumption.

A water crisis is looming as potentially 75 per cent of the world's population could face freshwater shortage by 2050, with global water shortages already threatening economic growth and geopolitical stability. The water crisis in South Asia in particular is gaining increasing attention, with major implications for stability in the region. It is inevitable that water is to become a likely source of conflict. The region's three major rivers, the Indus, the Ganges and the Brahmaputra, sustain water supplies for China, India, Pakistan and Bangladesh, all of which fall into a region classified as water-stressed, as the population here increases at the rate of 25 million people a year.

India, as both an upper and lower riparian country, finds itself in dispute with downstream neighbours, Pakistan and Bangladesh, which accuse it of attempting to dominate water flows. India fears the same of upstream China, which plans extensive dam-building projects over the Tsangpo River that flows into eastern India. The construction of Baglihar Dam by India in the disputed Kashmir region has triggered fierce opposition from Pakistan, which sees it as an effort to threaten, withhold and divert its rightful share of water. The view is that theBaglihar Dam creates a reservoir on a river coming into Pakistan and enables Indian control over the headwaters of the Indus, making Pakistan water dependent. The cumulative effect of the Baglihar Dam and other similar projects could give India the ability to store enough water to limit the supply to Pakistan at crucial times during the monsoon season. Therefore, these dams remain a source of significant tension.

India dismisses these allegations, stating that such projects merely delay river flows and considers itself to abide by the Indus Water treaty of 1960. Adding to the tension, more dams are being planned as India grows more power hungry, given its economic growth. The Indian Rajya Sabha reports 33 hydro projects in the border area with over 60 dam projects planned. Pakistan being downstream, is vulnerable as it is situated around a single great river, the Indus, which waters over 80 per cent of Pakistan's irrigated land that serves 180 million people.

More political row is certain in the future as both nations become water scarce and desperate for water access. India may keep dismissing Pakistan's concerns given that it is geographically situated upstream, however, it faces its own downstream concerns given its border with China.

Water shortage will become harder to manage as the region's population grows by 1.7 per cent yearly, creating more demand for food and causing further climate change. The effects of this can be seen already as weak river flows in several South Asian rivers are unable to subside waste. These river waters are becoming increasingly unsafe for drinking, cleaning and cropping, while encouraging parasitic diseases like Naegleria and deadly viruses such as dengue. Water tables are dropping and this is evident as the areas around the Ganges and the delta of the Indus in Pakistan are becoming semi-deserts. This results in more pumping of groundwater, which increases cases of arsenic poisoning.

The growing water shortage can be dealt with by governments collaborating to improve water management systems rather than sprinting to build dams and divert waters. As South Asia becomes increasingly water scarce, the potential for conflict will loom unless urgency and willingness is shown by governments to create multilateral arrangements and practices on inter-basin water sharing. Organisations such as the United Nations Water Agency and Saarc have a major role in promoting this agenda. Diplomatic dialogue and political cooperation is the only way forward in the hope of finding solutions.

THE INTERNATIONAL IMPLICATIONS OF CHINA'S WATER POLICIES

To determine the impact China's water policies will have internationally, China's foreign policy and its relationship with America, as the world's superpower, and India, as the regions other emerging power, need to be examined to understand possible international outcomes of these policies.

CHINA'S FOREIGN POLICY

Since the Cold War, Chinese foreign policies have primarily focused on promoting China's economic development and maintaining political and social stability within China. Main foreign policy objectives look to sustain an international environment that supports economic growth and stability by reassuring its neighbours and concerned international powers (particularly America) that China's rise is not an international threat. China, therefore, is willing to yield to international pressure on certain issues when resistance is seen to be detrimental to wider Chinese policies, and has accepted growing trends of multilateralism and interdependence in regard to economic issues.

However, China's poor record regarding human rights, intellectual property rights, product safety and its rising military presence has caused many (predominantly Western) countries to view China as a potentially destabilising influence in the international balance-of-power. This distrust is fed by China's demand for natural resources and its differing political and ideological views. This has resulted in the 'China threat theory' and is the dominant line of thinking in Western foreign policy discourse. Chinese leaders look to overcome this perception by promoting 'peaceful development' as its primary foreign policy doctrine, which involves commitment to multilateralism, peace and achieving a 'moderately well off society' through scientific development. Chinese leaders are therefore eager to avoid problems abroad and seek international cooperation as China develops and rises peacefully in international affairs.

However, China's rapid military modernisation makes it questionable how peaceful China's rise will be. China's military modernisation has made China the leading military power in Asia. This military development seems aimed at maintaining China's territorial sovereignty, especially in regards to Taiwan; preventing and protecting against potential attacks and dealing with 'local war' possibilities, such as territorial disputes with Japan or India. China's military capacity is increasing in capability, size and technology, enabling China to look further abroad in its deployment, and pre-emptively strike when protecting itself from perceived international threats. This seems at odds with Chinese policy of peaceful development and suggests the likelihood of China employing military force to achieve its national interests.

Chinese nationalism and security priorities highly affect China's foreign policy, as Chinese leadership is sensitive to national sovereignty and international security issues near China's borders. Therefore, in areas of security or political affairs, Chinese leaders are likely to view international relations in terms of balance-of-power. However, among Chinese leaders, there is a growing understanding of the importance of environmental protection for national security. The paradigm of environmental security, where environmental degradation acts as a 'threat multiplier' and so destabilises states, provides an alternative to the state-centric and military focused security theories, as environmental issues, particularly climate change, transcend national sovereignty and borders. Chinese leadership initially resisted the idea that issues like climate change could threaten national security, but increasingly recognise the importance of environmental conservation, as the associated security risks, especially exacerbating threats to security and social stability due to food and water availability, become more apparent. Environmental issues, such as water security, could therefore be perceived by Chinese leaders as issues of national security, to be dealt with in an uncompromising manner, which may threaten other countries' security interests.

The realist threat perception of China tends to overlook China's increasing engagement and cooperation internationally, and that international peace and stability are beneficial to China's development. Nevertheless, it would be naive to ignore China's assertiveness with respect to national interest priorities. Therefore, this paper aims to provide a balanced perception of the potential international consequences of China's water policies by highlighting possible areas of cooperation and tension internationally.

KEY CHINESE INTERNATIONAL RELATIONSHIPS

America

America's potential responses to China's water policies depend partly on the state of Sino-American relations. China's water policies will impact America through their potential effects on China's exports and impact on countries that America has close ties with.

Traditional realists generally view China's rise as a threat to US hegemony in the international system, and so believe that China must be contained. This view believes that rising powers tend to challenge the existing superpower so conflict between China and America is inevitable. Alternatively, from a constructivist perspective, China holds a positive perception of America and seeks to learn from its modernisation process, while America believes in having a special relationship with China. Therefore, both countries are predisposed to cooperation as the international system allows for both to realise their interests. Enhanced bilateral, regional and global cooperation has made it increasingly unlikely that the two will see each other as threats.

Interdependence between the two countries has grown, especially in their economic relationship. America is focusing on reviving its economy, which requires maintaining amicable relations with China due to China's position as the dominant emerging economy and holder of most of America's debt. Consequently, there is recognition that China with its surplus and America with its deficit, should cooperate to rebalance the global financial system, reinforcing the constructivist perspective of the need and desire for cooperation.

However, in issues of military, security and nationalism, Sino-American relations tend to follow a hard-lined realist approach. America authorising military sales to Taiwan angered China, and tensions are increasing at sea where US naval and military exercises with South Korea are concerning China. Additionally, America is opposed to China's territory disputes in the South and East China Seas, which has led to arms build-ups in both countries. America appears to be looking to India to counterbalance China, as India represents an alternative to Chinese hegemony in Asia. India's developing relationship with America chafes China and, as India is a democracy; its rise is accommodated by America. America, for example, has committed to upgrading defence cooperation, particularly in arms trade and technology transfer, with India to build a stronger defence and strategic partnership to reassure Asia against Chinese aggressive intentions.

Policymakers in China and America appear mistrustful of each other's intentions, especially in areas involving Taiwan, Japan and North Korea and any developments that could strain ties between them. Although cooperation has improved, a major increase in cooperation is unlikely in the short-term due to a range of conflicting interests and disputes. These centre on China's opposition to America's actions; such as American support for Taiwan, America playing a dominant role in the borders of Asia and aspects of American leadership in world affairs. America also views China unfavourably due to issues, including inequalities in the Sino-American economic relationship, American dependence on China financing its budget deficit, Chinese lack of enforcement of intellectual property rights, the build up of the Chinese military and the threat to US strategic interests in Taiwan, China's involvement in states that have a bad reputations internationally, plus China's poor human rights record. Currently, it remains doubtful that these differences will be resolved and these tensions could escalate in the future.

India

China's water policies include projects on trans-boundary rivers that could greatly impact India. As India is the other large developing nation in the region, Sino-Indian relations are examined to envisage potential outcomes of China's river policies.

Historically, Sino-Indian relations have been tense. Relations were minimal until China occupied Tibet in 1950, when the countries came to share a border. However, Communist China viewed India with wariness and suspicion as a capitalist reactionary country, and believed the Indian leaders were too influenced by Britain. The Indian Prime Minister of the time also believed Tibet should be independent, so was viewed unfavourably by the Chinese Communist party. Tibet, therefore, plays an influential role and remains relevant in Sino-Indian relations, especially as the Tibetan plateau is the source of many of the region's rivers.

After the Tibetan occupation, India and China had to engage diplomatically to establish an agreed Indian-Tibet border. India maintained that the McMahone Line, drawn up in the Simla Accord of 1914 between Britain, India, Tibet and China, was the border. China, however, refused to recognise the Line as, by doing so, it would cast doubt on the legitimacy of their takeover of Tibet. Recognising the validity of the Line would imply that Tibet was an independent state, not an inalienable part of China, and so China's occupation would have been an imperial conquest. Due to this, Arunachal Pradesh is still claimed by both India and China and is an area of frequent tension.

The Indian government granted the Dalai Lama asylum and provided refuge to many Tibetans after the Tibetan uprisings. These actions were seen as acts of provocation by China and the 1962 war over the disputed boundary further compounded the breakdown of Sino-Indian relations. As a result, India allowed the

Tibetans in India to form a government-in-exile, although this has never been formally acknowledged, and has also given the exiled Tibetan community significant assistance over the years.

Since 1976, Sino-Indian relations have begun to thaw but Tibet still remains a contentious issue. Tibet is an issue of national security for China as it provides a natural barrier between China and India, and is the origin of several major rivers. The legal foundation of China and India's border claims stem from the Tibet issue. China, especially after the 2008 Tibet uprising, is insecure about Tibet, and especially wary of India in this respect. India provides sanctuary to over 100,000 Tibetans and Tibet has always had a high degree of spiritual identification with India. The present Dalai Lama has also stated that India has a more legitimate claim on Tibet than China.

Despite tensions around Tibet, there are growing levels of political and economic engagement, which has helped stabilise the relationship and deter conflict. Economic relations, in particular, are viewed as an area of interdependence. Despite this perception, trade between the two has been described as superficial and uneven with India suffering from a widening trade deficit with China. India's exports to China largely consist of commodities and raw materials with little value-added, while China exports manufactured value-added goods to India. This disparity has led to India protesting and being the initiator of anti-dumping actions against China, which aggravate tensions between the two countries.

China's persistent relationship with Pakistan is a point of tension in Sino-Indian relations and considered a significant threat by India. China and Pakistan's close relationship grew from a shared hostility towards India and has remained strong due to China's concerns over energy security; ethnic unrest in China's western territories; and the need to counter India's potential as a future rival. India views these close ties as an attempt to encircle and contain it. Additionally, China and Pakistan have extensive defence ties, with China assisting to build Pakistan's conventional missile and nuclear capabilities. Pakistan is of strategic importance to China as it provides an alternative route for future energy supplies from the Middle East and the Persian Gulf. China uses its relationship with Pakistan mainly to advance its own interests, as demonstrated by China's varying stance over Kashmir and refusal to become militarily involved in Pakistan-India conflicts. China does, however, continue to supply Pakistan with military equipment and this is how analysts believe China intends to confine India's influence.

India's fears of containment are compounded by security concerns over China's 'String of Pearls' strategy. India fears that China's actions in increasing its geopolitical influence through extending its access to ports and airfields; developing special diplomatic relationships; and modernising military forces that extend from the South China Sea through the Malacca Straits across the Indian Ocean and to the Persian Gulf, is an attempt by China to gain a strategic foothold in the Indian Ocean and encircle India. While China claims that these ports are for trade purposes, India fears they could be used for military or strategic purposes, particularly if oil becomes scarce as India is positioned in the middle of China's supply route.

Recently, China has been developing a more balanced South Asian policy, which requires balancing support for Pakistan with improving Sino-Indian relations. Chinese leaders desire this as an Indian-Pakistan war would destabilise the whole region, but Pakistan still remains a sore spot in Sino-Indian relations. This conflict is exemplified by the issuing of unofficial visas by China to Indian residents of Jammu and Kashmir, implying that China believes these territories to be disputed. Similarly, in 2010, a visa was denied to the Indian army officer as he was considered to be commanding over a 'disputed area'. India responded by immediately cancelling defence exchanges with China. The Indian Foreign Secretary stated that India "has genuine concerns regarding aspects of the China-Pakistan relationship, particularly...China's role in Pakistan-Occupied Kashmir, China's [Jammu and Kashmir] policy and the Sino-Pakistani security and nuclear relationship". This has led analysts to suggest that China has undergone a policy reassessment towards India, possibly in response to India's closer relationship with America and its 'Look East' policy of forming close ties with nations also concerned with China's rising power.

CHINA'S WATER PROBLEMS

China is suffering from a lack of potable water, having to support 20% of the world's population on 5% of the world's renewable freshwater. The usable water resources that China possesses are under increasing strain and the Chinese Ministry of Water Resources has stated that water use has "already surpassed what our natural resources can bear". Water is vital to the economy, agriculture, industry, energy and people's livelihoods, and so is a hugely important resource and decreasing water resources are becoming a great concern to the Chinese government.

China's water resources are unequally distributed. China's northern regions are naturally water-scarce whereas the southern regions are water-rich. 19 out of China's 31 provinces, autonomous regions and municipalities have less water than the national average and these 19 account for 84% of the country's total industrial output and 67% of total agricultural output. Additionally, the water-rich south is losing water, increasing these concerns. Water pollution further adds to water issues: 78% of China's water is unfit for human consumption ; 90% of groundwater is polluted; and 19% of China's seven river basins and 35% of its 26 key lakes and reservoirs are too polluted for agricultural or industrial use. Polluted water is, however, still used due to huge demand and dwindling water resources, which leads to soil and crop contamination.

Agriculture

Water is the main constraint on food production and so water scarcity has an adverse effect on agriculture. When coupled with an increasing population, decreasing agricultural production threatens China's self-sufficiency. The Chinese agriculture sector is highly inefficient in its water use – it accounts for 66% of the water use in China but wastes over half of this, which further limits productivity. Water shortages result in water for agricultural use coming under increasing competition from industrial and municipal sectors.

Irrigation is heavily relied on to increase crop yields and is the largest water use in agriculture, relying mainly on groundwater extraction. This reliance on groundwater causes overexploitation and is unsustainable. Furthermore, China plans to increase its irrigated land by 2.7 million hectares by 2015 requiring more water. Due to the lack of water for agriculture, fertilisers are used to increase crop yields but over-use of fertilisers has the counter-productive effect of polluting water. Agriculture is the main source of water pollution in China, due to livestock farming, and fertiliser and pesticide run-off.

China has the largest population in the world to feed and its economic growth has resulted in an increasing affluent class. This has contributed to water scarcity as it has resulted in a dietary change towards meat consumption, which requires significantly more water to produce than crops, which has driven an increase in more water-intensive factory farming, especially of pigs.

Industry

The power sector is a major water user, as almost 96% of China's electric power generation requires water and in 2010, China became the world's largest energy consumer. China is reliant on energy from coal, which requires vast amounts of water to mine, wash and for cooling power stations. Furthermore, China plans to expand coal mines and power plants in its water-scarce northern and western regions, which could create a water crisis and drought in these regions. This expansion is aimed to meet government estimates that Chinese energy companies need to produce a billion metric tons more of coal annually by 2020, and the mining process to meet this demand requires 15 billion m^3 of water.

Although China has benefited economically from its position as the world's manufacturing factory, this requires potable water to produce goods, which are then exported to other countries – essentially exporting potable water in a virtual form. China is left with the pollution and wastewater from this manufacturing process, limiting its own supply of usable water. Chinese industries are inefficient in their use of water, generally requiring 10 -20% more water than industries in developed countries. The Ministry of Environmental Protection stated in 2009 that annual industrial wastewater discharge was 23.4 billion tonnes.

CHINA'S WATER POLICIES

Water management in China is, therefore, receiving increasing attention due to the worsening nature of the crisis. To attempt to address this, experts in China are pushing policies such as water pricing reforms, conservation, and recycling. Some of these are being enacted, but not enough as China's plans focus on major projects such as the SNWDP, which could result in additional economic and environmental costs.

China has implemented several policies that directly look at tackling water pollution or promoting water conservation, but several of its other policies have an effect on its water resources. These include a number of pollution and environmental policies, as climate change exacerbates droughts in the northern regions and the melting of the Himalayan glaciers limit river flows, energy policies, due to the interlinked nature of energy and water, as well as various economic policies, all of which effect China's water resources.

Recent reforms to address China's water problems, including the 11th Number One Document (which for the first time focused on water), have been heavily criticised for not going far enough to protect China's water resources. Fundamental changes are needed, rather than unattainable and difficult to enforce targets and consumption caps that do not address the reality that water resources are being polluted and overexploited without liability and accountability.

12th Five Year Plan 2011-2015

China's 12th Five Year Plan (12FYP) aims to address flaws in previous water policies and has been described as the "turning point to a brave new world". The 12FYP recognises China's water crisis and been described as the "most stringent water resource policies to date". The quotas and targets set in the 12FYP are now part of the Central Plan and its pollution and efficiency targets ensure these are met in the long term and not only during official inspections. The government recognises that water will be a choking point for economic development and so effectively has no choice but to address this issue. The 12FYP focuses on conserving and cleaning water resources and introduces a range of policies aimed to do this; however, the present paper is focused on Chinese policies affecting water under this plan that have potential international implications.

The measures under the 12FYP that will possibly have international implications include those that raise the cost of operating in China, as these affect the cost of Chinese goods and exports. These include measures to curb water pollution and encourage water efficiency; mainly through setting targets. These targets include reducing the Chemical Oxygen Demand, by 8% by 2015 and six new pollution targets that impact fertiliser use in agriculture. These targets include a 10% target for nitrogen oxides which is intended to encourage industries to move away from coal and implement pollution-reducing technology, reducing water use and pollution. Penalties will be applied to enterprises or public institutions that contravene pollution standards of any surface water bodies and groundwater. A country-wide system of imposing a levy on discharges and fines for any violations of the permissible standards has also been introduced. Water usage caps have been implemented to ensure that demand does not exceed supply, which means that enterprises will have to operate using less water, and if these quotas are exceeded the enterprise could have its business permit revoked.

Market-based policy mechanisms are increasingly employed to conserve water resources. Water prices will be reformed to reflect water scarcity and a progressive pricing scheme is planned for 2015. This means that the price of water will rise exponentially as water consumption increases. High water rates will be adopted for water-intensive industries and in rural areas a system will be implemented whereby discounts are given when water use stays within quotas, but water prices will rise if the quota is exceeded. Water tariffs, to encourage water efficiency and improve water management, have been significantly raised for urban and industrial use, although prices vary between provinces.

Export taxes have been placed on energy and resource-intensive goods, including a 5% export tax placed on coal, oil and coke, in order to discourage these goods being exported and to save scarce resources (including water in virtual form). Export tax rebates were eliminated or cut for 553 high-energy, pollution and resource-intensive products. Import tariffs on 26 energy and resource-intensive products were cut from 3-6% to 0-3%. There is also smaller export VAT refund on energy and resource-intensive goods. This policy is complementary to China's export tax policy and the two are designed to limit exports and increase the world market price of the affected goods. This policy seems to be effective as Chinese exports are less water-pollution intensive than Chinese imports and between 1995 and 2004, the water-pollution intensity of exports fell by about 84%.

South-North Water Diversion Project (SNWDP)

The government believes that water conservation alone will not meet the country's energy and water production demands. In the past, water shortages were dealt with by water-transfer projects; however, the government is planning a long-term permanent solution – the SNWDP. The SNWDP consists of building three giant canals to transfer water from southern to northern China. Construction began in 2002 and the Eastern and Central lines are to be completed by 2014 and will remove almost 36 billion m^3 of water annually from the Yangtze River basin and transport it to the north. The project will cost an estimated USD 62 billion. Authorities insist that the project "makes perfect sense" and is essential to developing the fastest growing cities in the northern and western regions of China, which are rapidly running out of water.

The Western line of the project is the most controversial of the three lines as it includes building a dam on the Great Bend of the Yarlung-Tsangpo, where the river curves into the Assamese plain of India and becomes the Brahmaputra. China is likely to construct a large hydropower station and storage dam in this area diverting 200 billion $m^3$of the Tsangpo's water to the Yellow River. China's exact plans for the SNWDP are difficult to ascertain due to conflicting sources, but several issues have caused it to be delayed, including, unstable geological conditions; freezing temperatures; technical challenges of the construction; diverting water impeding the capacity and operation of current hydropower projects downstream; and the mass relocation of villages, but this route holds the greatest potential water transfer.

Dam Projects

China's 12FYP calls for an increase in the use of hydroelectric power as under the 11FYP China only achieved 2/3 of its hydroelectric projects. China is damming trans-boundary rivers to achieve its hydropower targets, increasing its water-storage capacity and minimizing coal use; thereby reducing pollution and helping control climate change. China shares six river systems which originate from the Tibetan plateau in China with nine of its neighbours, which gives China an advantage utilising them. China has rejected the notion of national integrity over shared water resources (where states have the right not to be negatively affected by activities of upper-riparian countries), instead following a policy of absolute sovereignty. China has built more dams on its rivers than the rest of the world combined, and has no water sharing agreement or treaty with any of the states it shares rivers with. China is also not signatory to the 1997 UN Convention on Non-Navigable Use of International Water Courses.

China is already building eight out of a proposed 15 dams along the Lancang section of the Mekong River. Three of these dams are operational, but there has been little consultation with downstream countries. Similarly, China's Yunnan Provincial Government is proposing one of the world's highest dams on the Salween River, which flows into Myanmar and Thailand. This dam would be in an environmentally sensitive area according to the World Wide Fund for Nature, and the Provincial Government has not consulted Myanmar or Thailand.

China has also started its dam projects on the Tsangpo, with currently six hydropower developments, and the Zangmu dam, predicted to be fully operational in 2014. In total, China is planning to build 28 dams along the Tsangpo. All the hydropower projects will be run-of-the-river dams (i.e. will not have storage capacity), the largest of which will be at Motuo on the Great Bend near India's border, and will have almost twice the energy generating capacity of the Three Gorges Dam and the potential to form part of the Western line of the SNWDP

Despite complaints from lower-riparian countries, China has frequently stressed that dam building does not harm the environment and will bring regional benefits including improved navigation, flood and drought control.

'Going Global' Policy

The Chinese government recognises that these policies will probably not be sufficient to address their water issues and so have developed a 'going global' policy, to reduce dependence on imports of agriculture and raw resources. The government has encouraged investment in agricultural land, especially in Africa, Southeast Asia and South America, to produce agricultural products and import them to China (US International Trade Commission (USITC) 2011,p.4.3). Land acquisition is particularly popular, as access to land is essentially access to water which is often free and unregulated. Water scarcity, therefore, often compels investment in agricultural land as the water is considered more important than the land itself. The Chinese government has encouraged Chinese firms to 'go out' to seek resources by offering incentives. In response, Chinese corporations are controlling the supply of agricultural commodities and raw materials destined for China by investing in Russia, Brazil, Argentina and Canada among other countries. In the past five years, China has become a major player in the global land market to safeguard their domestic food security and has leases for agricultural land in Zambia, Tanzania, Zimbabwe and the Democratic Republic of Congo, and plans to invest USD 5 billion in African farming.

Policy Problems

There are, however, a number of problems with China's water policies, which cast doubts on the 12FYP, especially as China has a poor record when environmental policies conflict with economic policies. The complexity of China's institutional structures means that implementation and enforcement of environmental regulations is a challenge. Ministries have overlapping functions in planning, standard setting and monitoring that lead to conflicts of interest, and inefficiencies of policy implementation and legal enforcement. Once official crackdowns to ensure compliance with environmental laws have ended, "polluting industries can up pick up where they left off – as long as it will benefit GDP growth". China's environmental authorities are weak and the Ministry of Environmental Protection lacks financial influence and manpower compared to other agencies in China's Administration. The State Council recognises these problems, stating that "laws are not observed or strictly enforced, violators are not brought to justice; local protectionism, departmental protectionism and difficulties in law enforcement occur" and noting that government officials take bribes and bend the law, and abuse their power and authority to override the law.

The Central governments delegation of power to local governments causes difficulties in policy implementation and regulatory enforcement. According to a well respected Chinese environmental lawyer, barely 10% of China's environmental laws and regulations are enforced; and when they are, pollution fines are often less than the cost of adopting pollution control technology, so there is little incentive to reduce pollution. Even when local officials do collect pollution fines, they often only collect about 30% of the fine.

Market-based mechanisms, such as increasing water tariffs, generally result in increasing water use efficiency, but the implementation of water tariffs is problematic due to unclear responsibilities, poor collection-rates and institutional capacities. Additionally, an increase in water prices will not have a long-term effect if the demand for water is inelastic. In Beijing, for example, water prices are high, but water demand continues to grow. Ultimately, the end-users' income level and awareness affects how much water is saved.

The government has also issued conflicting policies, including plans to double the size of the economy in 10 years and urbanize another 350 million people over 20 years. Energy is needed to reach these goals and it is unlikely that the demand will be met by clean energy; therefore more coal will be required. Coal mining and use is highly water-intensive and it is unlikely that China's freshwater supply can meet this demand. Also, measures for addressing water scarcity need energy to operate, and national energy policies do not fully consider their impact on freshwater consumption, and vice-versa, which will create unsustainable outcomes. Government targets under the 12FYP to control pollution require energy to build and operate waste treatment plants, and achieving water targets also requires energy use, so reaching both of these targets increases energy demand.

Additionally, the Chinese government's preference for large projects prevents effective planning in managing water resources and there are problems with the SNWDP, which hinder its potential to address water issues.

The SNWDP will take at least 10 years to complete, so in the short–term, it will not alleviate water concerns, plus it will not transfer enough water to fulfil present, let alone future demand. The Ministry of Water Resources recognises this inability to meet demand, stating that the project will not solve China's water problem, but described it as a "'lifeline'".

There are also concerns over whether the water transferred will be clean enough to use when it reaches its destination. Extra treatment facilities are, for example, required for the Yangtze River's water, which currently is too polluted to be usable despite it already passing through over 400 water treatment plants and pollution control projects.

The majority of water transferred by the SNWDP is intended for industrial use, with a small percentage destined for agriculture, despite the concern that agriculture is in greater need of the water due to the risk of food shortages. Water from the project will be expensive for municipal and industry use, and probably prohibitively expensive for agriculture.

High water prices make desalination a cheaper alternative. There is also the issue of possible water shortages in the south due to the project, as the south is already losing water. Several transfer regions are concerned they will not be left with enough water to meet their demand, which causes conflict between the supply and transfer regions. The Western line's chief, however, believes the political and cultural resistance can be resolved and authorities maintain that the line will be built.

INTERNATIONAL IMPLICATIONS OF TRANS-BOUNDARY RIVER POLICIES

China's water policies include major projects on trans-boundary rivers, which will impact lower-riparian nations. China has built several of its dams on shared rivers, which has influenced downstream hydrology, causing sediment erosion of riverbanks and changing nutrient profiles. This has caused increased tensions between China and its neighbours, especially as information to assess the impacts of these dams is generally not available. Downstream countries are susceptible as China has strong political influence and access to capital, and so can manage its water resources in a manner contrary to the interests of lower-riparian countries. Furthermore, the SNWDP has the potential to divert water from the Brahmaputra River which is important to India, Pakistan and Bangladesh.

With respect to the Mekong River, Thai fishermen claim Chinese dams are responsible for the depletion of fish and the unpredictable flow of the Mekong since dam building started. Downstream states have frequently requested China to participate in multilateral consultation and have formed the Mekong River Commission (MRC), which China has refused to join. This reluctance to participate in regional, multilateral engagement is down to China's increasing water scarcity and worries of similar demands by other downstream states. A severe drought in 2010, however, caused China to become more willing to cooperate, with Chinese delegations participating in MRC discussions and data sharing. Nonetheless, the Chinese delegation emphasised that the drought was due to forces of nature and not China's hydropower development and assured the MRC that China's projects will not severely impact downstream water flow.

China's river plans could potentially affect Nepal, as some of its major rivers originate in Tibet, where China is contemplating more dams and diversion projects. This could also impact India, as tributaries from these rivers account for 46-71% of the Ganges River's water, creating problems for downstream India and Bangladesh. There is, however, little evidence that these plans are high on the political agenda, especially compared to China's plans regarding the Tsangpo.

China has no water sharing agreement or treaty with any of its lower-riparian states. Thailand, Laos, Cambodia, Vietnam and Myanmar have all been affected and expressed concerns over China's treatment of these shared rivers. These countries are, however, unlikely to have a significant effect on China's policies or stance towards trans-boundary rivers, as they probably will not form a united-bloc against China as they are fighting amongst themselves over their water issues and the power-dynamic remains in China's favour. However, India, as the other emerging regional power, is increasingly threatened by China's plans and may be able to challenge China, and so Sino-Indian relations with respect to China's designs over the countries shared rivers will be an important focus of this paper.

In terms of policies impacting Sino-Indian relations, China's policies regarding trans-boundary rivers are unclear. In 2010, Chinese Premier Wen Jiabao assured Indian leaders that China will not undertake projects that will affect countries downstream; similarly, the Chinese Foreign Ministry spokeswoman told India that "at present, the hydropower station on the Yarlung Tsangpo...will not lead to any big change in the downstream water levels or affect the harnessing efforts by the downstream countries". She stated that China "will fully consider impacts to downstream countries" and that "the dam being built on the Brahmaputra River has a small storage capacity. It will not have a large impact on water flow or the ecological environment downstream". Chinese specialists, however, maintain that the shrinking of the Himalayan glaciers will cause the Ganges, Yangtze and Yellow Rivers to have seasonal flows, making water security an issue of food and political security. Therefore, these threats dictate that China should exercise territorial sovereignty, exerting unlimited rights over resources within its territory.

The Tsangpo, or Brahmaputra, is important to India, as it is one of India's largest non-seasonal rivers and accounts for over a 25% of India's total water resources and 29% of the total run-off of India's rivers. The Tsangpo currently flows into Assam in India, where it forms the Brahmaputra and then joins the Ganges to form the world's largest river delta, providing water to over 300 million people. This river has largely escaped Chinese notice until recently, and, due to its importance to India and the region, China's designs have the potential to impact a huge number of people.

CHINESE DAM POLICIES

China maintains that the purpose of building dams along the Tsangpo is to generate electricity which will not require storage of water in large reservoirs. A senior engineer from the Zangmu dam's construction company stated that the river will not be stopped during construction and when operational, the water's flow will not be reduced. However, as demonstrated by China's dams along the Mekong River, India could still be affected in several ways.

Potential Impact on India

Any damming of rivers affects their flow, and China plans to build numerous dams on the Tsangpo. India believes that China's current dams on the river have had an effect on the Brahmaputra. In Arunachal Pradesh, it was claimed that the Brahmaputra almost dried up due to China's dams. If this is so, then the reduced flow will have an adverse effect on the economy and environment of India's north east. The Zangmu dam project, which is under construction, is reported to have the potential for 'flood control and irrigation,' which requires water storage and diversion and suggest that this dam could reduce the Brahmaputra's flow and have a greater impact on India than China claims.

Even if the dams do not have a significant effect on the Brahmaputra's flow, hydropower dams still impact downstream ecology by removing silt, which can block turbines, from the river before it enters the dam. This silt is nutrient-rich and vital for agriculture in India and Bangladesh. Most people living in the Brahmaputra's catchment area are farmers so the loss of this silt could adversely affect agriculture, especially if there is a reduction in water flow from the Brahmaputra, which raises concerns over India's food security. Pollution from the dams' construction will also be carried downstream, impacting farmland and depleting fish stocks, adding to food security concerns. Air pollution is also believed to contribute to melting the Himalayan glaciers, further depleting the regions rivers. The great potential for food shortages could cause social instability in India.

There are concerns that these dams pose geological risks, especially dams built on the Great Bend, which could cause seismic activity. In a worst-case scenario, the dams could collapse, creating a giant wave and destroying anything in its path, which may cause a domino effect, destroying downstream dams, which could be devastating to Arunachal Pradesh.

Potential Indian Responses

China's dam projects may not have a significant impact on India, but due to India's fears and mistrust of China, India will probably take action to ensure its water security. India feels threatened by China's advantageous position as the upper-riparian state and will try to safeguard its water resources. India, in the short-term, will look to take preventative action against China to halt its dam projects, through aiming to increase cooperation and decrease mistrust between the two and through this, secure a water sharing agreement from China.

India is looking to use principles of international water law, such as "no significant harm" and "prior notification of works", to increase its legitimacy as the lower-riparian state and enhance its bargaining position. However, India recognises that China is unlikely to cooperate voluntarily given its unpromising relations with other lower-riparian states and the MRC, and so will need to incentivise China to engage in water issues, while safeguarding against the possibility of hostile damming from China. India aims to achieve this through the de-securitisation of water resource management and by taking a river basin approach.

De-securitising water resources is important as it limits the potential for conflict, and for water to be used as a political weapon against India. River dialogue must be isolated from military and political concerns. To help defuse tensions, this separation can be achieved by presenting the issue as one of improving resource management with China. This is already underway, with the sharing of hydrological flood data between China and India, which has helped build trust. India could seek to engage China in cooperating over issues that are not politically sensitive and that are mutually beneficial, such as collaborating on improving water use in the agricultural sector, which will hopefully lead to cooperation on more contentious water issues.

However, China has rejected offers to join the MRC for managing river disputes and continues to develop its dam projects on the Mekong without consulting downstream countries. This reinforces the view that China wants to consolidate the greatest amount of control over its water resources and will continue to treat them with absolute sovereignty, making it difficult to find areas where cooperation is mutually beneficial. India encouraging cooperation may lead to a slight easing of tensions with China, but it is unlikely to halt China's plans on the Tsangpo, especially as China considers solving its water problems to be in its national interests.

From an Indian perspective, including Bangladesh in the engagement of China in this area is critical to finding a long-term solution. It benefits India to protect Bangladesh's interests, as water shortages in Bangladesh will likely cause migration to India. If Bangladesh is excluded, then it may feel that its sovereignty is being threatened and raises the potential for future conflict. China has signed a provision of flood season hydrological data with Bangladesh so will be unable to dismiss Bangladesh's interest as illegitimate. Collaboration in these areas will create a more amicable political climate and increases the likelihood of an agreement being reached.

However, India's claims against China's water projects lose legitimacy when India's actions as an upper-riparian state with regard to Bangladesh are considered, as India is planning 168 large hydropower projects in Arunachal Pradesh. India has, therefore, effectively been acting in a similar manner as China by exploiting its water resources to Bangladesh's detriment. Given the volatile nature of the Indian-Bangladeshi water relationship, it is questionable if Bangladesh will want to side with India against China. Given that India has failed to solve water disputes with a friendly state, it seems overly optimistic that raising concerns with

China will benefit India. China, therefore, will probably dismiss India, as it has the MRC states, and proceed with its water projects.

In the international arena, tensions have already surfaced through disputes over Asian Development Bank (ADB) loans to India that China attempted, or managed, to block, as they included funding for water projects in the disputed Arunachal Pradesh. Situations like this are predicted to become more common as water becomes increasingly scarce in the two nations.

If India fails to engage China on their proposed dam projects, and the projects prove to be highly damaging to India, then India's response will probably be combined with its response towards the proposed Western line of the SNWDP. The Western line's effect on India will likely amplify the impact of China's dam projects, as diverting the river will reduce its flow even more and have greater potential environmental consequences.

THE SOUTH-NORTH WATER DIVERSION PROJECT

The Western line of the SNWDP is the line that will have the most impact on India. This line is also the most controversial, as it is difficult to determine the likelihood of the line being built due to the lack of transparency and reluctance to share information from China. In response to Indian concerns, Beijing denies that it is considering diverting the Tsangpo, with China's Minister for Water Resources stating that the diversion of the Tsangpo is "unnecessary, unfeasible and unscientific". Authorities close to the government, however, say the line will be built and it has been approved in China's 12FYP. Many commentators also believe it is a matter of when, not if, the line will be built.

Potential Impact on India

If the Western line proceeds, it will divert 200 billion m^3 of the Tsangpo's water north and could cause drastic water shortages in the north of India. This could result in India becoming dependant on China for the Brahmaputra's flow, giving China political leverage. By reducing India's water supply, China could effectively halt India's economic growth and India would be at China's mercy during the dry season, and for flood protection during the rainy season. Reduction in the Brahmaputra's flow will affect India's utilisation of the river for its own projects. India's hydroelectric power potential will be reduced by roughly 40%, discouraging potential investors in this area and limiting India's clean-energy plans. India is suffering from a scarcity of potable water and has devised its own transfer project, the 'National River Linking Project' to divert water from the Himalayas to basins in south and peninsula India. The project is not currently underway, but if it proceeds, it will depend on water from the Brahmaputra. Reducing the rivers flow would thwart this project and deny India a potential solution to their own water crisis.

The diversion of the Tsangpo will adversely impact Bangladesh and could cause mass migration to India due to water related issues. Such a migration will create a human security issue and add to present ethnic conflicts, destabilise the region, and could strain Indian-Bangladeshi relations. There could be a greater reduction in agricultural production under the diversion of the Tsangpo than through China's dam projects due to the reduction in the rivers flow and silt, increasing the threat to food security and social stability. This threat to food security may be exacerbated by India's growing population and the influx of migrants from Bangladesh.

There is, however, the belief, mainly among Chinese scholars and analysts, that the diversion of the Tsangpo would not have a significant effect on the Brahmaputra's flow. This is as the majority of the Brahmaputra's water is collected from tributaries on the Indian side of the border and are a more significant source of the rivers waters than the shrinking glaciers.

Potential Indian Response

The best outcome for India, and the region as a whole, with respect to China's SNWDP would be to prevent China from implementing the Western line, as once China has diverted the Tsangpo it will be difficult for India to change the flow back. As proposed above, India will probably adopt a strategy to de-securitise water and encourage a basin-wide approach. There are, however, several other strategies India may employ in the hope of securing their water resources and stabilising the region.

Chinese and Indian leaders recognise that water security is a matter of national security, which legitimises the use of exceptional action. The water dispute is an issue that will probably be exacerbated with time and is believed to be the "biggest potential point of contention between the two Asian giants". India's foreign policy is developing a harder line against China, and water disputes will potentially be escalated by existing tensions between the two. Furthermore, it is believed that internal disputes over water will result in governments taking a stronger stance on external water disputes, especially as water security is likely to become an issue of political security. China believes water security is vital to its national interests so may go ahead with all its water plans on the Tsangpo taking full advantage of its position as the upper-riparian state to ensure its own water supply. While this is seemingly beneficial to China, it could be highly destabilising for the region and detrimental to downstream states with the potential to cause a humanitarian and environmental crisis.

Water Sharing Treaty

India desires a water sharing agreement with China, similar to those it has with Pakistan and Bangladesh, which could prevent the Western line of the SNWDP being built and stop some of China's hydropower projects. These existing water agreements have survived numerous conflicts, provide clarity over water rights and use, and provide mechanisms for dispute settlement. Such an agreement with China could reduce China's leverage as the upper-riparian state and provide a dispute settlement mechanism so disagreements can be worked out in a straightforward manner. India could attempt to obtain a treaty with China through continually engaging and opening channels of communication with China; building on previous agreements on sharing hydrological data for flood control and any mutually beneficial collaborations. India could also attempt to influence Chinese water plans and secure a water agreement by playing on China's insecurity over Tibet. India keeps the Tibet issue an international issue and its support of the Tibetan community in India has allowed the survival of their language, tradition, culture and nationalism. India's policies in this area, therefore, contradict China's claims that Tibet is an inalienable part of China and adds to Chinese insecurity over Tibet. In the past year India's policy towards Tibet has taken a harder line, with India implying to China that it will not concede to China on its core issue of Tibet, as long as China refuses to concede to India on their core issues. India, in 2010, publically and explicitly mentioned India's concerns over China's plan to dam Tibetan rivers that impact India, as an Indian core issue. Therefore, it would be political suicide for any Indian government to give ground to China on Tibet without an equal concession in return. Thus, this may be an area where India could politically manoeuvre to obtain a water sharing agreement.

India could look to the example set by Kazakhstan in their dealings with China over shared rivers. China has been diverting water from the Irtysh River since the 1990s and planned, by 2020, to double the volume of water diverted from the river. Diverting the river has led to reduced flow and increased pollution in Kazakhstan, leading the Kazakh press to publish a series of unfavourable articles that induced China to negotiate and resulted in agreements being signed over sharing water quality information in 2006. In 2007, Russia and Kazakhstan managed to bring water usage and rights of international rivers as a discussion topic to the Shanghai Cooperation Organisation (SCO) Forum and eventually, in 2011, an Agreement on Water Quality in Transboundary Rivers was signed. Kazakhstan's success in getting China to negotiate may be attributed to the value of its copper and oil to China, and success in bringing the issue to the SCO Forum to exert pressure on China. India, conversely, only has observer status in the SCO and is not rich in copper or oil, but could raise the issue of water sharing in alternative international forums to pressurise China to sign an agreement.

India has mainly pursued a bilateral approach with respect to trans-boundary rivers, but believes that Pakistan, Bangladesh and Nepal should be involved in countering China's water diversion plans as they also share rivers with China. Bangladesh has proposed joint basin-wide management of the Brahmaputra with China and India, which is hoped, will draw China into deeper engagement with lower-riparian states and set the basis for a water basin agreement. Furthermore, India aims to start a broader coalition, including Nepal, Bangladesh and Bhutan, on the Ganges-Brahmaputra-Meghna river system, which combined with increased international awareness, will induce China to formulate a river basin approach with the lower-riparian states.

However, China seems unwilling to enter into a water sharing agreement with India as Chinese local media believe that such an agreement would be "humiliating". As China is exercising the principle of absolute sovereignty over Tibetan rivers it is unlikely to let Indian concerns prevent it from fulfilling its perceived national interests. China is also unlikely to partake in a water sharing agreement, or become signatory to the 1997 UN Convention as China was 1 of only 3 countries that voted against the convention. This makes the resolution of potential problems complex and gives China leverage. Additionally, there are worries in India that once water problems become more serious, it will be increasingly difficult to engage China in water treaties, as China will be unwilling to compromise its water security. This makes it difficult to solve water disputes peacefully and increases the likelihood of conflict and tensions between the two countries.

China's track record regarding its involvement in river basin committees is not encouraging. The MRC, which is backed by Japan and the ADB, has been unable to prevent China's aggressive river projects. The Commission can only request China to "make amends" and this has not had any effect on China's projects, therefore India's desire to involve China in a river basin management scheme regarding the Brahmaputra will likely yield similar results.

Cooperation and Conflict

India and China already cooperate on several energy issues and share a similar stance on climate change responsibilities. If both nations are able to de-securitise the water issue then contentious border issues could be avoided. Tensions that surround the McMahone line will, therefore, not escalate the water disputes, which will make cooperation or a water sharing agreement more likely. Cooperation over water resources is desirable as it would stabilise the region and promote better management of resources, so ensuring long-term sustainable river management and mitigate some of the negative effects of climate change on river systems. China can benefit greatly by having a positive relationship with India, due to the potential for trade expansion; increasing economic ties; and promoting peace and stability in the region. Therefore, cooperation and shared management of the Tsangpo/Brahmaputra should be possible, especially given recent cooperation in Sino-Indian relations.

Keeping Sino-Indian border issues separate from water disputes is, however, unlikely as the current Indian government is too weak to compromise on issues of 'national honour'. Any concession to China on border issues, or failure of the government to take action against China diverting the Brahmaputra, will likely be greeted with strong public opposition. China will probably look to use water as a tool to pressurise India and gain concessions on boundary issues. Separating these issues is also complicated by the Brahmaputra supplying water to Arunachal Pradesh, which both China and India claim. China refuses to recognise Arunachal Pradesh as part of India, instead referring to it as 'Southern Tibet'. China's assertion means that it claims almost 200 million feet^3 s$^-$ of water resources in the state. Therefore, a water dispute in this area could easily turn into a wider dispute about territory, where tensions are already high. Both countries have increased their military presences at the border, which increases the possibility of a minor dispute in the area escalating into a full scale conflict.

India will probably become more possessive over its water resources due to China's hydrological advantage. India believes that as there are no water treaties, it must establish user's rights, essentially first in time, first in right. Therefore, India may try and harness the Brahmaputra's potential in the lower regions of Arunachal Pradesh to marginalise China's intentions on the river. Water projects in Arunachal Pradesh would become of national priority and have the maximum possible storage capacity to cope with possible water shortages caused by China. However, China is unlikely to be deterred by India's claims that it has user's rights on the Brahmaputra, especially as there is no international law or mechanism where India can defend this right. This right is only defensible if there is a water sharing agreement and China's dealings with the MRC demonstrate that China does not recognise the principle of first user's right. India will, therefore, be unable to rely on this right to protect its water resources.

China's water projects are likely to put additional strain on India's already increasing water shortages, leading India to divert more water from Pakistan. This increases the chance of conflict between the two countries and India is already preparing for the possibility of a "two front war" against China and Pakistan. China's constant support for Pakistan, and its military and nuclear assistance, would indirectly implicate it in any Indian-Pakistani conflict. Furthermore, China, India and Pakistan are all nuclear powers, so conflict between any of these nations could have disastrous consequences. Worryingly, although India and China are signatories of the no-first-use doctrine of nuclear weapons, China does not consider the use of nuclear weapons in its own territory as a violation of this doctrine. This means that China could potentially threaten to use nuclear weapons in water or border conflicts regarding Arunachal Pradesh, although the possibility of a nuclear conflict is unlikely, even in a worst-case scenario.

India's water plans in Arunachal Pradesh do not bode well for Bangladesh, which is highly dependent on the Brahmaputra's waters. India may go ahead with these projects even if the Western line is never developed, which could spark a humanitarian crisis in Bangladesh by significantly reducing their water and food supply, and increasing migration from Bangladesh to India. Indian actions in this respect would be highly detrimental to Indian-Bangladeshi relations and could result in conflict as well as increased instability within both countries.

India has also proposed to counter China's diversion plans by planning a South Asian-China-ADB power project at the Great Bend, although how this will solve India's water fears regarding the Brahmaputra is unclear. Rather, it seems dangerously counterproductive as it justifies China's proposals that will potentially have the greatest negative impact on downstream countries. It may be that India believes that if it cannot prevent China's plans, it can at least benefit from a share of the energy the project will generate.

International Pressure

India hopes to raise international awareness of the humanitarian importance of Tibet's water to almost 2 billion people, to convey the principle that Tibet's water resources are for everybody and not just China's benefit. India could raise awareness through the 'UN-Water' mechanism, which devises effective strategies for integrated management of water resources and use this raised awareness to exert international pressure on China. China has faced strong opposition from 263 NGOs over its dam construction projects on the Lancang River. These NGOs are worried about China's ability to use the Tibetan rivers as a political weapon and want a moratorium on the lower Mekong dams for at least 10 years. China Power Investment's plan to build a dam, similar to that of the Three Gorges Dam, in Myanmar (the Myitsone mega-dam project), which would supply 90% of the electricity produced to China, has been suspended due to opposition from local villagers, community groups and international NGOs. The Myanmar government, to China's shock, decided that it had to "listen to the people" and suspended construction. Therefore, it is possible that India could work with international NGOs and awareness groups to bring China's projects under similar pressure and slow down or halt construction.

International Influence

Both countries are competing to increase their influence in Asia to strengthen their international positions. India has signed a Comprehensive Economic Partnership Agreement with Japan, which will make each country the other's largest trading partner. India has signed bilateral trade agreements, or comprehensive free trade agreements, with Nepal, South Korea and 10 ASEAN member countries. Together with agreements with Sri Lanka and negotiations with Bangladesh, India has the majority of Asian economies covered, increasing its economic influence in the region. Furthermore, many South East Asian countries hold a greater dislike and mistrust for China than for India, due to India being a democracy, and China has aligned itself with countries that internationally are of poor repute, such as Pakistan, Myanmar and North Korea.

India's 'Look East' policy is another way to enhance its international position by increasing its influence in China's backyard. An Indian official stated that "our challenge will be to build our own leverage", so relationships with America, Japan and South East Asian parties are very important. India is likely to gain momentum in this respect, which will bring it into conflict with China's traditional resistance to an expanded Indian international role. India is currently pushing for a seat on the UN Security Council which all the Permanent Members, aside from China, have explicitly endorsed. India, therefore, is likely to be favoured regionally and internationally over China, which may lead to China curtailing some of its more controversial water plans due to concerns over international repercussions.

Tensions between India and China in the international arena have already surfaced and are likely to worsen if China diverts the Tsangpo. Although India is building up its international influence through its 'Look East' policy, it is unlikely that it will gain a permanent seat on the UN Security Council, especially as China can veto India's attempts. This could be problematic if India tried to bring an action to the Security Council, as China can veto any potential international action against it. India is, therefore, likely to strengthen its ties with America as it looks to gain support for its water grievances. India is of strategic importance to America's plans to reassert itself in the region and to contain perceived Chinese aggression. America is likely to offer India capacity building assistance in anticipation of the challenges China poses to India in this area. Therefore, Sino-American tensions are likely to increase as America will probably view China's water actions unfavourably due to the potential humanitarian, and destabilising, regional consequences. America may, therefore, counter China's actions through greater political, economic and military influence in the region and thereby increase the growing Sino-American rivalry.

India and China are both vying for regional and international influence, which, with deteriorating relations and rising tensions between them, could produce external alliances. This could generate new alignments and polarise Asia, compromising each countries internal options and could result in a regional 'Cold War' type situation.

RESULTING SITUATION

As a result of these factors, the most likely scenario is where China will be unwilling to sacrifice its sovereignty over shared rivers, and while it is difficult to ascertain if the Western line of the SNWDP will be built, it is probable that China will continue with all its dam projects on the Tsangpo. Given China's increasing energy demand it may also undertake the giant hydropower project on the Great Bend. Furthermore, if China decides that its national interests demand the projects to go ahead, it is unlikely to let lower-riparian states, or even international law, deter its interests.

Water is held to be a long-term threat to Asian stability and, given the generally dire relations between South Asian countries, water clashes will be more likely then cooperation. This is especially true as the Chinese and Indian governments will probably be unable to isolate water issues from those of security and national honour, which will confound cooperation on water issues. Climate change will make the water situation in both countries worse and exacerbate points of tension, making it more probable that China will fully exploit the Tsangpo. China's continual lack of information and transparency is unlikely to change in the short-term, so India will remain mistrustful and fearful, and continue to push its own water plans, causing concerns in Pakistan and Bangladesh. India may be able to engage China, to an extent, in areas that China deems to be beneficial to its national interests, but is unlikely to be able to dissuade China from actions perceived to be in these interests. This situation seems likely given China's track record of doing what it pleases, and India's history with Bangladesh and Pakistan undermining its grievances.

However, a full-scale military conflict, especially in the short-term, is unlikely due to the integrated nature of the region ; both countries being nuclear powers; and regional stability being beneficial to both. Tensions are, however, likely to dramatically increase, with "verbal skirmishes" likely between the two. There could also be an increase in strategic competition, which may have a destabilising impact on the region and result in polarisation and resource competition.

India will be forced to take action if China follows through on most of its trans-boundary river policies, as they could be devastating for India. India will try to exert its growing regional and international influence to place pressure on China and limit its ambitions in other areas. Strategic competition as a whole will also increase, with America taking increasing action to contain China, and China responding through its 'String of Pearls' strategy.

INTERNATIONAL IMPLICATIONS OF POLICIES IMPACTING INTERNATIONAL TRADE

In 2010, China became the world's largest exporter of merchandise and second largest importer. China's export success has been based on strong price competitiveness in the world market. China has a comparative advantage in its labour force and a disadvantage in land, water and other natural resources. China has become the 'world's factory', which has come at a cost to its environment and water resources. Due to China's position in the global market, and as the world's second largest economy, policies to conserve water and reduce water pollution are likely to have a notable international impact.

Water scarcity poses significant risks to companies looking to operate in China as it can limit companies' direct operations and their supply chains, and so affects their operational costs, profits and future growth. These risks generally materialise in four forms: physical risks, caused by the lack of water; reputational risks where competition for limited usable water can lead to conflict with other water users, including local communities; regulatory risks, where water scarcity results in increasingly stringent regulations and increased costs; and financial risks as water shortages lead to higher energy prices, increased insurance and credit costs and lower investor confidence. Businesses in China currently face all these risks but regulatory and financial risks are those most likely to have an international impact and so will be focused on.

Inflation

Water tariffs and increasingly stringent water pollution regulations will increase the cost of manufacturing in China, especially for water and energy intensive industries. Export taxes placed on energy and pollution intensive goods will further raise costs of Chinese goods. A study of the effects of a Chinese policy to reduce sulphur dioxide found that the policy resulted in a decline of pollution and energy-intensive exports. Therefore, policies aimed to conserve water will likely have a similar effect and so less water-intensive goods will be exported, causing prices internationally to rise.

Elevated costs of Chinese goods due to increased water costs could raise concerns internationally. America is the second largest importer of Chinese goods. America is concerned as the increased costs of imports are directly passed on to consumers, or enter into production of domestic goods as intermediate inputs, and add to American producer costs. This puts American producers under pressure to increase the price of their goods, therefore, contributing to America's Consumer Price Index and shifts inflationary pressures. There are concerns that more expensive imported goods will allow external and internal competitors to also raise their prices, and thus increase inflationary pressure. The global demand for Chinese exports, and their increasing costs, may cause America's or another country's prices to get out of control, as workers demand raises in response to rising consumer prices, resulting in an inflationary spiral. This could particularly impact China's trading partners who rely on China for the majority of their consumer goods, especially as it will take time for companies to build up manufacturing in cheaper countries.

However, mass inflation does not appear likely in America and countries with high unemployment, as unemployment undermines the bargaining position of workers. Governments can address rising costs of Chinese imports by importing alternative, less-expensive, goods from China or other countries and local competitors can be encouraged to keep their prices low to gain market share and offset some of the inflationary pressures. Additionally, increased Chinese export taxes will probably be applied to similar goods as EU and American carbon taxes, which will prevent carbon leakage concerns, and stop Chinese goods from losing some of their competitiveness. Therefore, Chinese goods should remain comparatively cheap.

China itself is under inflationary pressures and although inflation has recently slowed, China still remains at risk due to rising prices of food imports; weak international demand for Chinese exports; and rising costs of goods locally. Global food prices are increasing and this will probably continue due to the current drought in America. China has been increasing its imports of certain agricultural products, as it is equivalent to importing water, and is currently the world's largest importer of soybeans. A significant amount of China's imports come from America, and so it is likely to be effected by increasing prices of agricultural goods. China is planning on increasing its maize imports, and so may be further affected by increased global food prices. The rising costs of Chinese exports due to increased costs of water and water-intensive resources, may contribute to weakening demand in Europe and America, and so will probably adversely affect China's export-dependent economy. There is also the risk that consumer inflation within China may rebound from its recent easing after August due to seasonal factors and the rising labour and resource costs

There are concerns that these inflationary factors will constrain China's efforts to fix its economy. If inflation increases then the government will be less able to increase the money supply and fuel growth. This is a concern as sluggish Chinese economic growth could slow global recovery. China's continued economic growth is vital for driving the world out of recession and a lack of Chinese growth could threaten global political stability. Some analysts are, however, doubtful that China's inflation rate will be pushed back up,. Therefore, in the short-term, rising costs due to China's water policies are unlikely to stall China's growth, but future rising costs could have a detrimental effect on China's economy and in a worst-case scenario harm global recovery.

Relocation

Rising labour costs and increasing resource costs are causing some companies to move out of China to other South East Asian countries, which are becoming popular with European and American businesses. Relocation is more prominent in textiles and low-technology labour intensive industries. Rising costs associated with having to comply with pollution regulations and water tariff increases could serve to exacerbate this trend.

Relocation of companies is starting to lift some declining economic hubs, such as Penang, out of their economic slumps as it brings in foreign investment and jobs. Rising production costs in China has led to a reduction in the competitiveness of Chinese products in international markets and an increase in the industrial competitiveness of several Asian countries, who are starting to gain shares of China's labour-intensive products in the European, Japanese and American market. This trend could be positive for the economies of the countries where companies are relocating and will help dispel concerns over inflationary pressure caused by increased prices of Chinese exports. There is, however, the potential that local environments will be damaged and local resources endangered, causing similar problems to those China now faces, which could increase operating costs.

However, it is unlikely that relocation away from China will occur en masse, as there are advantages to operating in China not present elsewhere. These include China's reliable and sophisticated supply chain; its large labour force; and the increasing productivity of Chinese workers. Additionally, Bangladesh, Cambodia, Thailand and Vietnam may not be feasible alternatives to manufacturing in China, as China's plans regarding the Tsangpo and the Mekong give China the potential to limit the water supply of these states. In the short-term, therefore, it is likely that there will be a diversification of manufacturing across Asia, with some low-tech labour-intensive industries leaving, but the majority of companies remaining in China. This makes it possible that the costs of consumer goods will continue to rise, which could contribute to inflationary pressures mentioned previously.

The Chinese government wants to shift towards high-technological manufacturing and is encouraging industries to relocate to China. By doing this China could become a "strong manufacturing country" and regain market shares from losses caused by companies relocating to other Asian nations. Some believe that China's restrictions on rare earths, vital to many high-technology industries, are partly aimed to encourage these industries to relocate to China. However, high-technology manufacturing industries require a large amount of ultra-clean water in order to make semiconductors, so it is questionable how feasible this goal is given China's water situation. Furthermore, companies in this area have reservations about relocating to China due to poor intellectual property law enforcement and technology transfer. This desired shift towards high-technology industries clearly conflicts with water conservation policies and the desire to reduce water pollution and so could be problematic in the future.

WTO TRADE DISPUTES

China's export policies which limit water, highly polluting or energy-intensive goods being exported have international implications; this includes the exportation of rare earths. Rare earth mining is highly water-intensive and causes environmental devastation, especially to water supplies as it is highly polluting and so limits the availability of usable water in the area, and so adversely affects livelihoods and crop production. The Chinese government is looking to clean up this industry, requiring rare earth enterprises to increase their investment in environmental protection and improve production technology; increasing water efficiency and decreasing water pollution. The government has further imposed production caps, stricter emissions standards and is consolidating the industry to stop illegal mining. Together with the increased price of water, these measures mean the end to cheap rare earths on the global market. China has also introduced export duties on rare earths as well as export quotas, and these measures have become increasingly restrictive with quotas being reduced more drastically for foreign investors. China claims the restrictions are necessary to meet increasing domestic demand, conserve its resources and protect the environment. These export restrictions have, however, created global shortages of certain rare earths and dramatically raised international prices, giving Chinese domestic companies a competitive advantage and shifting the terms of trade in China's favour. Rare earths are particularly important in renewable energy and defence industries so restrictions raise national security and energy concerns. Domestic prices are significantly lower than export prices and some analysts predict the situation will get worse as China will not be able to fulfil its domestic demand for rare earths, and so further restrict exports.

Restrictions and high prices have resulted in some manufacturers relocating to China to take advantage of lower domestic prices and more ready supply. Several companies are switching to alternatives to reduce their dependence on China, while others are curtailing production. For many companies, relocating to China is undesirable, due to worries about intellectual property infringement and that Chinese companies would benefit from the resulting technology transfer and become direct competitors. This worry is of particular concern for companies involved in national security and defence. Additionally, some countries are considering stockpiling certain rare earths to protect against future Chinese restrictions, which will also contribute to rising global prices and demand. In response to China's rare earth export policies, America, Japan and the EU have brought a WTO case against China on the grounds that China's restrictive policies were "resulting in massive distortions and harmful disruptions in supply chains of those materials throughout the global marketplace" and "violated international trade rules and must be removed". China responded that their export quotas and duties were necessary for the protection of the health of its citizens and to conserve exhaustible natural resources.

This case is not presently resolved, but the facts are similar to a previous case brought against China by America in 2009, where China was found to be in violation of its WTO commitments.

Due to the similarities between the two cases, it is unlikely that the WTO will rule in China's favour, however, it is questionable if China will honour the spirit of a WTO ruling against it, or if it will impose additional restrictions in replacement of those that it would be required to remove.

China's handling of its rare earth resources has led to worries about the potential of China to use rare earths as a political weapon due to China's virtual monopoly and rare earths' industrial importance. Rare earths could be used as a bargaining tool to gain advantage over another country, such as China's rare earth embargo against Japan due to a territory dispute. China denies that it intends to do this but countries remain concerned. The 2012 WTO case has been initiated by some of the world's largest economies and China's largest trading partners. The case indicates to China how seriously these countries view China's rare earth restrictions and implies that these countries may be willing to form a united front and take actions against China beyond the WTO.

International disputes may also emerge over preferential treatment given to state-owned enterprises in China. State ownership of enterprises mitigates some of the effects of environmental policies, allowing these companies to continue high pollution or energy-intensive activities, and ultimately export more pollution and energy-intensive goods. This gives state-owned firms a competitive advantage over foreign and privately owned firms. This discriminatory treatment will probably be viewed unfavourably by foreign firms who may put pressure on their governments to bring actions against China.

Food Security

China has almost 20% of the world's population but only 7% of its arable land and 5% of the world's renewable freshwater resources. Therefore, China has concerns over food security and has addressed this issue by growing grain domestically at all costs. However, a rising population, more sophisticated diets, and dwindling water resources mean that China is unable to produce enough food domestically and so must resort to alternative solutions.

Increase in Imports

China became the second largest agricultural importing country in 2009 and imports are expected to increase as domestic demand increases. China is also a key global exporter of many agricultural products; due to this, China's water scarcity has global pricing implications.

China's aims for food self-sufficiency, particularly in grains, conflicts with its water conservation policies as grains require more water per hectare than alternatives. By increasing imports of water-intensive agricultural products, China is effectively importing water and saving its own resources. However, there are concerns that China's water problems, measures being taking to address them, and growing demand will increase food shortages in China, resulting in China becoming a major food importer. It is feared that this will accentuate the global food crisis and is especially problematic as it is predicted that China may not be able to feed itself by 2030.

Water prices are set to rise in China, and will probably increase substantially to encourage water savings and efficient irrigation, however, a farmer's ability to pay increased irrigation costs is low. Even when the SNWDP is complete there will still be a lack of available water for irrigation as the transferred water will be prohibitively expensive for most agricultural users and the majority of water transferred is destined for industrial and urban use. High water prices will result in lower crop production, especially water-intensive grain crops. Chinese farmers have come to rely on fertilisers to increase output under limited water resources; however, fertiliser runoffs are highly polluting and the government has imposed restrictions on fertiliser pollutants further decreasing agricultural output. These policies, therefore, could threaten national food security.

Global food security is a rising concern, particularly in terms of feeding Asia. In 2011 the Food and Agriculture Organisation announced that global food prices had reached record highs, due to poor weather conditions causing bad harvests. Pressures on the price and availability of rice and wheat will further rise if India and China increase imports. This could have negative consequences for social stability as, when prices of local staple foods rise, consumers tend to react badly. Furthermore, it is predicted that prices will continue to rise for grain, cereal, vegetable oil and sugar, and governments could respond similarly to previous spikes in food prices and begin stockpiling grain, which will exacerbate the situation. Some countries may benefit from China increasing its imports, such as South America and potentially America, but it is more likely that food prices will continue to rise globally due to China's huge demand.

China's increase in imports of soybeans for livestock feed in the 1990s triggered a dramatic agricultural transformation, converting 30 million hectares of rainforest and farmland in South America to soy plantations to supply China. This caused the loss of local food systems and an increase in pesticide use, causing a higher cancer rate amongst the locals. China is set to increases its maize imports to 5 million tonnes in 2012, which is more maize than China has imported in the last 25 years combined, and is affecting global food prices. China long regulated maize as a strategic crop for food security and opening up its markets to imports will likely have a similar effect as with soybeans, resulting in more local loss of land and food production, as well as environmental damage. The increase in China's soy imports, and its likely increase in maize imports is, however, beneficial to transnational agribusiness companies, grain traders and feed processors and so governments will likely overlook the negative environmental effects of increased production in the short-term due to the political influence of these corporations.

African exports of agricultural goods to China are increasing, and as Chinese diets become more sophisticated it is likely this relationship will grow (Mobius 2011, para.2). However, Africa may not be able to continue to export agricultural products to China as it may come under pressure from its population if food available for local consumption decreases, which is already a problem in parts of Africa. Additionally, as China's investment in Africa is generally in outward-bound, export facilitating transportation projects, and African exports to China consist primarily of raw commodities while China's exports to Africa are finished value-added goods, China has been criticised of neo-colonialism.

China is in a difficult position in respect to agriculture, as if it continues business-as-usual, over-exploitation of water resources, droughts and floods will serve to limit productivity and increase imports. The impact on the Yellow River Basin of a 30% or 50% reduction in water availability by 2030 will result in a 17% fall in cereal products, which would increase global food prices by 10% for maize, 9% for wheat and 6% for rice. Chinese policies in this area aim to promote efficient water use to ensure continual production, but China's rising population and increasingly affluence are creating a greater demand for food, and even with these policies it is unlikely that this demand will be met domestically. It is questionable whether these policies will have the desired effect, as increased irrigation costs have caused some farmers to switch to more water-intensive cash crops, rather than more efficiently farming grain crops.

Therefore, export taxes, increased domestic demand, and resource scarcity are likely to slow export growth in China due to a greater focus on meeting domestic needs. This will probably be coupled with increasing imports, so raising global food prices and shortages; and placing pressure on import dependent countries. This could lead to a similar situation as in 2008 where the price of food spiked causing riots in 36 countries as well as loss of life due to starvation.

CHINA'S 'GOING GLOBAL' POLICY

Importing agricultural products is, essentially, importing water in virtual form and so appears a viable policy option to combat water scarcity. China is, however, unlikely to take a positive outlook to increasing agricultural, especially grain, imports as it will become dependent on other countries. There are only a small number of countries that have a large number of virtual water trade connections to other countries, which gives them a reliable supply of virtual water, even if some of these connections may be compromised due to drought or political instability. The majority of countries, including China, have few connections so are vulnerable to market forces, and may have to pay more for imported food, threatening food security and local stability. The current drought in America highlights this, as China has already been affected by the global increase in soybean prices caused by this drought. If China becomes more dependent on the US for maize, then China's food sovereignty could be at greater risk. So, while imports to China will increase, the Chinese government will also look for alternative policy options to address food concerns caused by water scarcity.

South America

Originally, China looked to South America as a source of resources outside Asia and 77% of Chinese foreign investment went to South America in 2003. Chinese investment is highly concentrated in natural resources so involves extraction and mining, which are highly water-intensive, and agriculture.

China is looking to buy vast amounts of land in the region, which has left many locals feeling uneasy. To ensure a long term supply of soybeans and iron ore, amongst other commodities, China has increased its lending to South American countries. China's investments in commodities like soybeans are very important to Argentina and Brazil's economies, and some analysts have suggested that a neo-colonial relationship is developing. In 2010, about 84% of Brazil's exports to China were raw materials, while 98% of China's exports to Brazil were manufactured products a trend evident in China's relations with the majority of countries in the region. This gives China leverage over these countries as they become economically dependent on exporting to China.

By expanding its trade and investment in the region, there are concerns that China will gain a stake in the region's politics and become involved in the region's security affairs, a possibility of particular concern to America. China's influence in South America may also make it a powerful competitor for America in the region. Furthermore, Chinese involvement may result in economic displacement and political unrest as China competes in the same market as many industries in South America and normally undercuts these local industries. This could lead to increased corruption, poverty and unemployment.

Africa

Africa is the primary target of international land acquisition. The International Land Coalition calculates that from 2002, 1.7% of the world's agricultural land has been acquired by foreign investors for agriculture production and of this, 60% of these deals have been in Africa. Aside from land, China is interested in African oil, mined primary commodities and timber all of which are water-intensive.

China started to look for foreign sources of oil and minerals relatively recently and so many foreign reserves were already controlled by large multinationals. Leaving those that are located in less developed or volatile nations, which are generally avoided by Western firms due to problems of dealing with unstable and undemocratic governments, has led to three of China's biggest African trading partners being Sudan, South Sudan and Angola.

China's investments in Africa are concentrated in natural resources so involve mining and smelting, therefore, Chinese firms tend to have a negative impact on the environment and often violate international environmental standards. The UN Commission on Trade and Development's World Investment Report found that non-OECD, especially Chinese, investors that operate under a 'non-interference in domestic affairs' doctrine, often undermine governance standards; engage in poor labour practices; employ corrupt habits; bribe officials and ignore or bypass best-practice environmental standards. African political elites allow Chinese firms to extract resources with limited accountability to Africa's political, economic, environmental and social structures. By pursuing water-intensive and water polluting activities abroad, China is able to conserve its own water resources.

Potential Consequences

Chinese land acquisitions and investments can be problematic for targeted countries as Chinese investments are found in countries that are receiving aid from the UN World Food Program and are already struggling with issues of land and water access. Furthermore, in 2011 a German government official accused China of causing the famine in the Horn of Africa, although this was strongly denied. Chinese land acquisition reduces the land available for producing food for domestic markets and deprives indigenous people of access or ownership of land. These land deals could deprive millions of access to water and risk draining freshwater sources in these regions. Investing in land in order to grow bio-fuel crop is especially problematic, as it displaces farmers and food production, and causes famine among the local population. China also tends to export its workforce to work on the acquired land with the Chinese Ministry of Commerce estimating that there are over a million Chinese farm labourers in Africa, so there is no local benefit of increased employment.

This can lead to resentment against China, especially within Africa, and contributes negatively to the global food situation by helping to driving up global food prices. China's growing unpopularity within Africa could limit its quest for resources in the country. Chinese involvement in the region contributes to worsening poverty as the flood of Chinese imports into local markets cause many local factories to collapse as they are unable to compete with Chinese products, causing unemployment and anti-Chinese sentiment. However, African nations are eager for Chinese investments and Chinese companies are often financially integral to the community, so officials are unlikely to insist that Chinese companies comply with environmental regulations, instead simply urging Chinese firms to "be clean".

These issues make land and resource-induced conflict likely, particularly as land acquisitions generally occur in nations already suffering from conflict. The combination of land and food uncertainty and poverty could spark further conflicts in the region. Raised tensions between foreign investors and the local population are already evident and there have been clashes between foreign investors and locals over diverted water and land resources. Additionally, there is no reason to expect an end to investment in overseas resources. As factors such as population growth, high global food prices, unpredictable commodity markets, water shortages, and a decrease in arable land are prevalent, these act as incentives for countries to acquire foreign land. Plus, the fact that resource security is becoming an issue of national security, makes it probable that conflicts will increase in frequency and violence.

In response to these concerns, several governments are taking steps to prevent Chinese land acquisitions. Argentina has passed a law which will place a 20% cap on the amount of land available to foreign landowners; and of this 20%, no single nationality can own over 30%, as well as limiting the amount of hectares that can be bought per buyer. Brazil is contemplating introducing measures that will ban Chinese purchases of land, so China will have to continue buying commodities from the Brazilian market. As China does not permit foreign land ownership, countries can justify limiting or banning the amount of land China can buy. If more governments respond in this manner than China could be forced to become import dependent.

China's actions overseas are viewed unfavourably by the West. In Africa, many Western policy makers, politicians and business leaders view China's engagement with condemnation. They criticise China of cheaply extracting Africa's natural resources and exploiting Africa's weak political institutions for their own economic gains. As China becomes more dependent on Africa's resources, its influence in Africa becomes increasingly significant, with China providing infrastructure support and debt relief in many African states. This concerns international observers, as China's relationship with non-democratic states, such as Sudan, has undermined Western efforts to promote and protect human rights and good governance. China has, for example, readily replaced Western investors when they withdraw for political reasons. Chinese practices that undermine good governance have led the World Bank to ban some Chinese companies from bidding for tenders in Africa. There is a lack of information regarding China's commercial engagement in Africa and these issues set China on course for a potential conflict with Western countries if it continually fails to give proper consideration to the international community's concerns.

An international challenger to China's foreign policies in this area could be America due to perceived competition; the China threat perception; and the geographic proximity of South America.

There are several probable short-term soft-policy options that America can employ if it decides that China's increased involvement requires a response to offset or to compete with Chinese involvement. These include reviving American involvement around the world to counter China's increasing influence, which can be achieved by increasing American bilateral cooperation, trade and military relations with Africa. America can seek to be granted observer status in institutes such as the SCO, East Asia Summit, and advocate China and African countries to create observational status within the Forum on China-Africa cooperation, giving America insight into the group's policy priorities and the ability to participate in consultations. Therefore, China's greater involvement in South America and Africa could be met with increased American engagement in the same areas, creating the potential for Sino-American cooperation, but more likely, American involvement will be viewed by China as competition so could contribute to tensions between the two.

Japan, Korea and India share China's concerns over food security and are engaging in similar practices to support their companies in securing a steady supply of food. This could lead to future clashes over land and resources, especially as the countries that are currently providing these hungry nations could get more protective over their food supplies in the future, as demonstrated by the South American countries considering laws prohibiting land acquisition.

The West traditionally considers Africa and South America as its own trading partners and China's increasing involvement and influence in these regions is causing "deep nervousness" in the West. In 2009, China replaced America as Africa's biggest trade partner, and African trade with the EU and USA has fallen over the last 10 years. America is sensitive and uneasy about China's increased influence in Africa as it highlights America's declining influence as a world power, and China's rising prominence. African countries now have the power to choose among their investors, improving their bargaining position and making it difficult for Western countries to deal with them from their usual position of attaching conditions to aid and investment.

In South America, America remains the dominant power due to its strong historical and geographical ties with the region, but China is gaining a major share of South America's trade and taking a relative share of the USA and EU's trade. In a few years, China could replace the EU as the region's second largest trading partner. This has caused America and the EU to speed up negotiations and signing of free trade and association agreements with countries in the region to combat expanded Chinese presence and influence, potentially increasing competition in the region. There is the fear that due to China's increased influence there is the potential for the growth of a pro-China voting bloc in UN agencies and other international institutions.

China's acquisition of resources is causing political concerns that China could be buying up supplies that affect countries' national security, cornering the market, and increasing prices. Chinese moves to secure raw materials may be exacerbating global problems of strong demand by tying up supplies of natural resources; gaining preferential access to available output; and extending control over the world's extractive industries; and could give China a potential monopoly over these resources.

MOST LIKELY SITUATION

In summary, the likely consequences of China's water policies in terms of international trade is increased competition for raw resources and agricultural products, therefore, an increase in trade disputes and a worsening of the global food situation. China's water policies could contribute to a worsening global food situation due to decreasing agricultural productivity, and so increasing agricultural imports and global food prices.

Chinese involvement abroad will likely continue and expand in scope, especially in Africa. This involvement could create tensions within Africa and internationally, especially as China remains insensitive to the international community's political concerns regarding the region, and China's actions contribute to poverty and instability. This will ultimately result in tensions between China and the West, as well as the potential for a humanitarian crisis due to famine.

Inflationary pressures caused by increased prices will largely be offset in the short-term, partly by some companies relocating and through unemployment preventing an inflationary-spiral occurring. The effect of increased prices of Chinese goods will probably, therefore, be minimal. Several Asian economies will get a boost from the relocation of some companies, which will be positive for the region and result in increased regional trade. This is also likely to be minimal compared to the potential international consequences for trade disputes, increased agricultural imports, and consequences of Chinese involvement abroad.

Conclusions

The aim of this paper was to assess the potential international implications of China's water policies. This was achieved by investigating the water situation in China; the policies the Chinese government is implementing to address water problems; and, based on China's foreign policy and international relations, examining the casual effects these policies could have to determine the impact they may have on other countries.

China's management of its decreasing water sources will probably have a notable impact internationally due to China's prominence in the international arena, and will contribute to exacerbating several global issues. Water security has become an issue of national interest so the Chinese government will ultimately take any actions necessary to secure its water resources. If this can be achieved within the international framework and following international norms, China will do so, but it is unlikely to be constrained in this way.

The most probable outcome will be where China's relationships with lower-riparian states deteriorate as China becomes increasingly possessive over trans-boundary rivers. While this is unlikely to result in direct conflict between China and its neighbours, it could create several flash points for conflict in the region; including potential Indian-Pakistan conflict; renewed Sino-Indian border disputes; and instability within countries. China's relationship with India will deteriorate if China diverts water from the country and could spark a humanitarian crisis in parts of India, Bangladesh and Pakistan due to droughts and famine. Rising food prices will exacerbate this and lead to further instability. Worsening Sino-Indian relations over water resources may result in acute rivalry between the two countries, proving destabilising for the region and could result in the polarisation of Asia.

China will be unable to locally fulfil its demand for agricultural products and water-intensive resources. Many countries are, however, eager to gain access to the Chinese market, so imports to China will increase in the short-term, proving beneficial to the economies of the exporting countries.

However, this may have a negative impact on the exporting countries due to destruction of the local environment and local displacement. In the longer-term, destructive environmental methods used in countries to meet Chinese demand, or by Chinese companies abroad under China's 'go out' policy, could contribute to worsening climate change, which could cause heat waves, droughts and floods, destroying crops and so decreasing agricultural supply and increasing prices.

India, Pakistan and Bangladesh, amongst other countries, will probably increase their agricultural imports if China deprives them of water from shared rivers, and it is unlikely that this demand will be able to be met. Coupled with China switching to being a predominately agricultural importing country, this could result in massive food price hikes and governments may resort to stockpiling grain, causing political instability and famine in countries.

Growing competition over resources and agricultural goods will increase international tensions as countries vie to secure resources. This will result in greater competition for acquisition of land and resources abroad, while targeted countries try and guard their resources or 'play countries off' each other to secure the best investments.

While some countries like those in South America will pass increasingly restrictive laws making land acquisition by Chinese companies near impossible, resource exploitation in countries like Africa could hinder their development and increase conflict and instability within the region. There could also be a rise in armed conflict between local populations and foreign companies involved in land acquisitions. Trade disputes may increase due to countries looking to hold on to their own resources and increasing demand from other countries, particularly as China seems to be buying-up strategic resources and tying-up supplies, giving them a potential monopoly.

There is, however, the argument that the outcomes outlined above could be mainly due to China's economic and population growth, and so it is these issues, rather than its water policies per se that are driving these potential international impacts. China's rising population contributes to increasing agricultural pressures; resulting in China increasing agricultural imports and 'going out' for resources; and economic growth is fuelling China's quest for resources and hydropower.

Furthermore, if China did not address its water issues, the outcome internationally, especially in terms of food security, could be the same as the situation that could occur after implementation of their water policies, as both scenarios would result in decreased agricultural productivity and a greater demand for resources.

However, the Chinese government has introduced policies specifically addressing water issues to continue feeding its population and grow its economy in a sustainable manner to alleviate the worst potential outcomes. These issues ultimately boil down to water availability.

China's economic growth cannot continue without a sufficient supply of water and China cannot grow crops to feed itself without water for irrigation. In the short-term, some of China's water policies may have a similar outcome to those if the government was inactive. The fact that the government is taking action, however, will have a decisive impact and prevent the country from grinding to a halt, which in the long-term would be undesirable internationally. Projects such as the SNWDP are aimed solely at treating China's water shortages. International tensions caused by interfering with trans-boundary rivers can, therefore, be attributed to the fact that diverting rivers to meet water shortages is how China has historically dealt with its water deficits. While China's regional water imbalance has been exacerbated by rapid urbanisation and industrialisation, the SNWDP is seen as the logical permanent solution to solving the traditional water imbalance between the north and south.

Ultimately, it seems China's water policies will have a potential two-fold impact internationally; being highly destabilising to the region and increasing international tensions; but at the same time, potentially preventing China's economy from stalling, which could be destabilising to the entire international system.

6

India-bangladesh: 21st Century Battle for Water Sharing

Three major rivers of the region, namely the Ganges, the Brahmaputra and the Meghna/Barak (GBM) have a common terminus into the Bay of Bengal and thus form a river system. About 10 per cent of global population is living in the Ganges-Brahmaputra delta. Sediments carrying by the rivers transforming the landscpe to one of the most fertile lands of the world.The Ganges-Brahmaputra- Meghna river system carries over 2.9 billion tonnes sediments (one third of global sediment transport to the world ocean, Milman et al., 1983) into the Bay of Bengal. Thousands of years of civilisation flourished along the Ganges-Brahmaputra rivers. About 18 kilometrs of sediment thus deposited in the sinking basin (which still do today) making the world's deepest sedimentary basin of the world. The Bengal basin is tectonically active.

Brahmaputra River is Tibet's longest and the world's highest inaltitude. This 2,057km long river drains an area of 240,000 sq.km and provides irrigation for some of Tibet's major agricultural regions. Tibetans call it "Mother River".

The remaining two countries, India and Bangladesh, depend heavily on the waters from the GBM system. Thus, the dwindling supply of water in the dry season has become one of the key issues between India and Bangladesh. The situation is particularly critical for Bangladesh, as about 80% of its annual fresh wtersupply comes as transboundary inflows through 54 common rivers with India.

The Brahmaputra River shifted its course dramatically at the turn of 19th century, when it abondoned the old Brahmaputra, and took a new, more westerly path. Perhaps ready for a further major shift, which must not be provoked by ill-judged works on the river.

This river system falls in a number of countries in the South Asia region, including China, India, Nepal and Bangladesh. Of these, China contributes solely to the flow of the Brahmaputra, and Nepal to the flow of the Ganges. Both China and Nepal are upper riparian countries and the tributaries originating in these countries contributing to the GBM system are not yet fully utilised. As a result, these countries do not face any contentious water issue with their lower riparian neighbours.

The Ganges delta covers 1,093,450 km2 in total of which Bangladesh shares 46,000 km^2, Indian 861,400 km^2, Nepal 146,000 km^{2}and Tibet shares 40,4000 km^2. Bangladesh though accommodates only 4.0 percent of length but the Ganges delta covers 36.0 percent area of Bangladesh and meets 20.0 percent of fresh water requirement.

The three major rivers such as Ganges, the Brahmaputra and their tributaries. Bangladesh, as a tropical country, faces cyclones and floods every year causing havoc to the lives of millions of people.

Thus the paradox of water goes on; water is the source of life but it can also be the end of life. For us especially, water is vital for our thirsty crops, yet floods can often wash them away along with our very lives while droughts in our neighbouring countries cause untold miseries. Meanwhile, unplanned urbanisation and encroachment of our water bodies, has ensured that there is an acute shortage of water for drinking and other essential purposes. Unchecked polluting of our lakes and rivers has contaminated our water supplies, threatening our health and again, our lives. There is no doubt that human negligence and abuse has resulted in this pathetic state of being where water is either too much or too little but somehow never just enough. The workshop may not solve our water paradox but it does raise the point that there is so much we can do to ease the crisis. We must clean up our water bodies and stop polluting them or filling them up with our greed; We must save the water we have and refrain from wasting it whether in terms of not letting the water run while we brush our teeth to collecting the water from the heavens when it pours. For many it may mean adopting less wasteful lifestyles, using less energy, being a little more restrained. There is a lesson to be learned for every nation, whether rich or poor, to make sure that the pure relationship of man and water is once again, restored

In this dramatic view of the northern Indian subcontinent, the Brahmaputra River courses from the top of the image (east) through Bangladesh to the Bay of Bengal while the Ganges proceeds from the west also to the Bay. The Himalayas lie along the left side of this SeaWiFS image. The earliest deltaic arcs in Recent times are two simultaneous development called the Ganges Delta and Brahmaputra delta. The present Ganges-Brahmaputra delta, where much of the sediments accumulates, is represented onshore by a low lying flood plain covering more than 90,000 sq. km of present day Bangladesh and India, which is characterized by its dynamic growth.

The Early Bramaputra Delta , in the south of Shillong Massif (Assam, India) and Early Ganges Delta, in the districts of Kustia, Jessore and Khulna evolved from the north and northeastern part of the country. These two rivers are then diverted and have built a third delataic arc. The Early Meghna Delta: .

The Present Day Delta is actively and rapidly pushing into the eastern side of the Bay of Bengal (Landsat Imagery, Morton and Khan, 1979). Between 1972 and 1977 3,600 hectares were added to the Bay of Bengal. If no human intervention occurs, it is possible to reclaim land of about 5 to 10 thousand square miles mostly in the central coastal region.

The delta and offshore fan complex associated with the major rivers form one of the world's major depositional systems (Colman, 1969). The modern delta is a product of a large number of complexity interacting factors. The Ganges Brahmaputra delta began to adopt its modern form at about 10. 5 Ma. Sediments accumulated in response to subsidence in a delta plain to delta-front setting, which resulted in the highly channeled succession visible on the seismic data. Folding of the Brahmaputra-derived sedimentary strata in the east in late Pliocene to Holocene, in reponse subduction and inter-plate movement had a profound effect on the course of the Brahmaputra River. The Ganges-Brahmaputra delta is thus composed of a very large complex body sediment which has been subjected to a number of variables relate to two processes: plate tectonic and eustacy.

Sediments of the confluent Ganges and river today are deposited predominantly in the huge subaerial delta of these rivers. The present tectonics of the bay of bengal region have important implications for the future orogenic fate of the continental rise and fan sediments underlying the bay.

Present relative plate motion between the Indian plate and the Asian plate apparently in a northeast-southeast at a rate of convergence between 5 and 6 cm per year. Tectonics of this region are more complicated when examined in the light of major plate motions. India is still moving northeasterly into Asia.. Seismic activity continues along the Sunda Arc up to eastern Himalayan sytaxis, across the Himalayan Mountains, under the Tibetian Plateau and southern China. Since thermal subsidence of the passive margin is still active, sedimentation delta complex continues to be considerable.

HIMALAYAN DAMS POSE THREAT TO BANGLADESH

India, Pakistan, Nepal and Bhutan have planned a total of 552 hydropower projects in Himalayan region, of which some have already been built and some are under construction, that may have far-reaching impacts on downstream Bangladesh, informed sources said. Himalayan region is the centre point from where scores of small and large Asian rivers originated and run through. The Indus, Ganges, Brahmaputra, and Irabati are some of those. Bangladesh shares water of 54 rivers with India and 3 with Myanmar.

"If those upstream countries divert normal water flow through these dams, it will dry up many Bangladeshi rivers ruin irrigation system, kill lives in the water bodies. On the other hand, if they do not manage water properly it will inundate a big part of the country during rainy season," Joint River Commission (JRC) Member Mir Sajjad Hossen told The New Nation. A study of the 'International Rivers', an US based non-governmental organisation that protects rivers and defends the rights of communities, revealed that India has already built 74 dams, Nepal 15, Pakistan 6 and Bhutan 5 in Himalayan region in the recent years. It also found that 37 Indian, 7 Pakistani and 2 Nepalese dam are under construction in that area. The study also identified that India has planned to build 318 dams, Nepal 37, Pakistan 35 and Bhutan 16 more dams in this region to add over 1,50,000 Megawatts (MW) of additional electricity capacity in the next 20 years.

Sajjad Hossen said that the proposed and under construction dams, Tipaimukh dam is one of those, will change downstream flows, affecting agriculture and fisheries and threatening livelihoods of many people in Bangladesh. "These countries are supposed to share information with Bangladesh before taking any such step of building new dams, but they are not doing so. We have asked them for information. What we can do if they do not obey the river interlinking rules," said Hossen expressing helplessness against upstream powerful countries.

The author of the 'Mountains of Concrete: Dam Building in the Himalayas' Shripad Dharmadhikary wrote: "If all the planned capacity expansion materialises, the Himalayan region could possibly have the highest concentration of dams in the world. This dam building activity will fundamentally transform the landscape, ecology and economy of the region and will have far-reaching impacts all the way down to the river deltas."

Bhutan is planning a capacity expansion of about 10,000 MW in the next 10 years. Among the projects being planned for the near future are the 1,095 MW Puntansangchu-I and the 600 MW Mangdechhu projects.

Nepal is planning to install hydropower capacity of 22,000 MW in the coming years. For its own needs, Nepal plans to add 1,750 MW by the year 2020-2021, mostly through small and medium projects. Rest, mainly from the bigger projects, is planned for selling power to India. Pakistan has plans to add 10,000 MW through five projects by the year 2016. Another 14 projects totalling about 21,000 MW are under study for construction by 2025. The government is pushing for the immediate implementation of the massive 4,500 MW Diamer-Bhasha project.

India declared its intentions with the launching of the "50,000 MW Initiative" on May 24, 2003. This initiative fast tracked hydropower development by taking up time-bound preparation of the Preliminary Feasibility Reports (PFRs) of 162 new hydroelectric schemes totalling around 50,000 MW. India has plans to build this capacity by 2017 and then, in the 10 years following, to add another 67,000 MW of hydropower. Construction is ongoing for many of the projects including the 2,000 MW Lower Subansiri project, the 400 MW Koteshwar project and the 1,000 MW Karcham Wangtoo, to name a few. Many of these projects are already under construction. Due to various obstacles of dams, barrages and hydropower projects in Himalayan region, the source of water of rivers, Bangladesh get lesser water in rivers flowing throughout the country. The lean water flow in the rivers has already cast negative impact on ecology, aquatic life, and irrigation.

According to the Ganges treaty, signed in 1996, Bangladesh and India will equally share water if water flow is up to 70,000 cusec or less in the Farakka barrage point. Bangladesh will get 35,000 cusec of water and India will get the rest if water at Farakka point is between 70,000 and 75,000 cusec.

If water at Frakka point reaches more than 75,000 cusec, India will get 40,000 cusec and Bangladesh will get the rest. But India never followed these terms and conditions of the accord and released meagre quantity of water for Bangladesh, it was alleged.

The JRC statistics shows that Bangladesh did not get its proper share of water since signing of the treaty. In 1999 Bangladesh got 1,033 cusec of water at Teesta barrage point against its normal requirements of 10,000 cusec of water. After JRC meeting in 2000 the water flow rose to 4,530 cusec, in January 2001 it reduced to 1406 cusec, in January 2002 to 1,000 cusec, in January 2003 to 1,100 cusec, in November 2006 to 950 cusec, in January 2007 to 525 cusec and in January 2008 to 1,500 cusec.

Due to less quantum of water supply through Teesta barrage thousands of acres of land in the country's northern districts lack irrigation posing threat to Boro rice cultivation. Around 15 small rivers are also drying up and about to die due to the same reason. The Teesta River itself becomes a thin canal for less volume of water supply from the upper riparian Indian part. The rivers include: Kortoa, Dudhkomol, Jingira, Dhorla, Bangali, Ghaghot, Atrai, Akhira, Manas, Katakhali, Ichamoti, Punorvoba, Burighora and Dhauk also drying due to less water supply. WDB officials said sustainability of these rivers is impossible unless India supplies adequate water through the barrage.

Habitat and Ecosystems

Over 73% of the Brahmaputra River watershed's originial forest is gone. The remaining forests are disappearing at 10% per year. Currently only 4% of the land is in protected areas. The area supports 4 endemic bird habitats and one RAMSAR-listed wetland.126 fish species also call the Brahmaputra basin home (WRI).

The ecoregion covering the Brahmaputra River in northeast India harbors India's largest elephant population (Rodgers and Panwar 1988), the world's largest population of the greater one-horned rhinoceros, tigers (*Panthera tigris*), and wild water buffalo (*Bubalus arnee*) (WII 1997). The ecoregion overlaps with a high-priority (Level I) ecosystem that extends north to include the subtropical and temperate forests of the Himalayan midhills.

The known mammal fauna consists of 122 species, including 2 near-endemic species. Of these, the pygmy hog and the hispid hare are confined to the grassland habitats. At present, twelve protected areas cover about 2,500 km^2 of intact habitat, or 5 percent of the ecoregion. Of these, Manas, Dibru-Saikowa, Kaziranga, and Mehao are the larger and more important reserves. Mehao extends over two other ecoregions and is only partially within this ecoregion. Kaziranga has the world's largest population of the greater one-horned rhinoceros, estimated at 1,100 individuals. Because of the large number of wide-ranging large vertebrates in this ecoregion, additional protection is urgently needed. Specifically, habitat connectivity should be provided within the Buxa-Manas complex and the Barail-Intanki-Kaziranga complex to allow elephants to disperse and migrate (Rodgers and Panwar 1988).

The ecoregion represents the swath of semi-evergreen forests along the upper Brahmaputra River plains.Assam Valley semi-evergreen forest, Assam alluvial plains semi-evergreen forest, eastern submontane semi-evergreen forest, sub-Himalayan light alluvial semi-evergreen forest, eastern alluvial secondary semi-evergreen forest, sub-Himalayan secondary wet mixed forest, and Cachar semi-evergreen forest. But most of the ecoregion's original semi-evergreen forests have been converted to grasslands by centuries of fire and other human influences. Only small patches of forests now remain.

THE BRAHMAPUTRA'S CHANGING RIVER ECOLOGY

The Ganga-Brahmaputra, one of the world's largest river systems, is first in terms of sediment transport and fourth in terms of water discharge. A detailed and systematic study of the major ion chemistry of these rivers and their tributaries, as well as the clay mineral composition of the bed sediments has been conducted. The chemistry of the highland rivers (upper reaches of the Ganga, the Yamuna, the Brahmaputra, the Gandak and the Ghaghra) are all dominated by carbonate weathering; (Ca + Mg) and HCO_3 account for about 80% of the cations and anions. In the lowland rivers (the Chambal, the Betwa and the Ken), HCO_3 excess over (Ca + Mg) and a relatively high contribution of (Na + K) to the total cations indicate that silicate weathering and/or contributions from alkaline/saline soils and groundwaters could be important sources of major ions to these waters.

The chemistry of the Ganga and the Yamuna in the lower reaches is by and large dictated by the chemistry of their tributaries and their mixing proportions. Illite is the dominant clay mineral (about 80%) in the bedload sediments of the highland rivers. Kaolinite and chlorite together constitute the remaining 20% of the clays. In the Chambal, Betwa and Ken, smectite accounts for about 80% of the clays. This difference in the clay mineral composition of the bed sediments is a reflection of the differences in the geology of their drainage basins.

The Ganga-Brahmaputra river system transports about 130 million tons of dissolved salts to the Bay of Bengal, which is nearly 3% of the global river flux to the oceans. The chemical denudation rates for the Ganga and the Brahmaputra basins are about 72 and 105 tons· km - · yr $^{-1}$, respectively, which are factors of 2 to 3 higher than the global average.

The high denudation rate, particularly in the Brahmaputra, is attributable to high relief and heavy rainfall (The Ganga-Brahmaputra river system transports about 130 million tons of dissolved salts to the Bay of Bengal, which is nearly 3% of the global river flux to the oceans. The chemical denudation rates for the Ganga and the Brahmaputra basins are about 72 and 105 tons· km - · yr $^{-1}$, respectively, which are factors of 2 to 3 higher than the global average. The high denudation rate, particularly in the Brahmaputra, is attributable to high relief and heavy rainfall. The Ganga-Brahmaputra river system transports about 130 million tons of dissolved salts to the Bay of Bengal, which is nearly 3% of the global river flux to the oceans. The chemical denudation rates for the Ganga and the Brahmaputra basins are about 72 and 105 tons· km - · yr $^{-1}$, respectively, which are factors of 2 to 3 higher than the global average. The high denudation rate, particularly in the Brahmaputra, is attributable to high relief and heavy rainfall.

Ganges-Brahmaputra river system, sediment discharge is estimated to be 109 t/yr at gauging stations 300 km inland of the coast, but little has been known of the downstream fate of this material. Geochronological, geophysical, and stratigraphic investigations of the lowland flood plain, delta plain, and shelf help to delineate the extent of Holocene fill and allow calculation of a first-order sediment budget.

Results reveal that 1500 × 109 m^3 of sediment fill has been sequestered within the flood plain and delta plain since ca. 7000 yr B.P., or about one-third of the annual discharge.

The remaining load appears to be apportioned between the prograding subaqueous delta (1970 × 109 m^3) and transport to the deep-sea Bengal fan via a nearshore canyon. Modern (less than 100 yr) budget estimates based on short-term accretion rates indicate a similar dispersal pattern.

River-linking plan not abandoned

BSS, NEW DELHI, October 7, 2004: Indian Water Resources Minister Priyaranjan Dasmunshi has told President APJ Abdul Kalam that the Congress-led UPA coalition government is committed to implementing inter-linking of South Asian rivers. The highly controversial project, adopted by the immediate past BJP-led NDA government, plans to divert waters of international rivers, which if implemented would drastically affect the region's co-riparian countries, particularly the lower riparian Bangladesh.

The minister informed Kalam that the new Indian government would give priority to the south-bound peninsular rivers in the first phase of the project. He also informed the president, an advocate of the project, that the Water Resources Ministry of India directed the National Water Development Agency to complete the full feasibility reports of 18-river links out of 30 by December next year. Dasmunshi told him that the ministry also set up a technical group of engineers for working out a consensus plan on "priority links" by October 31. The mega project, estimated to cost 5,60,000 crore Indian rupees, raised protests from India's neighbours, particularly Bangladesh, besides several Indian provinces as well as environmental groups, who consider it could spell disaster for the entire region.

IUCN to set up a Ganges, Brahmaputra and Megna Rivers Commission to conserve natural river systems

The IUCN World Conservation Congress adopted a resolution Wednesday to help set up a Ganges, Brahmaputra and Megna Rivers Commission to conserve natural river systems. Representatives of the government and nongovernmental organisations supported the resolution raised by Bangladesh although neighbouring India opposed it at the 3rd IUCN Congress in the Thai capital Bangkok.

India's controversial river interlinking project made headlines time and again in both the domestic and international press for the last two years. The $120 billion project designed to interlink 37 rivers including the Ganges and Brahmaputra to divert water, has been termed by the Bangladeshi experts as a 'death trap', which will cause an ecological and economic disaster in the lower-riparian Bangladesh.

India also plans to construct a controversial barrage on river Barak, upstream of Meghna, a major river system of Bangladesh. The IUCN resolution was raised by Hasna Jashimuddin Moudud. Opposing the resolution, the Indian delegates proposed to withdraw it saying, "The motion should be taken back as integrated water resource management as a bilateral issue." About 65 per cent government delegates and 88 per cent NGO delegates supported the resolution while 11 per cent government delegates opposed it.

Adopting the resolution, the IUCN congress called upon the civil society and governments in the Ganges, Brahmaputra and Meghna basins to promote dialogue and cooperation towards sustainable development of trans-boundary water resources. The congress urged the IUCN director general to promote basin-wise river management and regional cooperation in all international river basins and help of setting up a Ganges, Brahmaputra and Meghna Rivers Basin Commission to conserve natural river systems.

The congress also urged all bilateral and multilateral development agencies and government agencies to support a Ganges, Brahmaputra and Meghna River Basin Commission, to promote regional cooperation and sustainable management of water resources (New Age, November 25, 2004).

RIVER-LINKING A STATE VS PEOPLE CONFLICT

The people of South Asia must unite to fight the battle against the controversial plan to interlink trans-boundary rivers to withdraw water and to cordon rivers by constructing dams, said Medha Patkar, a celebrity activist leading the Narmada Bachao Andolan (Save the Narmada Movement) of India. 'You [people of Bangladesh] have to take the lead in the battle as you are the biggest victims since you are in the downstream,' she told New Age on Friday morning at the Osmani Memorial Auditorium in Dhaka.

'We also will continue to raise our voices in India as the project creates concern for people living in the river valleys there [India]', Medha said. She is visiting Bangladesh to attend a three-day international conference on 'Regional Cooperation on Transboundary Rivers: Impact of the Indian River-Linking Project' that began on December 17. Later, on Friday evening, she addressed a general session of the conference at the auditorium of the Institution of Engineers of Bangladesh.

Medha Patkar spearheads the Narmada Bachao Andolan, the 20-year-old struggle against the dam project that threatens the right to life and livelihood of the people of India's Narmada valley, which has grown into one of the world's largest non-violent social movements.

She has been at the centre of the struggle, gaining worldwide renown for sharp analysis and courageous activism that has included long fasts, police beatings and jail. The Narmada Sagar, one of the 30 major dams on the Narmada and one of the two biggest dams, is likely to submerge 254 villages.

Medha said that interlinking of rivers to divert one-third of the water of the river Brahmaputra, 60 per cent of which is used for irrigation and maintaining the ecosystem of the Brahmaputra basin, should not happen unless Bangladesh is consulted. 'Bangladesh should raise its voice not for information [about the project] only; Bangladesh should also be involved in the consultation to determine the feasibility of the project,' said Medha, who also leads an influential network of over 150 mass-based movements across India called the National Alliance of People's Movements.

Medha, a former faculty member of the Tata Institute of Social Sciences, also emphasised the need to involve other neighbouring countries, that are sharing the same river systems, in the movement against the much-talked-about project which, in her words, 'is the worst project one could ever think of'. 'The project is going to cause devastation, which many people are not able to understand, to the people of the region, many more times than the Farakka Barrage caused in Bangladesh and the Narmada Dam in India,' she said, in her warning about the dangers of the $120 billion project.

'It will destroy the ecosystem, which really supports the human habitat, the fish and also the forest. In Bangladesh, for example, the very large number of people who live in the Ganga, Brahmaputra and Megna deltas, may lose their life support system, that has already been disrupted by the Farakka Barrage, by destruction of aquatic wealth and causing huge floods without really supporting the flood-plain,' she said. 'Intra-state conflict will come up within India and regional conflict will be emerging within South Asia too,' Medha warned.

Medha, however, was less enthusiastic about the 'government-level dialogues' to resolve disputes regarding sharing the water of common rivers. 'I don't believe that a state can initiate a genuine dialogue as the nation-states in South Asia are more influenced and controlled by the global powers than the people in the countries.' 'The people to people dialogue can create the alternatives that could compel the states to include the issue in their political agenda and give rise to the right kind of intervention in ongoing politics which is exploiting the people,' she said. 'Unity of the civil society of South Asia has to be strengthened. River valley organisations of the region will have to come together to unitedly fight the battle,' Medha said. 'It should also be the concern of the human rights organisations and those who are fighting [against] the globalisation-liberalisation paradigm.

'I think, at the moment, we only can take a strong position against the impractical plan [river-linking], which is in a way the manifestation of a colonial tendency within the country [India] and within the region [South Asia] where people have always been and are being exploited,' she said. Medha told, 'We are facing the same kind of challenges, which have come up because of the states' wrong approach to natural resources management and at the cost of the common people - in favour of urban industrial societies within our own nation-states.' She warned that the 'conflict' should not be seen as an "India versus Bangladesh issue" at all. 'Rather it should be seen as "states versus people conflict" caused by the governments' wrong and anti-people position and 'state versus science, experience and conscience of the civil society at large'.

When asked about another one of India's controversial project, the Tipaimukh Dam, a multipurpose barrage on the river Borak upstream of the Meghna, a major river system of Bangladesh, Medha said, 'We are against the Tipaimukh dam.' 'The northeast of India has become the target now...which is clear because during the World Water Forum, held in the Netherlands, all of those who represented the Indian government were talking more about the northeast and the northeastern rivers than anything else,' said Medha, also a commissioner of the World Commission on Dams, the first independent global body formed to examine the water, power and alternative issues related to dams across the world. 'It is because many of the bilateral and multilateral agencies want to invest in the water sector in South Asia, although this kind of dam will ultimately destroy the natural ecosystem and the human population which is a part of that,' she said.

She criticised the role of the multinational lending agencies, including the World Bank, which, in her words, 'are keen to tap every river'. 'Whether it is exploiting the Tipaimukh or the Ganga or the Brahmaputra, they [lending agencies] will be involved in it,' Medha predicted. 'Are we really for this kind of privatisation of rivers?' she asked. 'Are we selling out our rivers, which will adversely affect the people's sovereignty?' (New Age, December 19, 2004)

BANGLADDESH CONCERNED BY INDIAN RIVER LINKING PROJECT

A Bangladesh parliamentary panel has expressed concern over India's funding its river-linking project. Bangladesh fears such diversions will affect the flow of the rivers in Bangladesh. India and Bangladesh share 54 common rivers. They have been engaged in disputes over sharing of Ganges water and the Teesta water sharing. The Indian river linking project will add further fuel into the water dispute between the two neighbours. The Indian mega project of river linking is aimed at diverting the waters of some of the common rivers to India's drought-hit regions by linking them with canals.

The new BJP government in India, led by Prime Minister Narendra Modi, on July 10 allocated 1 billion rupees in his maiden budget with a call for a serious effort regarding river interlinking project to expedite preparations for the Detailed Project Report.. Meanwhile, Bangladesh Parlia-mentary Committee on the Ministry of Water Resources decided at a meeting on Wednesday to seek details of the project from India.

"We have come to know from media that the new government of India allocated Rs 100 crore in budget to bring pace in the river interlinking project which will harm us. We will, therefore, ask the ministry to get clear picture about it," Romesh Chandra Sen, chief of the Jatiya Sangsad committee told reporters after the meeting at the Jatiya Sangsad. Terming it a grave concern for Bangladesh's environment and eco-system, Romesh, a ruling Awami League MP and former water resources minister, also said the committee will request foreign ministry to communicate with India to obtain information about its fresh move regarding the river interlining project.

Originally, the BJP-led NDA government of Atal Bihari Vajpayee in India had mooted the idea of interlinking of rivers to deal with the problem of drought and floods afflicting different parts of India at the same time. The succeeding Congress-led UPA government could not carry the project forward due to stiff opposition from environmentalist groups, but the Supreme Court, in Feb, 2012, ruled that the government could proceed.

The congress general secretary Rahul Gandhi said in 2009 that the entire idea of interlinking of rivers was dangerous and that he was opposed to interlinking of rivers as it would have "severe" environmental implications. BJP MP Rajiv Pratap Rudy suggested that Gandhi should do some research on the interlinking of rivers and its benefits and then arrive at a conclusion. Jairam Ramesh, a cabinet minister in former UPA government, said the idea of interlinking India's rivers was a "disaster", putting a question mark on the future of the ambitious project.[Meanwhile environment activists and scholars have questioned the merits of Indian rivers inter-link project. They also question whether the inter-linking project will deliver the benefits of flood control.

Other scholars have suggested to opt for other technologies to address the cycle of droughts and flood havocs, with less uncertainties about potential environmental and ecological impact. Meanwhile, water storage and distributed reservoirs are likely to displace people - a rehabilitation process that has attracted concern of sociologists and political groups.

Further, the inter-link would create a path for aquatic ecosystems to migrate from one river to another, which in turn may affect the livelihoods of people who rely on fishery as their income. Indian experts also feared that 50,000 ha of forest to be submerged only by peninsular link. - Intensive irrigation in unsuitable soils will lead to water logging and salinity. - Highly polluted rivers will spread toxicity to other rivers. - River system will be altered catastrophically creating droughts and desert (Holiday, July 18, 2014).

Tipaimukh dam

Tipaimukh Dam is not an isolated project; it is part of a comprehensive Indian plan of using rivers that flow from India into Bangladesh, and, hence, needs to be viewed in the general context of sharing of international rivers by these two countries.

In general, India has been using its upper riparian position and its economic and financial strength to take unilateral steps with regard to the flow of these international rivers. Most of these unilateral steps have been of diversionary character, diverting the water flow to destinations inside India and thus reducing the flow of water into the rivers of Bangladesh.

Glaring examples of such diversionary interventions are the Farakka Barrage on the Ganges and the Gozaldoba Barrage on the Teesta. India has undertaken numerous other diversionary and flow-controlling structures on most of the 54 rivers shared by Bangladesh and India.

These diversionary projects of India go against the international norms regarding sharing of international rivers. In particular, they violate Bangladesh's right to prior and customary use of river water. The entire economy and life in Bangladesh have evolved on the basis of rivers. Any major change in the flow of these rivers is, therefore, seriously disruptive for Bangladesh. Furthermore, river intervention structures affect the flow of sediments, which are vital for deltaic Bangladesh, which is facing submergence by rising sea level caused by global warming.

- First, Bangladesh does not yet have the necessary facts to assess the changes in Barak flow to be caused by Tipaimukh.
- Second, dams can also be a source of destabilisation, not only in the extreme situation of dam-break, but also in the often recurring situation when the excess water needs to be released to protect the dam from overflow. Such unplanned releases lead to unexpected floods. For example, the unusual 2008 floods in Bihar were caused by unexpected release of water by the dams that India has constructed on the Ganges tributaries near Nepal.
- Third, for Bangladesh to benefit from stabilisation of the Barak flow, it has to have a say in the release of water at Tipaimukh. This would suggest that Tipaimukh should be under joint control of India and Bangladesh. As of now, Tipaimukh will be entirely under Indian control, and the water release decisions will be made by India alone, putting Bangladesh at the mercy of the Indian officials operating Tipaimukh. Such a helpless situation is not in Bangladesh's interests.
- Fourth, river flow contains not only water but also sediments, which are very important for deltaic Bangladesh. One damaging impact of Tipaimukh will be reduced sediment volume in the Barak flow.
- Fifth, Bangladesh has to assess the costs and benefits for her economy of the seasonal changes in the Barak flow caused by Tipaimukh. For example, boro, which is cultivated in the haor areas that become dry in winter, is the main crop for many in the Surma-Kushiara basin. If Tipaimukh increases winter flow, cultivation of boro in these areas may not be possible. Without detailed studies it is difficult to say whether the net economic impact of the cross-season stabilisation of the Barak flow will be positive for Bangladesh.
- Sixth, there is also the issue of ecology to consider. The flora and fauna of the Surma-Kushiara-Meghna basin have

developed on the basis of a certain seasonal pattern of the river flow. Detailed studies are necessary to gauge the environmental and ecological impact of Tipaimukh.

Worldwide experience shows that large-scale interventions in rivers do not prove to be that beneficial in the long run. The hydropower generated often proves to be meagre and costly. The irrigation carried out on the basis of diverted water often proves wasteful and leads to salinity and deterioration of the soil quality, so that diversionary projects end up harming not only the basin from which water is withdrawn but also the area to which water is transported (at a great cost). The reservoir submerges large areas of land, destroying the ecology and displacing thousands of (often most vulnerable) indigenous people, causing permanent problems of alienation and insurgency. The reservoir also becomes a source of methane, undercutting the emission reducing potentiality of the hydropower generated. The reservoir and the upstream flow often become a cesspool of pollution. Dams obstruct sediment flow and the free movement fish stock. While many of the damages prove to the permanent, dams themselves become obsolete due to sedimentation, filling up of the reservoir, etc.

In view of these negative consequences many are now sceptical about dams, barrages and other large-scale river intervention projects. It is an open question whether Tipaimukh dam will be beneficial in the long run and in net terms even for India.

Many in India are opposed to the Tipaimukh dam. They include, indigenous people, state governments of Manipur and Mizoram, environmentalists, river activists, human right advocates, and even economists and social scientists. By providing various monetary benefits and offering free electricity, etc., the North East Electricity Production Company (NEEPCO), the current Tipaimukh implementing agency, has been able to pacify the state governments. However, in India, opposition to Tipaimukh continues.

India should not undertake water diversionary project (such as at Fulertal or at other points) on the Barak river under any circumstances. India should refrain from water diversionary projects on other rivers shared with Bangladesh. Bangladesh, India, and the other countries of the sub-continent should abandon the current commercial approach to rivers and to adopt the ecological approach.

Delhi set to build Tipaimukh dam

Amidst mounting protests both at home and in lower-riparian Bangladesh, India is going ahead with the plan to construct its largest and most controversial 1500 mw hydro-electric dam project on the river Barak at Tipaimukh on the common borders of three northeastern states of Assam, Manipur and Mizoram. Officials and experts in Dhaka fear the unilateral Indian move to construct the massive dam and regulate water flow of the Barak, which feeds both the Surma and Kushiara rivers in Sylhet, will have lasting adverse effects on livelihoods, ecology and environment in a vast region of Bangladesh. Moreover, people living in the vicinity of the hydro-electric project in Manipur, costing over 5,000 crore Indian rupee, fear submersion of vast areas on the Indian side too.

One of the largest river systems in Bangladesh — the Meghna with its distributaries — is fully dependent on the waters rolling down from the Surma and Kushiara. A massive construction on the Barak river will adversely affect the water flows of the Meghna and its distributaries. Against this backdrop, tension is growing over reports that the Indian prime minister laid the foundation stone of the project recently.

Meanwhile, people in greater Sylhet under the banner of Shahjalal Samaj Kalyan Parishad plan to hold a rally at Court Point in the divisional city today, protesting the Tipaimukh project. In India too, protests have been going on for years in the northeastern region as many people living in the Barak catchment areas fear permanent flooding of their areas due to the impact of the dam.

According to reports from across the border, the Naga Women Union of Manipur protested Manipur State Government's signing of agreement with the North-Eastern Electrical Power Corporation (NEEPCO) for constructing the project. It feared that due to the dam-induced submersion, 15,000 people would be rendered landless and homeless. The Naga People's Movement for Human Rights (NPMHR) also condemned the government decision of constructing the 162.8 metre-high dam. Tawhidul Anwar, a senior member of Indo-Bangla Joint Rivers Commission (JRC), told The Daily Star yesterday, "We have no confirmed reports about Manmohan Singh (Indian premier) laying the foundation stone during his recent visit to northeastern India. But we have come to know for sure India has started updating the Tipaimukh DPR (Detailed Project Report)" (Daily Star, November 27, 2004)

Bangladesh to issue formal protest against Indian dam project

Dhaka will formally protest against New Delhi's plan for construction of a dam which may adversely affect Bangladesh's ecology, after a new government takes over in India, a senior Bangladeshi minister said Saturday. Indian plans for construction of a multi-purpose dam on the Tipaimukh River might cause an ecological catastrophe for its downstream neighbour Bangladesh, Finance Minister AMA Muhith told reporters after a meeting in Dhaka. He charged that the proposed dam could lead to desertification in the northeastern region of Sylhet, while also drying up the Surma, Kushiara and Meghna rivers downstream. "We cannot allow this disaster to take place," the minister said, calling on Bangladeshis to campaign against the Indian project, which has also drawn protests inside India itself.

Bangladesh will send a delegation to visit the project areas after the new Indian government assumed office to see their plan and understand the possible impact. "We'll solve the problem through bilateral discussion," he said.

In April, Indian Foreign Secretary Shiv Sankar Menon in a surprise visit to Dhaka had requested Bangladesh to send a delegation at the project site to assess the impact of the project in the downstream.

Bangladesh has long asked India to refrain from building the dam, to be located at the confluence of the Barak and Tuivai rivers. India began soliciting international bids for the dam in early 2006. The Barak River feeds Bangladesh's Surma and Kushiyara rivers in the northeast, eventually flowing into Meghna, one of the three main rivers in Bangladesh. India plans to complete the project by

2012. Two senior cabinet ministers, who hail from the region (Sylhet), spoke about their plan to resist the construction of the dam at the Annual General Meeting of Jalalabad Association at Bangladesh Shishu Academy auditorium. "The dam will desert the greater Sylhet region," Finance Minister AMA Muhith told the meeting.

He said, the Tipaimukh dam will dry up the rivers Surma, Kushiara and Meghna as well as the haors. "It's the responsibility of every citizen to resist the dam," he said, adding that a plus point is that the Indian people in the surrounding areas of the project like Karimganj and Monipur are also against the project. Muhith said by implementing the project, India will withdraw waters from international river Barak for irrigation purpose, which will desert the land in Bangladesh's northeastern region. "We cannot allow this disaster to take place."(Daily Star, May 16, 2009).

Tipaimukh hydroelectric project

Even as Delhi is all set to begin work on the Tipaimukh hydroelectric project, a multipurpose high dam inclusive, upstream of a major river system of Bangladesh, Dhaka seems oblivious to all relevant developments. Manmohan Singh, the Indian prime minister, is scheduled to lay the foundation stone of the Tipaimukh project on November 23, a source in Indian state of Manipur said quoting chief minister O Ibobi. The Rs 5,163-crore Tipaimukh plan, which has been on the drawing board for nearly 40 years, is set to be built on the river Barak, which bifurcates into two streams as it enters Bangladesh as the rivers Surma and Kushiara.

The Meghna originates at the confluence of the Surma and the Kushiara. Goutam Chakraborty, the state minister for water resources, told New Age Sunday evening that the government did not know anything about the foundation stone laying of the Tipaimukh project.

"Earlier we had protested against implementing the Tipaimukh project through the joint rivers commission of the two countries," he said. "We have requested India to provide detailed information about the project. But they remain taciturn," Goutam said. Secretary to the water resources ministry, Omar Faruque Khan, said, "The government will look into the latest development regarding the Tipaimukh project." The Tipaimukh plant, which was delayed after the Manipur State Assembly had raised objections, has led to protests in India and its downstream neighbour Bangladesh as the project will cause economic, ecological and human catastrophes in both countries.

The residents of the Indian states concerned who are likely to be displaced and affected on account of the project have been staging protests and making representations to their respective state and the union governments, saying that thousands of people will suffer as the construction of the dam will submerge 73 villages, many sacred sites and cultivable land and violate their inalienable human rights. The people of the localities where the dam is proposed to be built have sought constitutional protection, particularly with a view to safeguarding the tribal people, their land, belief, culture and history.

Expressing grave concern over the possible consequences of the dam, the protestors said in a recent memorandum submitted to the central government of India, "Once the dam is built, the land, covering an area of 275.5 sq km, will be submerged permanently." Meanwhile, experts in Bangladesh have expressed their apprehension about the project that is sure to block the flow of the country's major riverine network in the northeast and have further disastrous consequences downstream. They claim that it could hit the country fatally, or have consequences of no less magnitude than the Farakka Barrage across the Ganges to the north-west of Bangladesh (New Age, October 18, 2004)

Tipaimukh to become another Farakka

Dr. Soibam Ibotombi of Dept. of Earth Sciences, Manipur University says that *the dam will be a geo-tectonic blunder of international dimensions: The site selected for Tipaimukh project is one of the most active in the entire world, recording at least two major earthquakes of 8+ in the Reichter Scale during the past 50 years. The proposed Tipaimukh HEP is envisaged for construction in one of the most geologically unstable area as the proposed Tipaimukh dam axis falls on a 'fault line' potentially active and possible epicenter for major earthquakes*

The Tipaimukh Hydroelectric Project is being constructed near the confluence of Barak and Tuivai rivers, in Manipur, India and within 100km of Bangladesh border. Costing Rs 6,351 crore ($1.35 billion) the 164 meter high dam will have a firm generation capacity of 401.25MW of electricity.

While Hydroelectric projects are typically considered greener than other power generation options in short term, it has significant long-term impact to the environment like changes in the ecosystem, destroying nearby settlements and changing habitat conditions of people, fish and wildlife. Especially in the densely populated countries like India and Bangladesh, where rivers are lifelines, projects like Tipaimukh will create adverse effect to a huge number of population and their habitats. No wonder right from the start this project faced protests from potentially affected people in India, and the recommendations of the WCD (World Commission on Dams)".

The people of Manipur have been fighting legally to stop the project but have so far been unsuccessful. The Indian government is going ahead with the plan. The Sinlung Indigenous People Human Rights Organisation (SIPHRO) of India said that "the process for choosing it (the project premises) ignored both the indigenous people and the recommendations of the WCD (World Commission on Dams)".

People of Zakiganj yesterday formed a human chain at Amolshid in the upazila protesting Indian move to construct a dam on the river Borak at Tipaimukh in the Indian state of Manipur. Acid Santrash Nirmul Committee, Sylhet, staged the protest against the controversial dam project, 100-km upstream of eastern border of Sylhet district. The river Borak bifurcated into two flows and entered Bangladesh as Surma and Kushiyara through Zakiganj border.

Zakiganj Pourasava (municipality) Mayor Iqbal Ahmed and Sylhet City Corporation Councillor Koyes Lodi also joined the human chain programme. On Friday night, Bangladesh Environmental Lawyers' Association (Bela) organised a discussion in Sylhet city in observance of the World Environment Day. Chaired by Sushasaner Janya Nagarik Sylhet chapter General Secretary

Faruque Mahmud Chowdhury, the speakers. The Indian government initiated the project about a decade ago, but could not go ahead in the face of widespread agitation from its own people at times. Even some 25 peoples' forums like that of Tipaimukh Dam Resistance Committee have been formed there to protest the move. With reference to some experts' opinion, the discussion meeting was told that implementation of the dam project mainly aimed at producing electricity would cause a disastrous situation in the Meghna basin, especially the greater Sylhet and Mymensingh region, during the dry season due to withdrawal of water in the upper stream. Also, they said, there are apprehensions of recurrent flooding during the monsoon due to possible release of water. It will be another Farakka, the speakers said, urging the people to resist the move (Daily Star, June 7, 2009).

India's secretive handling of Tipaimukh dam causing huge concern downstream

Ignoring its promise, India in the last four years has refrained from sharing technical information with Bangladesh about building the Tipaimukh Dam in the bordering Manipur state, triggering public uncertainty and outcry over its possible negative impact on the neighbouring country. While India has not started construction of Tipaimukh dam on the Barak river near Manipur-Mizoram border, it had floated international tender in 2005 and opened the bid in 2006 during the era of former BNP-Jamaat alliance rule.

In 2005, India promised to share with Bangladesh the project design, which is pending till date. Besides, the country also did not share any study report on the dam's impact on downstream regions. Experts told The Daily Star the construction of Tipaimukh dam would impose a great environmental threat to Bangladesh as four major rivers in the Meghna basin — the Meghna, Kalini, Surma and Kushiyara — lie downstream the Barak, locally known as 'Ahu'.

Amid such concerns, the prime minister has recently said an all-party parliamentary committee will visit India to know about the issue. The schedule of this visit has not yet been set. Indian response to Bangladesh's worries has so far been remained confined within officially informing the government that they have not started any construction yet. At a Joint River Commission (JRC) meeting in September 2005 held in Dhaka India formally assured Bangladesh that they would not divert any water for their irrigation project, he said.

Hiding any information by the upper riparian countries about the use of common rivers is considered as violation of the international water management convention. The expert warn of an increase in salinity in the Meghna-Surma basin, unusual floods in haor region, reduce in water flow in the Surma, Kushiyara and Meghna rivers in certain period, damage to the country's ecosystem and agriculture patterns in Sylhet region, among other impacts of the dam.

A chain of severe impacts is very likely as Bangladesh gets 7-8 percent of its river waters through the Barak. Negative impacts of any large dam are very widely known around the globe. A detailed study by the World Dam Commission published in 2000 says adverse impacts of any large dams are irreversible for the lower riparian region.

The study after reviewing 1,000 dams from 79 countries concludes in its report: "The environmental impacts of dams are more negative than positive ones and in many cases dams have led to irreversible loss of species and ecosystems."

Indian High Commissioner to Dhaka Pinak Ranjan Chakrabarti at a meeting with Communications Minister Syed Abul Hossain recently said though his country will have sole control over water flow at the proposed dam site, it would not make any barrage. He also said Bangladesh would not be 'affected' by the dam. However, experts fear once the dam is set up, it may reduce the natural monsoon flood patterns in the Sylhet region, adversely affecting cultivation and livelihoods on a vast scale.

"It will increase the risk of floods at the end of monsoon and hamper the agriculture patterns during winter," said Ainun Nishat, eminent river expert of the country. Rainfall patterns are changing due to climate change and a lot of rainfall takes place at the end of monsoon, said Ainun Nishat. If it rains at the end of monsoon, it will open the spillway gates of the dam and unusual floods will occur here, he added.

They would preserve the water during monsoon after building the dam and release it in winter, which will increase the water flow downstream. "The land downstream the Barak in Sylhet region is wetland, where people grow crops during winter when it gets dry. If they release water during winter the wetland will be inundated and it will be a great impact on our agriculture," Nishat warned.

An increase in water level in the winter will cause a major impact on the ecosystem if the wetland gets inundated, he added. He however said without checking every piece of information it is not possible to measure the total impact of Tipaimukh dam.

The experts fear India may hold up water flow during dry season and divert water at the proposed Phulertal Barrage 100 kilometres downstream Tipaimukh and 100 km upstream Amalshid in Sylhet. The Phulertal barrage would have a direct bearing on the Surma, Kushiyara and Meghna rivers due to diversion of water for irrigation purposes in northeastern India. On hydropower component and rock fill dam, India claims no damage would occur to Bangladesh, but Bangladesh fears upstream water flow regulation. Director General of Water Resources Planning Organisation (WARPO) Jalaluddin Md Abdul Hye said, "We don't have enough information to talk about the issue."

International Convention And Ganges Water Sharing Treaty, 1996

According to the International Convention on Joint River Water, without the consent of the downstream river nation no single country alone can control the multi-nation rivers. But India does not care for these international laws despite being a signatory of this convention.

If India constructs the dam without the consent of Bangladesh, it will also violate the article 9 of Bangladesh-India Ganges Water Sharing Treaty, 1996. Asked about a possible solution, Ainun Nishat said the solution has to be political. He added in the Ganges Water Sharing Treaty both the countries agreed to manage all the joint rivers on bilateral basis. "So under the Gages Water Sharing Treaty, both the country can resolve by sharing information and a joint team can study the adverse impacts on both the countries," Nishat added.

India handed over a number of primary project proposals to Bangladesh in 1979 and 1983. Later they conducted detailed studies about the project and completed the final design and environment impact assessment but did not share those with Bangladesh. According to the primary project proposals, the height of the Tipaimukh damn was fixed at 161.8 metres and length 390 metres to contain at lest 15.9 million cubic metres of water.

INDIAN CITIZENS ALSO PROTESTING THE DAM

Information surfaced in different websites says several Indian organisations and civil society bodies are protesting the dam considering its negative impacts. The websites also say the Expert Appraisal Committee (EAC) of India has found the design of the dam contains many errors, omissions, gaps, lacks in scientific rigour and falls far short of compliance of normative standards set by the scientific and academic community in India and the world.

The Action Committee Against Tipaimukh Dam (ACTIP), a platform protesting the dam, along with some other local committees from Manipur and Mizoram submitted a memorandum on March 14, 2007 to the president and prime minister of India in protest against the project. They mentioned in their memorandum that once the project is implemented, an area of 286.20 square kilometres land will go under water forever.

Eight villages situated in the Barak valley will be completely inundated leaving over 40,000 people landless and more than 90 villages, mostly in Tamenglong district, adversely affected. Besides, about 27,242 hectares of cultivable land will be lost. The Barak waterfalls and Zeilad Lake, which are connected with the history of the Zeliangrong people, an indigenous community in India, will go forever underwater. All folklores and legends will have no monuments' proof and it will become a makeup story for the next generation.

In the memorandum they said the mega-dam proposed in Tipaimukh will smother this river, change its age-old knowable and reliable nature, and drown them all in sorrow forever. The project is not for the common people, they said, appealing to the government to let the Ahu run free.

India plans to go ahead with river-linking plan, September, 2004

The Congress-led Indian government has decided to implement a controversial river-linking project for unilateral withdrawal of water from trans-boundary rivers despite widespread concern over and protest against the mega-project within India and in Bangladesh. The government will take up the issue for a comprehensive review any time this month, the Indian Supreme Court was reportedly told Monday. Indian solicitor general told the court that the government had decided to continue with the project, the New Delhi-based Times News Network reported Tuesday. The solicitor general told the court that the issue would be placed before the cabinet in September for a 'comprehensive review'. The Indian government sought six weeks time to get back to the court. The case is posted for further hearing eight weeks from now, the Times News Network added.

Dhaka, meanwhile, remains in the dark as the no detail communications have been made by New Delhi since the government of Prime Minister Manmohan Singh assumed office in May this year. The government is, however, aware of the Indian move, Water Resources Secretary Dr M Omar Faruque Khan told New Age Tuesday. "All of us in the lower riparian country should stand together against such a project irrespective of political views as the project may bring about ecological disaster."

Dhaka has already expressed grave concern over the project and called upon New Delhi not to implement it as it is meant for withdrawal of water from the rivers Brahmaputra, the Ganges and Barak, main sources of surface water in Bangladesh, ignoring the interests of other riparian countries. The move in the Indian court came within days of Congress MP Jairam Ramesh's statement that inter-linking of rivers could lead to severe ecological and rehabilitation problems. "The first requirement for managing floods on a long-term basis in East and North East is a viable, durable water-sharing agreement in the Ganga, Brahmputra and Barak basin involving the states of eastern India, Nepal, Bhutan and Bangladesh," he said while participating in a recent discussion in Rajya Sabha, the upper house of the Indian Parliament.

"As the river-linking project makes headway, more inter-state and inter-country dissensions are likely to surface," Dr Sudhirendar Sharma, who heads the Delhi-based Ecological Foundation and specialises in water issues, told New Age during his recent visit to Dhaka.

The Indian initiative would be another 'death trap for Bangladesh, even more deadly than Farakka.

According to the initial plan, 37 rivers will be inter-linked to transfer water to regions facing scarcity through 30 links across 9,600 kilometres, connecting 32 dams. Water from the Brahmaputra will flow into the Ganges, which will be connected to the Mahanadi and the Godavari. The Godavari will be linked to the Krishna, then the Pennar and the Cauvery. The Narmada will flow into the Tapi and the Yamuna into the Sabarmati. This huge inter-basin transfer is to be completed by 2016 with an estimated cost of $112 billion (New Age, September 1, 2004).

The concept of "surplus" or "unused" water

The most important question that needs to be addressed is whether or not there is any "surplus" or "unused" water in Brahmaputra River. The concept of "surplus" or "unused" water is an ironic one. The water that flows in Ganges-Brahmaputra-Meghna (G-B-M) basin is the reason why there exists the deltaic country called Bangladesh to start with. The sediments laid down by these rivers built the delta over millions of years that we call Bangladesh today.

Needless to say that there is a very complex ecosystem, including the Sunderbans, that is supported by the freshwater flow in these rivers. Any diversion of water also means proportional diversion of sediments. Any lack of sediment flux to the delta and coastal plains will cause accelerated drowning the coastal region in the face of rising sea-level.

In essence, it is already happening due to the impact of Farakka Barrage and will certainly accelerate if other barrages (e.g. the proposed Ganges Barrage, and Mowa Barrage).

The people of Bangladesh, India, and Nepal living in the Ganges-Brahmaputra-Meghna basin share common history, heritage, and friendship that go back to the time immemorial. India as the largest country in the basin has the responsibility to protect the interests of her own people, as well as the interests of all her neighbours. The Govt. of India should take initiatives to develop an integrated water resources development plan based on the principles of equity and respect of her neighbours, which in turn will strengthen the regional stability, security, peace, and prosperity (M. Khalaequzzaman, Dept. of Geology & Physics, Lock Haven University, 2003)

CHINA'S MOVE TO DIVERT TIBETIAN RIVERS

CHINESE leaders are drawing up plans to use nuclear explosions, in breach of the international test-ban treaty, to blast a tunnel through the Himalayas for the world's biggest hydroelectric plant. The proposed power station is forecast to produce more than twice as much electricity as the controversial Three Gorges Dam being built on the Yangtze river. The project, which also involves diverting Tibetan water to arid regions, is due to begin as soon as construction of the Three Gorges Dam is completed in 2009.

China will have to overcome fierce opposition from neighbouring countries who fear that the scheme could endanger the lives and livelihoods of millions of their people. Critics say that those living downstream would be at the mercy of Chinese dam officials who would be able to flood them or withhold their water supply.

China's state-run media reported that the project would form part of a national strategy to divert water from rivers in the south and west to drought-stricken northern areas. The reports said that a 38 million kilowatt power station at Muotuo on the Yarlung Zangbo river in Tibet would harness the force of a 9,840ft drop in terrain over only a few miles.

The capacity of the station would make it the world's largest power generation facility, much bigger than the 18 million kilowatt plant at the Three Gorges. The cost of drilling the tunnel through Mount Namcha Barwa has not yet been announced, but appears likely to surpass £10 billion.

At the bottom of the tunnel, the water will flow into a new reservoir and then be diverted along more than 500 miles of the Tibetan plateau to the vast, arid areas of Xinjiang region and Gansu province. Beijing wants to use large quantities of the plentiful waters of the south-west to top up the Yellow River basin and assuage mounting discontent over water shortages in 600 cities in northern China.

Yang Yong, a geologist who has explored the river, said the dam could become an embarrassing white elephant amid growing signs that the volume of water flowing in the Yarlung Zangpo could shrink. He said: "Environmental conditions in the upper reaches of the river continue to deteriorate, with glaciers receding and tributaries and lakes going dry." (The Canada Tibet Committee. Issue ID: 00/10/23; October 23, 2000.]

Tibetan activists have warned that the plans are likely to devastate the lower reaches of the Yarlung Zangbo, which flows south where it becomes the Brahmaputra. This river irrigates the northern plains of Assam state in India before flowing through Bangladesh and emptying into the Bay of Bengal.

LARGE DAMS AND LOCAL POPULATIONS

River linking - A Millennium Folly?

Considered to be the "mother of all projects", interlinking of rivers is projected as the one and the only solution to all water problems - droughts and floods. Never before has any proposal won the unstinted support of the apex court, the first citizen and the chief executive of the country, all at the same time. The book is a collection of articles by experts who dissect and analyze the proposed project from various angles

Amongst other issues, the book brings into the focus the question of the rights of the riparian countries. Authors assert that riparian rights are not being taken cognizance of and that a unilateral decision by India without a fully consulted prior consent of the concerned countries can injure the already fragile political atmosphere in South Asia.

The idea of interlinking of the rivers of India is described by - from the President down to local leaders in the less water endowed areas - as the perfect win-win solution for addressing the twin problems of water scarcity in the western and southern parts of the country and the problem of floods in the eastern and northeastern parts. The claims and statements of politicians, do not, however, substitute comprehensive scientific assessment, so that one can know whether by the proposed interlinking, the right quality and quantity of water would be stored and delivered at the right time in the right places...and all this would be achieved in the most cost-effective manner. For this, what is needed is sound professional assessment of the technical proposals based on the latest interdisciplinary systems knowledge.

Unfortunately, as far as the proposal for interlinking is concerned, there is little information available to the open world of science, beyond some lines drawn on the map of the country. Unless the scientific basis and technical details of the proposal are made available for open professional assessment, the justifications that are being propped up for the project will remain mere exercises in the act of guessing on the part of the people, and professing on the part of the water resource officials. Such silence about the technical details of the proposals also has other implications. For example, in contrast with the official prescription for interlinking of rivers, there are strong opinions that India's water crisis is caused by the mismanagement of water resources and the solutions do not lie in supply side augmentation. Iyer (2000), a former Secretary of Water Resources of the country corroborates this fact, with the view that:

Large scale supply side augmentation has been prescribed by the engineers as the only way for the satisfaction of water requirements of the developing countries. As a result, political leaders at all levels have sold the idea of solving the water problem by harnessing the huge monsoon run-off.

The reductionist view of engineering is unable to recognise the ecological significance of the unhindered flows in the river as critical to drainage, transportation of sediments, recharge of groundwater, maintenance of the delta and highly productive estuarine ecosystems and related biodiversity. Hence, it finds little difficulty in locating 'surplus' river basins!

Disastorous for the Whole Region

The withdrawl of waterfrom the major rivers will be disastorous for the whole region:

- Loss of plankton flora and fauna i.e. dramatic decrease of fish in delta front (beyond Sri Lanka).
- No new land will be reclaimed from the Bay of Bengal. The Bengal delta which has been built since millions of years will begin to erode.
- Coastal erosion, saline water intrusion i.e. the upstream water diversion in Bangladesh include saline ingress through the lower Meghna, which could be as far as the haor basin of Sylhet (northeast Bangladesh).
- Almost all cities, industries and agriculture of Ganges-Brahmaputra basin dispose of untreated effluents to rivers. Without fresh water influx a poisonous coctail of biological and inorganic poison will displace ten per cent of global population.
- Flood and tidal storm will displace millions of population.
- The reduction of flows in Atrai, Karatoya and Teesta could spell disaster for the rainfall-deficit Northwestern hydrologic region. Wetland and groundwater recharge capacity would also decrease in the Brahmaputra Dependent Area.
- The decrease in the flow of Brahmaputra (Jamuna) within Bangladesh would adversely affect the flows of the distributaries in the North-Central hydrologic region. The amount of Jamuna water reaching the Canges at Goalundo would also diminish, thus adversely affecting the distributaries of the South-Central hydrologic region

- Extiction of Sunderbans (Flora and Fauna), the world's largest mangrove forest of the world.
- Unknown ecological disaster as we have very small scientific knowledge on tropical rivers and consequnces due to plate movement (seismic activities) and water withdrawl.

POLLUTION IN THE GANGES BRAHMAPUTRA DELTA PLAIN

Indian 'Green Lady' and former environment minister Maneka Gandhi was worried that in early 21st century the Indian provinces may be involved in battles due to irrational water sharing.

National Water Development Agency (NWDA) of India to carry out 560,000,000,000,00 Indian rupee (50 Rupees= 1 US Dollar) a project to link 37 rivers through similar number of canals and 32 dams. Indian Prime Minister's personal initiative helped prioritise this project, while the President directed a 'Task Force' in August 2002 to complete the project within 10 years.

India is apparently stressing on the Hormon Doctrine, which originated in the United States in 1895, but has never gained universal acceptance. It is conveniently forgetting various provisions of the Montevideo Declaration of American States (1933), the views of the 1977 UN Water Conference held in Mar del Plata, the decision of the Lake Lanoux Arbitral Tribunal in the dispute between Spain and France and those of legal experts from the International Law Commission.

The Indian plan envisages transfer of water of the Ganges and its tributaries to Maharashtra, Rajasthan and Gujrat. Similarly, it also plans to divert the waters of the Brahmaputra and its tributaries to the Ganges and from there to the Godavori, Krishna, Pennar and Cauvery basins through Subrnarekha in West Bengal and Mahanadi of Orissa.

Again the Brahmaputra and the Teesta would be connected to take waters from the former to the latter and from the latter to the Farakka Barrage. For this purpose they need some 30 connecting canals which (if joined) together would be around 10,000 km in length. Besides nine big and 24 small dams—four of them in collaboration with Bhutan and Nepal—would also be built as required in the master plan.

India also plans to produce 34 million KW (kilowatt) waterpower under the same project. The policymakers, moreover, in India believe this river-link project is worth the huge expenditure as they take the multi-faceted benefits from this project into consideration.

Another thing that added motion to the Indian government's initiatives in materialising the project is a verdict of the Indian Supreme Court. The court verdict, which came after a public interest case was filed with it, ordered the government to realise the project by December 31, 2016. Indian President APJ Abdul Kalam has spoken in favour of this project recently while the BJP govt. has been calling it "Indian's dream project" and promising to materialise it for quite some time now

Notable water expert, Tauhidul Anwar Khan, Member of the Joint River Commission has also very correctly pointed out that India's unilateral move to inter-link the trans-boundary rivers contravenes existing Articles of the 1996 Treaty between Bangladesh and India with regard to the sharing of the Ganges Waters at Farakka. According to him, such a scheme would be contrary to the body and spirit of Articles 2(2) and 9 of this Treaty and would affect providing of due share of common river's water to a co-riparian.

Consequences for Bangladesh

Such steps would have disastrous impact on the economy of Bangladesh, its ecology, the livelihood of its people, its eco-system. It will also in the long run lead to internal displacement of millions of its citizens. Specialists have also pointed out that implementation of such a project would most certainly lead to more severe flooding in the monsoon and worse droughts in the lean season. Such vagaries would also contribute to increased salinity across the country and sharp fall in sweet water levels. These factors would juxtapose to eventually destroy the largest mangrove forest in the world, the Sunderbans. According to a Washington Times report on September 20, the Indian plan would cause severe flooding during the monsoon rains and worse drought during the dry season in Bangladesh.

Centre for Development and Environment Policy at the Indian Institute of Management in Kolkata as saying that once the Indian plan is implemented, the world could lose the richest fisheries in south Asia. Bandhopadhyaya points out that salinity would also make inroads into the region, affecting thousands of hectares of arable land [and] affecting the lives of millions of people living on agriculture in Bangladesh. Mangrove forests too, he says, will be disastrously affected as they depend on the steady rise and fall of tides for their roots to breathe. Arresting the natural flow of rivers could be a death knell for the world's largest remaining coastal forest a World Heritage site shared by the delta regions of Bangladesh and India.

The wisdom of linking up rivers is not beyond question because more than 70 percent of Indian river water is polluted by linking them and then allowing them to enter into Bangladesh will poison all our water bodies, human beings and wildlife.

The International Law Association (ILA)'s Helsinki rules-1967 and the International Law Commission (ILC)'s second report on the Law of Non-navigational Uses of International Water Courses-1986, both prohibit co-riparian states from altering the flow of an international water course, so as to cause either substantial or appreciable harm to another. Both adopt the equitable balance approach with regards to sharing the waters of an international drainage basin.

Similarly, the Salzburg Resolution of the Institute of International Laws in 1961 stated that the right of a sovereign state to use the waters of a shared river is limited by the right of utilisation of other states interested in the same water course. In it's general commentary the ILA states that "Any use of water by a basin state, whether upper or lower, that denies an equitable sharing of uses by a co-basin state/states, conflicts with the community of interests of all basin states, in obtaining the maximum benefit from the common resource. Certainly, a diversion of water that denies a co-basin state an equitable share is in violation of International Law".

While Farakka barrage alone has adversely affected our 40,000,000 (four crore) people of Bangladesh, crippled our agriculture, fisheries, navigation, hydro-morphology, industry, forestry, poultry and other relevant sectors; the Mohanada and the Teesta barrages that were not left uncommissioned by India. By and large Farakka, Mohananda and Teesta barrages together have resulted severe ecological and climatic degradation in Bangladesh resulting in the desertification of the north and north-western parts of the country, destroying the Sunderban forest, the largest mangrove forest of the world, including its flora and fauna, posing serious threat to Mongla Port, and intensifying flood, flash flood, cyclone and draught.

Facing endemic arsenic contamination

According to WHO study, the prevalence of arsenic in drinking water (60mg/1) is much above the permissible limit (0.05mg/1) and this supports the fact that some 80 million people are affected with some degree of arsenic contamination in Bangladesh.

This monster silent killer is also spreading fast affecting more and more people with the passage of time making it an endemic health problem in the country.

Most of the people depend on tube wells across the country for safe drinking water and this makes them vulnerable to the threat. Most of these tube wells are installed at about 120 feet deep below the surface where the arseno-pirates charged underground water level exists. As a result, people are naturally being affected silently by arsenic drinking water from these tube wells. Safe water from tube wells thus has turned to be a nightmare. People are being affected by painful skin diseases, cancer and gangrene due to long term intake of arsenic contaminated tube well water across the country.Studies suggest that unilateral withdrawal of water from the trans-boundary rivers is causing rivers and canals to die fast. In fact, the North and Southwest part of the country have now turned into a veritable desert. Due to the severe scarcity of water in the dry season the ground water level dropped sharply and that cannot be recharged sufficiently resulting in further drop of underground water level. Pumping out ground water for irrigation and other uses makes the situation worse further.

Experts suggest that tube wells should be reset at 350 feet deep underground to avoid arsenic contaminated underground water level. For a sustainable solution to this problem, the government should put pressure on the neighboring country not to divert water from common rivers unilaterally. It should take initiatives to ensure proper treatment of arsenic related diseases and complications under one umbrella.

A holistic effort needs to be initiated throughout the country to stop downward turn of underground water level. Mass awareness through anti-arsenic campaign should also be taken where the media - both print and wire - should play a dominant role (Daily Sun, Editorial,31-03-2014).

Hilsa Fish (*Clupeidae Tenualosa Ilisha*)

Imagine a scenario hundred years from now. The curator of Dhaka-Museum is showing a skeletal remains of Hilsa fish, a recently extinct species, to the visiting school children. The once glorious novelty and mouth-watering delicacy Hilsa fish — a delectable entrée of any common Bengali's dinner — is completely lost in oblivion.

The extinction of Hilsa and a great many other fishes and aquatic lives would be a fait accompli, if a wrong decision is executed by the Indian leaders. According to the recent media reports, a grandiose River Linking Plan is being seriously considered by the ruling BJP leadership of India.

The plan's formal announcement is not yet made. Neither is the detail released to the public domain. The would-be affected neighbouring governments of Bangladesh, Nepal and Bhutan are ignored and not even consulted. Sifting through the sketchy information from Indian NGOs and western news media, we can sense some aspects of the River Linking Plan and its horrific consequence on India itself and other co-riparian neighbours, especially Bangladesh.

Because of its gargantuan negative consequence on Bangladesh, we should voice our serious concern over this notorious plan and do everything necessary to stop this project. In this article I will address the following questions: what is the project all about and what would be its impact on aquatic life, especially the Hilsa fish of Bangladesh?

Hilsa *Clupeidae Tenualosa Ilisha* - Bengalis most Favourite Fish

Our mouthwatering Hilsa fish (scientific name: *Clupeidae Tenualosa Ilisha*) is a rare anadromous species in tropical water, and it migrates from the Bay of Bengal upstream about 30-60 miles in Bangladesh for spawning during monsoon and a short period in winter. Hilsa shad live most of their lives in the Bay of Bengal.

They count for almost one-third of fish production of Bangladesh. Approximately three million people's livelihood as fishermen depends on Hilsa. Hilsa eggs are hatched in fresh water at about 73 degrees Fahrenheit. This fish initially feeds on zooplankton, and then on phytoplankton. Large scale impounding of water in upstream lakes and later discharging will lower the temperature in spawning rivers in Bangladesh, thereby hatching will be impeded significantly. The forthcoming controlled structures in the upstream India will increase the silt content, thereby obstructing the spawning migration in Bangladesh.

The change in river load will drastically change the ecosystem of Bangladesh, wrecking havoc. The runoff from the Indian agricultural land will be contaminated with herbicides, insecticides, and fertilizer. The wastewater disposal from Indian industries will unleash chemical contaminants in downstream rivers, and Bangladesh will be in the receiving end. The diversion of one-third water from the eastern river system will dry-up and silt-up many rivers in dry season, and then over discharge from Indian dams during monsoon will flood the silted rivers. The over-all scenario of Bangladesh will be a cancer alley where death and destruction will loom with impunity, and our favourite Hilsa will be a shadow of the past.

Indiscriminate catching of *jhaktas* (tiny fishes) in Bay going on

The indiscriminate catching of jatka in the Bay of Bengal has been going on due to lack of awareness among the fishermen. The coast guards launched campaign in the coastal areas not to catch jatkas. The dishonest fish warehouse owners are instigating the fishermen to catch more jatkas for earning more profit. Jhatkas are seen everyday in the coastal area markets, fish warehouses and pickup vans which carry Jatkas to different places of the country.

The mass awareness about the destruction of national wealth through media will check the killing of Jatkas. In the deep sea fishing trawlers are using current nets to catch jantkas. If jatka killing continues in this manner one day the children will forget the reality of their poem *"Elish Bhaja Khete Maja Garam Garam Holey"*.

No hilsa fishing for 2 months 20km stretch in Padma to be declared sanctuary

A 20km stretch of the Padma is to made sanctuary for hilsa as the government has decided not to allow catching of the kingly fish in March-April every year. The decision came at a meeting held at the fisheries and livestock ministry yesterday chaired by its Secretary Mohammad Shah Alam. This will be the fifth hilsa sanctuary. The area has been selected on the basis of research, said an official of the ministry. The areas of the fifth sanctuary include Bhomkara, Kachhikata, Tarabuniya and Beparipara of Shariyatpur.

The production of hilsa has increased by around one lakh tonne after four sanctuaries were declared and putting a ban on catching jatka (hilsa fry), the official added. In 2001-2002 the hilsa production was 1.99 lakh tonne, which went up to 3 lakh tonne in 2008-2009, said Dr GC Halder, director research of Bangladesh Fish Research Institute.

The production has shot up because of the ban on catching hilsa from their breeding grounds that include Hatia, Sandwip and Dhalchar for 10 days from October 15 to 24 last year. This year 95 percent hilsa fish laid eggs, which was only 5 percent last year, he continued. He said the number of jatka has increased in plenty this year. There is also a ban on catching, transporting and selling of jatka (up to 23cm) from November 1 to March 30 as per the Fish Conservation Act-1950, he said. The first sanctuary is a 100km long stretch in the Meghna River and its branches from Shatnol of Chandpur to Char Alexander of Lakshmipur. The second one is a 90km long Shahbajpur channel of Meghna confluence including Madanpur of Manpura, Char Ilisha, Char Pial of Bhola district. The third sanctuary covers 100km long Tentulia river from Bheduria of Bhola to Char Rustom of Patuakhali while the fourth is 40km long Andharmanik river route under Kalapara upazila in Patuakhali. Fishing in the first three sanctuaries is prohibited from March to April while in the fourth one the ban comes into effect from November to January, said an official of the ministry.

He said they have a target to increase the production from 3 lakh tonne to 6 lakh tonne in future and 4 lakh to 4.5 lakh tonne within a few years. The announcement of the new sanctuary is part of their campaign to achieve the target. Meetings will also be held at local level to grow awareness among fishermen so that they themselves do not fish during those times, he said (Daily Star June 10, 2009).

But we do not know whether this campaign will work.

Hilsha still too dear

The government decision to ban hilsha fish export for the next six months is yet to make any impact on its wholesale and retail prices during the last 48 hours in Dhaka markets. A moderately big-size hilsha was selling at Tk 300 per kg at Karwan Bazar yesterday. The ban on hilsha export has failed to contain the price in Khulna and Bagerhat markets also, reports our staff correspondent from Khulna.

Md Yusuf Sikder, secretary of the Barisal Fish Exporters Association, attributed the recent increase in price of standard-sized hilsha to the rise of catching cost as prices of fuel and spare parts of the fishing trawlers and daily expenses of the fishermen increased and the catch of standard-sized hilsha decreased.

In Bagerhat, a section of sellers are allegedly cheating the customers in weight by inserting small iron pieces into hilsha fish, he added. However, hilsha price fell by 15-20 per cent in Barisal.

The stopping of the legal way of export may lead to increased smuggling of hilsha from the points of catching in the Bay, they said, adding that the matter will also affect national economy, trade balance as well as foreign relationship. Following the government decision taken on Wednesday, customs officials in Benapole land port on Thursday sent back the trucks loaded with hilsha from Barisal that were scheduled for export to India. Supply from different hilsha mokams (procurement centres) to Barisal exporters decreased while the exporters are now preserving their stocked fish in cold storages of Khulna and Jessore, reports our Barisal correspondent. The amount of hilsha export from Bangladesh was 3,414 tonne in fiscal year 2006-07 and 4,495 tonne in 2005-06 (Daily Star, 07. 07. 07).

The abrupt decision of the government to ban exports is the very reason behind the dearth and thus the increasing price

According to economists and fishmongers, the abrupt decision of the government to ban exports is the very reason behind the dearth and thus the increasing price. 'The government should have contemplated the consequences and the alternatives before taking this decision. A rash decision like this is going to complicate things than solve them,' says Anu Mohammad, Professor, Department of Economics, Jahangirnagar University, to Xtra when asked about the crisis. 'By things,' he continues, 'I am talking about the overall price mechanism. Most fish traders are very likely going to hoard fishes for the next six months, until the ban is lifted.' According to recent reports and fishmongers, the trend has already began as supply from Khulna and Barisal has decreased drastically.

He goes on to explain that the ban will also encourage smugglers to smuggle Hilsas to neighboring countries at a higher price. 'The move has, therefore, also increased their chances of higher profit,' he says. Motin points out that although the government has imposed the ban, they will never be able to stop the smugglers. 'This group has their own resources and with most border patrol authorities on their payroll, Hilsa will be smuggled out of the country,' he says.

He further points out that the second reason behind the unnatural price of Hilsa is the dominance of the middlemen. 'There is a huge difference between the prices at which the fishermen sells the Hilsa and at the prices at which we receive them. This is due to the unnatural and somewhat, unethical profit that the middlemen are making,' he says. M M Akash, Professor, Department of Economics, explains that besides the dominance of middlemen and smuggling, government also needs to look at the transportation and storage costs involved with the Hilsa trade.

'The fish is a perishable good and therefore, it needs to be stored in freezers, whose maintenance is very expensive. Plus, the rise in fuel prices, trawler parts and other variable costs are indirectly increasing the selling price,' he says. He further points out that the export ban, besides harming the economy, will also affect trade relations with neighbouring countries. 'Already, India has threatened to stop export of rice to Bangladesh due to this move. The government should have seen this coming before making the decision,' he says. He points out that India's retaliation is quite obvious as even before the ban on export, on each weekday over 40 tonnes of Hilsa were exported to the country through the Benapole land port. Around 20 importing firms of West Bengal purchased an amount of Hilsa that dragged around Tk 250 crore into Bangladesh last year.

'We cannot sustain such a retaliation and this move will only encourage smuggling as it wont really help our economy in any way,' he says. He urges the government to cut down the dominance of middlemen and the costs related to Hilsa fish trade. Anu, on the other hand, wants the government to delve into the broader aspect of the country's 'food security'. 'If past governments were a bit more careful, we would not have had to be hostages in the hands of these countries in such a way. It's about time, that we try to replenish our lost edge in food items like rice, Hilsa and others,' he says.

The Hilsa Shad

Hilsa shad, one of the most important tropical fish of the family clupeidae under the genus*Tenualosa* and species ilisha is anadromous in nature, not a common phenomenon in tropical water compared to temperate and arctic regions, lives in the sea for most of its life, but migrates at least 1,200 km up in some river system in Indian sub-continent for spawning behavior. Distances of 50-100 km are more typical in Bangladesh.

Hilsa shad contributing 30 % of total fish production of Bangladesh, and about 40 % fishermen or 2 % of total population of the country earn their livelihood depending on Hilsa fishery directly or indirectly. Therefore economic contribution from this single species of fish is very high, in an agricultural based country like Bangladesh.

Three separate species of Hilsa Shad are found in Bay of Bengal, they are Hilsa kelee, Hilsa toli and Hilsa ilisha now Tenualosa ilisha. Tenualosa ilisha is considered as anadromous species while the other two species are restricted to marine environment. And in this report we are dealing only with anadromous stock.

During the commencement of the south-west monsoon and consequent flooding of all the rivers, Hilsa shad starts its spawning migration upstream. A mature Hilsa shad with a length ranging from 30-55 cm lays 0.1-2.0 million eggs, the eggs are deposited in fresh water, and hatching takes place in about 23 to 26 hours at an average temperature of 23oC. The newly hatched larvae is recorded as 2.3 mm in size and the larvae and juveniles make their way downstream to the sea during a period of several months, feeding and growing on the way. At this stage of their life cycle they are locally known as "Jatka". Jatka the juveniles of Hilsa shad from 4-15 cm are widely available during the period from February to May in the foreshore and riverine water of Padma, Meghna and other deltaic rivers of Bangladesh.

Usually *Jatka* grazes for five to six months age in fresh water before they migrate to seawater. They are caught in large amount using current nets of small mesh size during their grazing period in rivers as well as in sea shore by artisanal fishermen to sell them in local markets, calling them "Chapilla" instead of "Jatka", which is a different species of fish, and thus exploiting this resource in a way, According to a report published through Bangladesh Fisheries Research Institutte,over 3700 metric tons of Jatka are caught annually during their nursery season from inland rivers.

Jatka is usually a plankton feeder preferring zooplankton, and the rate of food intake is comparatively very high at this stage, but with the age and seasonal variability it changes its food habitat, and becoming bigger changes to phytoplankton feeder. And during maturation Hilsa shad decreases its food intake and cease feeding for the duration of spawning migration. After growing for 1-2 years in sea, Hilsa shad matures and reaches an size of 32-55 cm prior to their spawning migration towards inland rivers, and the cycle continues.

During their upstream migration these brood fish are caught by fishermen in huge amount in estuarine rivers using gill and seine net, moreover construction of dams, weir, anicuts in the rivers to impound water for irrigation, (specially in India) had topped the fish in their migration. Not only did this interfere with migration but it also rendered stock prone to excessively heavy exploitation at location where migration was impeded, the barriers are so many and the fishing methods so efficient that the potential breeders are ruthlessly exterminated, during the past 20 to 25 years in India. As a result the stock is available in huge amount in Bangladesh. But unfortunately once more this particular stock is being exploited, with over fishing and natural barrier in their migratory route due to heavy siltation in inland rivers. Therefore conservation and management of this population in Bangladesh has become important for utilising this resource in future

Migration of Hilsa shad is not limited to monsoon only, but it also migrates for a short period during winter. In other words it can be said that Hilsa shad is available in the river through out the year. But the peak catch periods are during upstream migration in monsoon and winter. During the peak catch period, due to shortage of sufficient storage facilities and ice availabilities, in addition to high temperature and poor transport facilities to northern part of the country, huge quantity of caught Hilsa shad is destroyed each year. Therefore steps should be taken to promote the export of fish, which could not be locally consumed during the peak catch periods.

"Ram Mandir" and the 'River-link project'

Amid this kind of ongoing disaster, the Indian authority has again undertaken a huge project to linking all the rivers within her country surrounding Bangladesh. This project prominently concerns Bangladesh, and to some extent Nepal and Bhutan. The project has been designed to transfer waters from all the 57 water channels falling from India into Bangladesh. While many of the Indian experts remain skeptical about the outcome of this project, the authorities decided to go ahead with the programme.

"Ram Mandir" and the 'River-link project'

In fact, political analysts in India are of the view that "Ram Mandir" and the 'River-link project' issues are going to be used as trump cards in the upcoming national election by the rightist fundamentalist Bharatiya Janata Party. Now, if India goes ahead with this project — it now appears to be a strong possibility — the fallout will be devastating for Bangladesh. The proposed river-link project is worked out depending on the two major rivers of the region — the Ganges and the Brahmaputra.

As for India these two rivers are also of equal significance to us, whose flow provide and determine to a large extent the flow of other small rivers and tributaries. Now, when the river-link project comes into Operation, India will start withdrawing water from both the Ganges and the Brahmaputra and instantly water flow of the rivers in our north-west, north-middle, south-west and south-middle areas will fall sharply. Consequently different types of water bodies like beels, canals, wet lands of those area will go dry. The deadliest effect however will be the increase of salinity to a dangerous level.

But if the waters coming from the Brahmaputra decrease because of withdrawal of water in the upstream, waterflow will also fall in the lower Meghna and consequently saline water will get inside and spread up to the mid-point of the country. That is exactly what happened to our south-western part of the country because of Farakka. In that case it was the Gorai river which suffered from low flow of water.

ROSY FOR INDIA, UNFORTUNATE BANGLADESH

River-linking Mega Project Of India

Study on ecological impacts before implementation: An Indian expert has said that his country would not proceed with the implementation of the planned river-linking mega project if there is any possibility of ecological disaster in the region. Professor Shishir K. Dube, who is actively involved in the much maligned project, said that a study on ecological and other impacts would be conducted prior to kicking off the project. "If the study reveals that the project may harm the ecosystem of the region, we won't go for its implementation," he said while talking to New Age at the Hotel Sheraton on Tuesday.

Professor Dube has been assigned by the India government to assess the ecological impacts of the project on its neighbouring nations. He came to Dhaka to attend a seminar on "Tropical Cyclones and Storm Surges in the South Asian Region and Agricultural Application of Meteorology" and talked to New Age before leaving for India on Tuesday afternoon.

When Bangladesh's apprehension of the likelihood of an ecological disaster if the project is implemented was brought up, he replied, "The project is still in a preliminary stage. We must consider how all concerned parties may be affected by the project before finalising it." In this regard, he said two meetings involving high officials have so far been held, where they had discussed the prospects and potential impacts of the project.

Professor Dube, who is involved in several decision-making bodies formed by the Indian government, said that the feasibility study would resume soon, and once study ended, they would look into the project's engineering aspects. Replying to a question, he said that the ultimate objective of the project is to transfer water from one place to another in the country. "There are some places that have excessive water while there are places suffering from drought. So our plan is to transfer the excess water to the drought areas in our country."

Asked about the protest from several Indian states and some other countries, including Bangladesh, he said, "We will not only study the impacts on the neighbouring countries sharing rivers with India, but will also examine the impacts on different Indian states." He also said that the India government is very much aware of Bangladesh's concern over probable environmental disaster. "But the question arises only after we go for its implementation," said Dube, who is also the director of the Indian Institute of Technology in Kharagpur. (New Age, December 24, 2003).

The ruling BJP passed a resolution in its National Council at Nagpur on August 27-28, 2000, in which the BJP wants to link thirty major rivers including the eastern river Brahmaputra all the way to the southern river Kaberi of Deccan peninsula. The linking distance between Brahmaputra and Kaberi is more than 2,640 kilometer. This is equivalent to bringing water of river Mekong of Vietnam to Nepal irrigating land through Cambodia, Thailand, Myanmar, Bangladesh, India, Bhutan, and Nepal.

This can also be compared to artificially channeling water of river Tigris of Iraq to Madhya Pradesh of India distributing water through Iraq, Iran, Afghanistan, Pakistan, and Indian province of Rajasthan. With a price tag exceeding 112 billion US dollars, this plan also includes digging hundreds of reservoirs and more than six hundred canals; diverting one third water from Brahmaputra, Ganges, and other eastern rivers; irrigating 135,000 square miles (more than double the area of Bangladesh) of almost un-arable land of India; generating 34,000 megawatts of hydroelectricity.

All these appear rosy to Indians, but at whose definite peril and destruction? The sacrificial lamb would be unfortunate Bangladesh. In fact, this is a lose-lose situation. India too will be a loser in the long run because of the nature's wrath that would be unleashed by the destruction of the entire ecosystem of India.

The devastating change to the eco-system of Bangladesh, especially to her fisheries as a result of the India's River Linking Plan, could be learnt from two relatively smaller projects in USA involving the Colorado River and the Columbia River.

Riparian Rights

"Control over water has again and again provided an effective means of consolidating power within the human grouups-led, that is, to the assertion by some people of power over others (Worster, 1985).

From S. Vombatkere, River Linking A Millennium Folly, 2004:

International relations and inter-State relations within India need to be carefully considered.Bangladesh has raised objections to the proposal to divert water from Brahmaputra and Ganga or their tributaries in terms of international law.

The effect of India's going ahead with the project in spite of such objections can only lead to increased friction and tension. Bangladesh cannot be faulted if it applies the logic of the Supreme Court of India that has categorically ruled that Karanataka (upper riparian state) has to release water to Tamil Nadu (lower riparian state) and cannot keep the water for it self.

Consequences of Farraka Barrage

The Farakka Barrage built in 1974 across the Ganges about 17 kilometers from Bangladesh border already limits water flow by half at certain times of the year. The result is the non-availability of irrigation water to adjoining Bangladeshi districts of Kushtia, Jessore, Pabna and Faridpur. The construction of the Barrage has damaged the ecosystem of the Sundarbans, the largest mangrove forest of the world.

A Panos study says that Bangladesh has been maintaining that the reduced natural flow of water in the Ganga has affected agriculture, fisheries and navigation. The lower riparian claims that the Gorai, a distributary of the Ganga, has all but dried up causing increased salinity and endangering the freshwater mangrove forests, the Sundarbans, in the delta. The dispute was even taken up to the United Nations by Bangladesh. The Farakka Barrage built in 1974 across the Ganges about 17 kilometers from Bangladesh border already limits water flow by half at certain times of the year. The result is the non-availability of irrigation water to adjoining Bangladeshi districts of Kushtia, Jessore, Pabna and Faridpur. The construction of the Barrage has damaged the ecosystem of the Sundarbans, the largest mangrove forest of the world.

The gradual exclusion of water from the Ganga, the Teesta and the Mohanada has increased our sufferings since many years. Our natural ecosystem has been gravely damaged by this iniquity, and its reflections can be viewed in all spheres of our life-significant number of jute mills are closed, news print and paper mills shuttered, desertification process began in north and north-western districts, Sunderban mangrove forest shrunken, large number of birds and animal species diminished, many species of fishes at the verge of extinction and above all the increased intensity of flood, flash flood, cyclone, draught etc. At this point in time India's huge project of diverting waters from all the river channels failing into Bangladesh will further caused damage to Bangladesh with infinite natural and human catastrophe.

Colrado River

The Colorado River's headwater is in Colorado's Rocky Mountains and the river ends at the Gulf of California. The construction of Hoover Dam across its course started in 1930 and was completed in 1935. By 1950 seven more dams were built. These dams with associated reservoirs and control structures drastically changed the ecosystem of the entire Colorado River basin.

The dams replaced the silt-laden, turbulent, and seasonally warm water flow of the Colorado River by less silty, less turbulent, and colder water flow in smaller discharge necessitated by the diversion of water for irrigation, hydroelectricity, and civic needs in large cities. The result is the near extinction of fishes such as the bony tail and the razorback sucker, which were the proud inhabitants of the Colorado River and were considered a delicacy by the Hopi Indians, the indigenous people of the Colorado River basin. Moreover, the increased industrial and agricultural activities in the upstream basin introduced innumerable chemical contaminants, parasites, herbicides, pesticides, fertilizers, and other wastes in the water, dramatically changing the ecosystem. The draconian changes have also been made in Columbia River ecosystem since 1972 by constructing dams, diverters, and controlled structures along the course of this majestic river. The salmon, a delicacy of international repute (raised to its celebrity status by Somerset Maugham's short story, Luncheon), is now becoming a dying fish in its one of the best abodes, the Columbia River.

From the above experience we can evaluate the fate of eco-environment of the Gangetic delta if India's River Linking Plan is implemented. Especially its impact on our favourite Hilsa fish is unthinkable. India's project will be much more humongous and devastating than the Colorado and Columbia projects.

WATER WARS MAY START AFTER OIL WARS

The idea of water wars to follow soon in the wake of oil wars has been around as another doomsday scenario for a while. But a dismissal of the scenario as something that has not materialised, and will not, has meant also an under-rating of the potential for conflict that continues to float around water sharing.

"We need to make a distinction between violent conflict and conflict itself," Mark Zeitoun, researcher with the London Water Research Group, a part of the Centre for Environmental Policy at King's College and the London School of Economics told IPS. "There are no examples of states engaging in violent conflict strictly over water resources. But water is often an element in violent conflicts, and there are conflicts that fall short of war. Absence of war does not mean absence of conflict."

At the sub-national level there are many instances of violent conflict over water, he said. "In Chad, in Western Darfour, you have different tribes, sometimes members of the same tribe fighting over limited resources of water."

There is a conflict between Ethiopia and Egypt over the Nile waters, he said. "Ethiopians in the highlands are unable to irrigate their land and develop hydroelectric projects as they would like to. Israelis and Palestinians are not fighting over water, but Israel controls 90 percent of trans-boundary flows that Palestinians have very little ability to control, and there is deep resentment over this on the Palestinian side."

Water issues are always subordinate to the larger political context, he said. "Turkey is building dams on the Tigris and Euphrates, to the detriment of the interests of Iraq and Syria. But relations have been improving between Turkey and both Syria and Iraq, and there is more cooperation than there was three years ago, even though Turkey continues to build the dams whether Iraq and Syria want them or not." Privatisation of water spilled over into political conflict in Bolivia. "People took to the streets, there were some very difficult moments, and several people died in the violence," Vicky Cann from the World Development Movement, an independent research and campaigns group told IPS. "Water has a political dimension in many ways," she said.

"There is enough fresh water to go around, but access to it can be a political issue, and privatization is worsening that situation."

Conflicts over water are "very definitely an issue, and will only grow when you think in terms of the impact of climate change in the future."

Water is often at the core of development, and that relates directly to levels of people satisfaction-a deeply political matter for any government in its dealings either domestically or with other countries. An earlier report by the Overseas Development Institute (ODI) warned of the potential for conflict that may arise in the Awash Valley in Ethiopia.

The report by Alan Nicol of the School of Oriental and African Studies, with Yacob Arsano of the University of Addis Ababa and Dr Joanne Raisin of the University of Bradford looked at a wide range of risks of violent conflict which the EU may need to address in the Horn of Africa.

The report does not hold out scenarios of water wars, but says that access to natural resources can exacerbate tensions. The caution came in the context of a difficulty with Egypt over sharing of Nile waters. In the long term, it says "competition and ensuing conflict, whether actual or latent, may exacerbate environmental degradation further, increasing future risk of conflict, particularly during periods of drought."

Violent conflicts A strong link between droughts and violent civil conflicts in the developing world bodes ill for an increasingly thirsty world, say scientists, who warn that drought-related conflicts are expected to multiply with advancing climate change, writes Stephen Leahy from Brooklin, Canada. "Severe, prolonged droughts are the strongest indicator of high-intensity conflicts," said Marc Levy of the Centre for International Earth Science Information Network at Columbia University's Earth Institute in New York.

These are internal conflicts, not between countries, and involving more than 1,000 battle deaths, Levy said at a press briefing in Washington last week. Such conflicts tend to occur about a year after a "severe deviation in rainfall patterns", he said. Levy and colleagues used decades of detailed precipitation records, geospatial conflict information and other data in a complex computer model that overlays all this onto a fine-scale map of the world.

"Major deviations from normal rainfall patterns were the strongest predictor of conflicts," he said. "I was surprised at how strong the correlation is." Levy is careful to say that droughts don't directly cause conflicts but are more likely triggers in regions where already tensions or low-level conflicts exist. For example, in the recent civil conflict in Nepal, the parts of the country where most of the fighting occurred experienced low rainfall for several years and then a severe drought in the late 1990s.

Farmers may have simply given up hope of farming and joined the local rebellion as a way of sustaining themselves and their families, he hypothesised. And rainfall appears to have a pacifying affect. The wet areas of Africa, for instance, have far fewer years of violent internal conflict than the dry regions, he said.

Areas with a high risk of conflict this year due to extremely dry conditions last year, according to his model, are Cote d'Ivoire, Sudan, Bangladesh, Haiti, and Nagaland and Manipur in India. While the idea makes sense, "you can't predict how people will act", said Robert McLeman of the University of Ottawa, who studies the relationship between environmental extremes and human migration.

Africans have been dealing with drought for thousands of years. Currently cities serve as an outlet so there is seasonal migration during the dry season. And more and more people are staying in cities where presumably they can meet their needs more easily than in the countryside, he said.

Normal droughts can usually be accommodated, but significant and rapid environmental changes are more likely to lead to societal instability, forced migration and inter-group violence, says Nils

Petter Gleditsch of the Centre for the Study of Civil War at the International Peace Research Institute in Oslo, Norway.

"Drought in Hungary is not the same as drought in Ethiopia" in terms of the state being able to buffer the impacts, Gleditsch added at the briefing. About 1.5 billion people are estimated to be suffering from severe water stress around the world, and that number is expected to increase with population growth and climate change. "Climate change is likely to lead to a greater frequency of civil wars," Levy said.

Inequity is at the heart of most conflicts, said Satish Kumar, director of programmes at Schumacher College International Centre for Ecological Studies in Britain.

"There is growing anger that the rich are the cause of global warming but it's the poor who will suffer the most," Kumar told IPS. "I've heard people make this connection in regard to the unprecedented droughts in parts of India."

The lifestyle of the average North American produces 12 times the amount of greenhouse gases compared to that of people in poor countries, according the U.N. statistics, Kumar points out. Increased conflict, violence and social unrest is inevitable as global warming makes life even more difficult for many of the world's poor and they become aware that the rich of the world are responsible, Kumar added.

Only urgent action to reduce greenhouse gas emissions and to address economic and social inequities can stave off the worst. And he warns against neo-liberal solutions: "Capitalism is shrewd enough to use shortages of resources like water to make even more money for the rich."

7

Water, Power, and Competition in South Asia

THE FUTURE OF OUR WORLD WILL BE determined by several factors. One critical factor is adequate access to natural resources. The sharpening geopolitical competition over natural resources has already turned some strategic resources into engines of power struggle. Water, mineral ores, and fossil fuels like coal, oil, and gas are resources of the greatest strategic import. They hold the key to human development and, in the case of water, to human survival.

Food production is closely intertwined with water and energy, whereas water and energy are closely connected with each other. Water is essential for energy extraction, processing, and production, while energy is vital to treat, distribute, and supply water. Moreover, water is intimately linked with climate change. Human-induced changes in the hydrological cycle contribute to climate variation, and global warming, in turn, affects water resources, creating a vicious circle in the process.

Access to potable water is becoming a major issue across large parts of the world because of rapid demographic and economic expansion. Lifestyle and dietary changes have spurred increasing per-capita water consumption in the form of industrial and agricultural products. Freshwater, although a renewable resource, is a finite commodity whose quantity has virtually remained the same since the dawn of civilization. In fact, less than 1% of the world's water is usable because 97.5% of it is ocean salt water while another 1.6% is locked up in polar icecaps, glaciers, and permafrost.

Asia is attracting international attention more than ever before, in large part because of its reemergence on the global stage after a two-century decline. Asia is now the world's largest creditor and main economic locomotive. Asia's rise, however, has been accompanied by an insatiable appetite for natural resources. This has set off a sharpening resource competition between Asian economies within Asia and far beyond in other continents.

Although able to secure fossil fuels, mineral ores, and timber from distant lands, Asian economies cannot import the most critical resource for their socioeconomic development—water. Water is essentially local and prohibitively expensive to ship across seas. To compound the continent's challenges, some of the world's worst water pollution and shortages are found in Asia, promoting environmental degradation and creating a potential for conflict over shared waters.

A little-known fact is that Asia, not Africa, is the world's most water-stressed continent. Water stress is internationally defined as the per capita availability of less than 1,700 cubic meters per year. Not only is Asia's per capita water availability the lowest of any continent, but its water stress has also been exacerbated by its dramatic economic rise. The rapid economic growth, coupled with breakneck urbanization and the changing lifestyles of Asians, has made an already difficult water situation worse. Much of the world's coming expansion of urban population is projected to take place in Asia, with the portion of the global population living in urban areas expected to jump from slightly over half in 2011 to more than two-thirds in 2050. Asia's rapid urbanization is driving increased water demand both for municipal supply and for the industrial and agricultural products in demand in cities.

This essay analyzes how shared water has become an instrument of power in interstate relations in Asia, stoking underlying tensions, fostering competition, exacerbating impacts on ecosystems, and impeding broader regional collaboration. It examines cases of both upriver and downriver hydro-hegemony, which is water-resource capture or control at the basin level achieved through coercive or diplomatic means by exploiting and reinforcing regional power asymmetries. And it analyzes the security-related water trends in Asia, now the center of global water challenges. In doing so, the essay opens a window to the nature of interstate water competition and conflict, its wider impacts, and its management.

ASIA'S RESOURCE CHALLENGES

Natural-resource constraints in Asia raise troubling questions about the region's future growth trajectory. Asian economies facing a domestic resource crunch are being forced increasingly to rely on imported mineral ores, timber, and fossil fuels, bringing international supplies under pressure and triggering price volatility. Yet Asia, paradoxically, remains the world's economic locomotive. Its growing resource constraints raise the issue of whether it can continue to spearhead global economic growth in the coming years.

Asia's rise has fueled an insatiable appetite for resources it does not have. Unlike North America and Europe, which are well endowed with natural capital, Asia is the world's most resource-poor continent in per-capita terms. Its resources are also unevenly spread. Its energy resources, for example, are largely concentrated in the desert lands of Central and West Asia, while its water resources are concentrated in the mountainous hinterlands, yet 95% of Asians live in the plains or coastal regions. Even as resource-wealthy countries such as Australia, Brazil, Canada, and Russia enjoy commodity-export booms, Asia's resource struggle has brought it to a treacherous point of growing external dependency, geopolitical tensions, and environmental degradation.

Asia's overexploitation of its own natural resources has spurred an environmental crisis, which, in turn, is furthering regional climate change. Asia thus confronts three interlinked crises—a resource crisis, an environmental crisis, and a climate crisis—that threaten its future. From Asian cities dominating the list of the world's most-polluted cities to many urban areas reeling under serious water shortages, Asia faces increasing resource-related stresses. Meanwhile, sharpening Asian resource competition has aggravated disputes over resource-rich territories, including in the East and South China Seas and southern and central Asia.

Shortages

All the important Asian economies are in or near conditions of water stress.China supports 19% of the world's population on its territory with a 6.7% share of global water resources. The situation in India is grimmer: It has 17.8% of the global population but just 4.3% of the world's water.

A World Bank estimate placed the economic cost of water-resource degradation and depletion for China at 2.3% of gross domestic product (GDP), including 1% stemming from the direct impact of rampant water pollution. The health and non-health impacts of both air and water pollution in China were estimated at US$100 billion a year, or about 5.8% of GDP. China, with a per capita annual availability of 2,060 cubic meters in 2013, is not yet in the category of water-stressed states, a list that includes a number of other Asian economies. Water-scarce India and South Korea, for example, are seeing a greater impact nationally than China, with water shortages already beginning to reshape their economies, including the location of industries.

Asia's yearly per capita freshwater availability (2,816 cubic meters) is not even half the global average of 6,079 cubic meters. Yet Asia has experienced the world's most rapid growth in freshwater withdrawals from rivers, lakes, and aquifers in the period since it began rising economically. One international report, detailing the resulting steep declines in water availability for development in a number of Asian states since 1980, had this warning about the regional water situation: "Water shortfalls on this scale heighten competition for a precious resource and frequently lead to conflicts, which are emerging as new threats to social stability."

Asia's rate of utilization of freshwater already exceeds its renewable stocks. By digging deeper wells, further damming rivers, and transferring surface water across some basins, Asia is using tomorrow's water to meet today's needs, thereby accelerating environmental degradation. State policies, including the provision of irrigation subsidies as well as subsidized electricity and diesel fuel to farmers, have unwittingly contributed to water-resource depletion and environmental degradation.

The fact that Asia has one of the lowest levels of water efficiency and productivity in the world makes a bad situation worse. With water stress projected to cover two-thirds of the global population by the end of the next decade, up from about 50% today, the majority of the world's people living in water-related despair will continue to be in Asia.

Food

Asian economies are already facing a new problem on the food front at a time when agriculture's appropriation of the bulk of the water resources is coming under challenge from expanding cities and industries. Growth in crop yields and overall food production in Asia is now beginning to lag behind demand. Rising prosperity and changing diets, including an increased preference for animal-based protein, are compounding Asia's food challenges.

While new technologies, including genetic engineering, can serve as tools to enhance agricultural productivity, a way has not yet been found to reduce the dependence of crops on large amounts of water, except by installing expensive micro-irrigation systems. Unlike the large conglomerates that own much of the cropland in North America and Europe, most farmers in Asia have small acreage, limiting their capacity to invest in new technologies and irrigation systems.

The fast-rising Asian consumption of meat has by itself turned into a major driver of water stress. After all, production of meat is as much as 10 times more water-intensive than plant-based calories and proteins. In a reflection of the larger Asian trend, meat consumption quadrupled between 1980 and 2010 in China. The ecological footprint of Asia's increasing livestock population is compounding environmental and resource stresses. The only silver lining for India in an otherwise dismal water situation is the fact that a sizable percentage of its population remains vegetarian.

Asia needs to grow more food with less water. To be sure, the region has come a long way in addressing its food needs. Up to the 1960s, it was troubled by food shortages and recurrent famines. Then, on the back of an unparalleled expansion of irrigation, Asia emerged as a net food exporter in just one generation, opening the door to its economic rise. The total irrigated cropland in Asia doubled between 1960 and 2000 alone. Now, Asia boasts 72% of the world's total acreage equipped for irrigation, with irrigation mostly concentrated in its most populous subregions.

The irrigation-spurred farming boom, however, has come at a high price. Asia channels 82% of its water resources for agricultural use. This level is not sustainable. With the world's most rapid industrialization and urbanization, Asia is witnessing the fastest increase in water demand from its industries and municipalities. It thus must make major water savings in agriculture to quench the thirst of its booming industries and expanding cities. This challenge is compounded by the slowing growth in crop yields at a time when Asian food demand, for the first time in decades, is outstripping supply.

Poverty

How Asian states manage their resource challenges will shape their security and economic trajectories in the coming years. For example, the biggest enemies of alleviating economic poverty are water poverty and energy poverty. Water and energy poverty keep the poor chained to economic poverty. Asia needs an energy-technology revolution that can deliver cheap, reliable power to those mired in energy poverty and help clean up polluted or brackish waters, chemically treat and recycle wastewater, and make ocean water potable. Otherwise, water pollution—largely an intrastate challenge at present—is likely to assume transboundary dimensions and compound inter-country tensions and discord.

ABSENCE OF COOPERATION IN MOST BASINS

Asia's water resources are largely transnational, making inter-country cooperation and collaboration essential. Yet the vast majority of the 57 transnational river basins in continental Asia have no water-sharing arrangement or any other cooperative mechanism. This troubling reality has to be seen in the context of the strained political relations in several Asian subregions.

The river basins in the Asian continent that have a treaty-based sharing arrangement currently in place are the Al-Asi/Orontes (Lebanon-Syria), Araks-Atrek (Iran-Russia), El-Kaber (Lebanon-Syria), Euphrates (Iraq-Syria), Gandhak (India-Nepal), Ganges (Bangladesh-India), Indus (India-Pakistan), Jordan (Israel-Jordan), and Mahakali (India-Nepal). Arrangements in some of these basins, such as the Gandhak, Jordan, and Mahakali, do not incorporate a formula dividing the shared waters between the parties but rather center on specific water withdrawals, transfers, or rights of utilization. An important arrangement in the Mekong Basin—limited to the lower riparian nations—is centered on the sustainable management of water resources but without any water sharing.

The only treaties in Asia with specific sharing formulas on cross-border river flows are the ones between India and its two downriver neighbours, Pakistan and Bangladesh. In addition, the Soviet-era water arrangements in Central Asia continue to hold, even if tenuously, through an interim agreement signed in February 1992. Such is the competition over scarce water resources that even sharing arrangements are not free of rancor and discord.

Central Asia

Consider the water discord among the five so-called "stans" of Central Asia. The interim agreement, signed shortly after these states gained independence, defined on an ad hoc basis the principles to govern the sharing of the waters of the region's two main rivers, the Syr Darya and the Amu Darya. Soviet Central Asia's internal rivers became international watercourses following the independence of Kazakhstan, Uzbekistan, Kyrgyzstan, Tajikistan, and Turkmenistan. The post-Soviet agreement, while stipulating that the principles would continue until the parties had worked out a new water-sharing arrangement, set up an Interstate Commission for Water Coordination (ICWC) to help develop a new but still-illusive regional water management system.

In the Syr Darya River Basin, where the total annual flows aggregate to 36.57 billion cubic meters, the share of Kazakhstan—

located farthest downriver—was set to be no less than 10 billion cubic meters downstream of the Chardara Reservoir. Uzbekistan, however, is the main consumer of the waters of both the Syr Darya and the region's largest river, the Amu Darya, whose average yearly flows total 78.46 billion cubic meters. In 1996, Uzbekistan and Turkmenistan reached a water-allocation accord between themselves to supplement the five-nation 1992 interim agreement.

The fact, however, is that rising nationalism and competition over water resources in parched Central Asia has impeded the development of a regional alternative to the Soviet-era water management system. The old system survives largely due to the threat of force. The three lower but militarily powerful riparians—Uzbekistan, Kazakhstan, and Turkmenistan—wield the threat of force against the small and weak Kyrgyzstan and Tajikistan, which are the sources of the Syr Darya and the Amu Darya, respectively. Most of the water flows in these two lifelines of Central Asia are generated in the mountainous parts of Tajikistan and Kyrgyzstan.

China

More broadly, Asia's water map stands out for the unique riparian status that China enjoys. China is the source of rivers for a dozen countries. No other country in the world serves as the riverhead for so many countries. This makes China the central driver of inter-riparian relations in Asia.

Yet China also stands out for not having a single water-sharing arrangement or cooperation treaty with any co-riparian state. Its refusal to accede to the Mekong Agreement of 1995, for example, has stunted the development of a genuine basin community. By building mega-dams and reservoirs in its borderlands, China is working to unilaterally re-engineer the flows of major rivers that are the lifeblood for the lower riparian states.

To be sure, China trumpets several bilateral water agreements. But none is about water sharing or institutionalized cooperation on shared resources. Some accords are commercial contracts to sell hydrological data to given downstream nations. Others center on joint research initiatives, flood-control projects, hydropower development, fishing, navigation, river islands, hydrologic work, border demarcation, environmental principles, "good-neighborliness and friendly cooperation," or nonbinding memorandums of understanding. By fobbing off such accords as water agreements, China creates a false impression that it has cooperative riparian relations. In fact, it is to deflect attention from its unwillingness to enter into water sharing or institutionalized cooperation to sustainably manage common rivers that Beijing even advertises the accords it has signed on sharing flow statistics with co-riparian states. These agreements are merely contracts to sell hydrological data, which some other upstream countries provide free to downriver states.

The plain fact is that China rejects the very concept of water sharing. It also asserts a general principle that standing and flowing waters are subject to the full sovereignty of the state where they are located. It thus claims "indisputable sovereignty" over the waters on its side of the international boundary, including the right to divert as much shared water as it wishes for its legitimate needs. This principle was embodied in the now-discredited "Harmon Doctrine" in the U.S. more than a century ago. This doctrine is named after U.S. Attorney General Judson Harmon, who put forth the argument that the U.S. owed no obligations under international law to Mexico on shared water resources and was effectively free to divert as much of the shared waters as it wished for U.S. needs. Yet, despite this thesis, the U.S. went on to conclude water-sharing agreements with Mexico between 1906 and 1944. China, in rejecting the 1997 United Nations Convention on the Law of the Non-Navigational Uses of International Watercourses (which lays down rules on shared water resources and constitutes the first move to establish an international water law), placed on record its assertion of absolute territorial sovereignty over the waters within its borders: "The text did not reflect the principle of territorial sovereignty of a watercourse state. Such a state had indisputable sovereignty over a watercourse which flowed through its territory." This indicates that the Harmon Doctrine may be dead in the country of its birth but is alive and kicking in China.

In this light, it is hardly a surprise that water has become a new divide in China's relations with riparian neighbours. This divide has become apparent as Beijing has increasingly shifted its dam-building focus from the dam-saturated internal rivers to international rivers, most of which originate on the water-rich Tibetan Plateau. Only three important transnational rivers—the Amur, the Irtysh, and the Ili (or Yili), which flow to Russia or Kazakhstan—originate in China outside the Tibetan plateau, whose wealth of water and mineral resources is a big factor in its political subjugation. China's water disputes with neighbours extend even to North Korea, with which it has yet to settle issues relating to Lake Chonji and two border rivers, the Yalu and the Tumen.

China's rush to build more dams promises to roil inter-riparian relations, fostering greater water competition and impeding the already slow progress toward regional cooperation and integration. By erecting dams, barrages, and other water diversion structures in its borderlands, China is setting up an extensive upstream infrastructure, thereby spurring growing unease and concern in downriver countries. Getting China on board has thus become critical to shape water for peace in Asia.

More fundamentally, the absence of water institutions in the bulk of transnational basins in Asia is hardly conducive for water peace because it increases the geopolitical risks from the sharpening resource competition and unchecked environmental degradation. These risks are accentuated by the lack of an overarching Asian security architecture and by weak regional consultation mechanisms. Asia is the only continent other than Africa where regional integration has yet to take off, largely because Asian political and cultural diversity has hindered institution building.

Integrated management of transnational water resources through interstate collaboration is essential to prevent their degradation, depletion, and pollution. Only robust water institutions, with rule-based cooperation and sharing, can create the right incentives for nations to sustainably manage and conserve water supplies and to refrain from actions at the expense or injury of a downriver state. When cooperative arrangements are absent in any basin, there is a strong incentive for an upper riparian to try to capture water resources before they flow out of its national borders.

WATER AS POWER

Just as the scramble for energy resources has defined Asian geopolitics in recent decades, the struggle for water seems set to define many inter-country relationships in the coming years. At a time when territorial disputes and separatist struggles in Asia increasingly are being driven by resource issues, water indeed is becoming the new oil. But unlike oil—dependence on which can be reduced by tapping other sources of energy—there is no substitute for water.

In what can be described as tacit hydrological warfare, the resources of transnational rivers, aquifers, and lakes have become the target of rival appropriation plans. The fusion between national identity and river or groundwater basins creates a sense of ownership and propels efforts to control water resources, even if they are internationally shared. Driving the rival appropriation plans and the accompanying water nationalism is the notion that sharing waters is a zero-sum game. This, in turn, has given rise to environmentally questionable ideas with transboundary implications—from China's Western Route to divert river waters from the Tibetan plateau to its parched north and northwest, to India's embryonic National River Linking Project that proposes to connect rivers across India to alleviate floods and shortages. China's Western Route plan is the third phase of its South-North Water Transfer (or Diversion) Project (Nanshui Beidiao Gongcheng), whose first two phases involving internal rivers—the Eastern Route and the Central Route—are already complete or nearing completion.

The danger that riparian disputes could escalate to overt conflict looms large on the Asian horizon, with important implications for Asia's continued rapid economic growth and water security. Water-rich areas, ominously, are at the center of geopolitical tensions in Asia. They range from Kashmir and Tibet to the Golan Heights and the West Bank. Such areas not only boast water wealth but also are strategically located.

Take Central Asia's Fergana Valley, whose control is divided among Kyrgyzstan (which holds almost two-thirds), Uzbekistan, and Tajikistan. The ethnic fault lines that run through the Fergana

Valley—a minefield of ethnic animosities—are the source of periodic clashes among the Kyrgyz, Tajiks, and Uzbeks. The 2010 bloody riots in the Fergana Valley, which left several hundred Uzbek citizens of Kyrgyzstan dead, were sparked in part by local ethnic Kyrgyz fear that Uzbekistan wanted to absorb the water-rich Kyrgyz part.

There is a similar tripartite political split over water-rich Kashmir. India controls about 45% of the original princely state of Jammu and Kashmir, Pakistan 35%, and China the remaining 20%. Because the largest rivers flow to Pakistan from the Indian-administered part of Kashmir, many Pakistanis—especially the military generals and their longstanding allies, the mullahs—have linked the Kashmir dispute with Pakistan's water security. However, only one of the six Indus-system rivers originates in Indian Kashmir; three have their source in India's Himachal Pradesh state and two in Chinese-ruled Tibet.

Even the Pakistani-held portion of Kashmir, paradoxically, has assumed water-related significance for Pakistan's unity and social harmony because the upstream Pakistani construction of giant dams on the Indus has created a deep divide between the downriver Sind and Baluchistan provinces and the upriver Punjab, which has appropriated the bulk of the river waters through hydroengineering structures, located largely in Pakistani Kashmir. This large-scale upstream diversion has reduced the Indus system's farthest downstream flows to a trickle, turning the Indus Delta into a saline marsh and inviting saltwater intrusion from the Arabian Sea into a once-fertile land.

However, to deflect attention from their water appropriation, the Punjabi elites that rule Pakistan have sought to scapegoat India, an increasingly water-stressed country that reserved more than 80% of the Indus basin waters for Pakistan under the 1960 Indus Waters Treaty. This pact remains the world's most generous water-sharing arrangement, under which India agreed to keep for itself only a 19.48% share of the waters. (The volume of waters earmarked for Pakistan—by way of comparison—is over 90 times greater than the 1.85 billion cubic meters the U.S. is required to release to Mexico under a 1944 treaty with that country.) India is wracked by increasingly bitter domestic water-sharing disputes that have defied settlement through judicial arbitration.

Significantly, South Asia is the only region, other than North America, where inter-riparian relations are governed by bilateral treaty arrangements, which involve India, Bangladesh, Nepal, and Pakistan. There are also project-specific water agreements between Bhutan and India. Yet water has emerged as a divisive issue in this region in both the inter-country and intra-country context, with dam building at the center of tensions and recriminations on the subcontinent. The India-Pakistan water relationship remains rife with disputes.

Pakistan, for example, invoked the Indus treaty's dispute settlement provisions in recent years to take two Indian hydropower projects separately for international adjudication. India has embarked on several dam projects in its part of Kashmir to address chronic electricity shortages there. While railing against the modestly sized run-of-the-river Indian dams, Pakistan has stirred local grassroots protests at home by embarking on much larger, storage-type dams such as the 4,500-megawatt Bhasha Dam (also known as Diamer-Bhasha) and the 7,000-megawatt Bunji Dam. While storage-type hydropower plants impound large volumes of water, run-of-the-river projects are located so as to use a river's natural flow energy and elevation drop to generate electricity without the aid of a large reservoir and dam.

Pakistan's new dams are centered in Pakistani Kashmir's northernmost Gilgit and Baltistan areas, where the Pakistan Army and Sunni jihadist groups have sought to suppress a long-simmering rebellion against Pakistani rule by the local Shiite Muslims. China's growing role in dam building and other strategic projects in Gilgit-Baltistan, along with the entry of Chinese military units to guard such construction sites, has made the situation there more complex and unsettled, as underscored by the June 2013 killing of nine foreign tourists, including three Chinese, by gunmen.

Kashmir, like other water-rich regions, is a key crossroads in the international geopolitical rivalry, with the Islamic insurrection in the Indian-administered part adding to the India-Pakistan tensions. Tibet is firmly under China's rule, while the Golan Heights (the source of the Jordan River's headwaters) and the aquifer-controlling West Bank remain under Israel's control since their capture in the 1967 Six-Day War. However, Kashmir, like the Fergana Valley, remains a divided and contested territory, with Pakistan averse to accepting the territorial status quo. For the foreseeable future, all the water-rich regions extending up to the traditional Kurdish homeland, which straddles the Tigris-Euphrates basin, are likely to stay potential flashpoints for water conflict in Asia because they seem ripe for further geopolitical jousting.

In fact, like arms racing, "dam racing" has emerged as a geopolitical concern in Asia, where the world's fastest economic growth is being accompanied by the world's fastest increase in military spending and the world's fiercest competition for natural resources. As riparian neighbours compete to capture the water of shared rivers by building dams, reservoirs, barrages, irrigation networks, and other structures, distrust and discord have begun to roil relations between upstream and downstream states.

Asia is already the world's most dam-dotted continent: It has more dams than the rest of the world combined. China, the world's biggest dam builder, alone has slightly more than half of the approximately 50,000 large dams on the planet. China's dam-building zeal began in the Mao Zedong era but picked up momentum after Deng Xiaoping emerged as the paramount leader in 1978. A succession of engineer-presidents in China—Jiang Zemin, Hu Jintao, and Xi Jinping—have supported grand water-diversion projects, including the Three Gorges Dam and the South-North Water Diversion Project.

The numerous new dam projects in China and elsewhere show that the damming of rivers remains an important priority for Asian policymakers. In the West, the building of large dams has largely petered out; the rate of decommissioning of dams indeed has overtaken the pace of building new ones in several developed countries. According to international projections for the next 10 years, the total number of dams in developed countries is likely to remain about the same. Much of the dam building in the developing world, in terms of aggregate storage-capacity buildup, is expected to be concentrated in Asia. Dam building on transnational rivers, however, is already stoking inter-riparian tensions in Asia.

ZONES OF WATER DISCORD

Water disputes in Asia center on four distinct zones: China and its neighbours; India and its neighbours; the countries of continental Southeast Asia; and the five "stans" of Central Asia. The dam-building competition involves even the lower riparian states because it is often driven by the doctrine of prior appropriation, which legitimizes the principle "First in time, first in right." Under this doctrine of customary international water law, the first user of river waters (whether an upstream or downstream state) acquires a priority right to the continued utilization of river waters, as long as those resources are diverted for "beneficial" applications, including irrigation, industrial or mining purposes, electric power generation, and municipal supply.

In the interstate context, water can be turned into an instrument of power through resource capture and control or by upholding inequitable utilization patterns. This usually necessitates either the construction of hydroengineering structures to reengineer transboundary flows or the perpetuation of unfair, pre-independence arrangements in the name of protecting "historical rights." The latter could involve implicit threats of use of force. Dam building, by intensifying water disputes and tensions across Asia, carries implications for regional stability.

The ability to fashion water into an instrument of control or manipulation, of course, hinges on regional power equations. Only militarily and economically powerful states can normally shape water into a possible political weapon, irrespective of whether they are located upstream or downstream. But if one party, even if lacking matching military and economic prowess, has sufficient capability and political will to mount an effective or strong challenge against a co-basin state, it crimps the latter's potential to use water as a weapon. Generally, downstream states have a tendency to be alarmist on an upper riparian's damming of a shared river. When the upper riparian is the preeminent regional power, it may have little incentive to enter into a water-sharing treaty with a downriver state, although the United States and India have concluded such pacts with weaker neighbours.

Central Asia

Central Asia serves as a good example of how water can be wielded as an instrument of power through downstream control, including through threat of force. The regional water competition pits the upstream interests of energy-poor Kyrgyzstan and Tajikistan against those of the larger and stronger countries that are the main water consumers: Uzbekistan, Kazakhstan, and Turkmenistan. The three hydrocarbon-rich countries not only use the bulk of the region's renewable water resources—estimated at 263 billion cubic meters per year—but also insist that their leonine share is protected under the norm of "historical rights."

The Central Asian downstream states, with their military might, have the capacity to prevent the upstream countries from building any new hydroengineering projects that could materially alter transboundary flows. This power has blocked the emergence of an equitable successor regime to the region's Soviet-era water-management system, which integrated water, energy, and agriculture under a federally run and highly centralized regional arrangement. The region's artificial political frontiers, which bear little resemblance to natural or ethnic fault lines, have also compounded water-sharing issues. The regional water competition indeed is fraught with major ethnic-rivalry dimensions. The intersection between ethnic identity and water insecurity in Central Asia has fostered deep-seated ill will among communities and occasionally spawned violent conflict.

The continued downstream production of cotton, a highly water-intensive crop, through intensive irrigation has exacerbated the regional water discord. In fact, the curse of cotton from the Soviet era has been an important contributor to the degradation of water and land resources in Uzbekistan, Turkmenistan, and Tajikistan. It has also led to the extensive retreat of the Aral Sea, which has shrunk to about one-fourth of its original size because of heavy extractions for irrigation from its principal sources, the Amu Darya and the Syr Darya.

In this tricky and risky situation, Uzbekistan, with 45% of the Central Asian population, consumes more than half the region's water supply and uses threats of military reprisals against upstream states to shield its appropriation of the dominant share of water resources. It remains embroiled in bitter water rows with Tajikistan and Kyrgyzstan over their dam-building proposals to boost energy production. Tajikistan and Kyrgyzstan contend that such dam building is imperative because the main water-consuming states located downstream are unwilling to supply them with hydrocarbons at concessional rates, as was the practice in the Soviet era. However, Uzbekistan's implicit military threats have stymied their plans to build large new hydroelectric stations and become renewable-energy exporters. The threats have compelled Tajikistan, for example, not to press ahead with plans to resume work on unfinished Soviet-era hydropower projects, including one on the Vakhsh River that was intended to be the world's highest dam.

China

China, however, serves as the best example of upstream water hegemony in Asia—and indeed the wider world. It has established a hydro-hegemony unparalleled on any continent by annexing in 1951 the Tibetan Plateau, the starting place of major international rivers. Another sprawling territory Beijing forcibly absorbed, Xinjiang, is the source of the transnational Irtysh and Ili Rivers. Given that China is at the geographical hub of Asia, sharing land or sea frontiers with 20 countries, no rules-based regional order can emerge without its participation in institutionalized cooperation. This challenge is most striking on transboundary rivers.

Not content with the large number of dams, reservoirs, barrages, and irrigation networks it has already built, the Chinese government in early 2013 unveiled plans to build new cascades of dams, many of them on major rivers flowing to other countries. The decision by China's State Council to ride roughshod over downstream countries' concerns and proceed unilaterally showed that the main issue facing Asia is not readiness to accommodate

China's rise but the need to persuade its leaders to institutionalize cooperation with neighboring countries.

Most of China's dams serve multiple functions, including generating electric power and supplying water for manufacturing, mining, irrigation, and households. Dam building in downstream countries, although stoking interstate disputes too, pales in comparison with the extent of China's dam building. For example, China's latest dam on the Mekong River, the 5,850-megawatt Nuozhadu, can alone generate more electricity than the combined installed hydropower capacity in the lower-Mekong countries at present. The 330-megawatt Indian dam project on the Kishenganga (Neelum) stream that prompted Pakistan to invoke international arbitration proceedings under the Indus Treaty in 2010 is of a size that Chinese dam builders would scoff at, considering it uneconomical as a stand-alone project unconnected to a cascade of dams. In fact, the largest dam India has built since independence, the 2,000-megawatt Tehri on the Bhagirathi River, is not large by Chinese standards. Tehri is capable of producing barely one-tenth of the electricity generated by China's Three Gorges Dam, the world's biggest.

By ramping up the size of its dams, China now not only boasts the world's largest number of mega-dams, but it has also emerged as the biggest global producer of hydropower, with an installed generating capacity of nearly 230 gigawatts. The serious environmental and social problems spawned by the Three Gorges Dam—which officially uprooted 1.7 million Chinese—have failed to dampen China's hyperactive dam building.

In its 2013 actions, China's State Council, seeking to boost the country's hydropower capacity by another 120 gigawatts, identified 54 new dams—in addition to the ones currently under construction—as "key construction projects" in a revised energy-sector plan up to 2015. Most of the new dams are planned in the biodiversity-rich southwest, where natural ecosystems and indigenous cultures are increasingly threatened. Among the slew of newly approved dam projects are five on the Salween and three each on the Brahmaputra and the Mekong. China has already built six mega-dams on the Mekong, the lifeblood for continental

Southeast Asia. The new damming plans threaten both the Salween River's Grand Canyon—a UNESCO World Heritage site—and the pristine, environmentally sensitive upstream areas through which the Brahmaputra and the Mekong flow. These three international rivers originate on the Tibetan plateau, whose bounteous water resources have become a magnet for Chinese planners. The Salween, which runs through Yunnan Province into Myanmar and along the Thai border for a stretch before draining into the Andaman Sea, will cease to be Asia's last largely free-flowing river once work is completed on the giant 4,200-megawatt Songta Dam in Tibet.

The State Council decision reversed the suspension of dam building on the Salween announced by Premier Wen Jiabao in 2004, after an international uproar over the start of multiple megaprojects in the National Nature Reserves, adjacent to a world heritage area—a stunning canyon region through which the Salween, the Mekong, and the Jinsha flow in parallel. The decision to resume work on dams along the rim of the Three Parallel Rivers World Heritage Area was consistent with the pattern established elsewhere, including the Yangtze: China temporarily suspends a controversial plan after major protests in order to let public passions cool and to buy time, before resurrecting the same plan.

China's new dam projects on the Brahmaputra, the main river running through northeastern India and eastern Bangladesh, have meanwhile prompted the Indian government to advise China to "ensure that the interests of downstream states are not harmed" by the upstream works. Water has emerged as a new divide in Sino-Indian relations. Then-Indian Prime Minister Manmohan Singh personally proposed to Chinese President Xi Jinping and Premier Li Keqiang in separate meetings in the spring of 2013 that the two countries enter into a water treaty or establish an intergovernmental institution to define mutual rights and responsibilities on shared rivers. Both Xi and Li, however, spurned the proposal. The Indian assumption that booming bilateral trade would make Beijing more amenable to solving the border and water disputes with India has clearly been belied.

Indeed, China is damming not just the Brahmaputra, on which it has already completed several dams, but also other rivers in

Tibet that flow into India. It has built a dam each on the Indus and the Sutlej and unveiled plans to erect a cascade of dams on the Arun River, which helps augment downstream Ganges flows and is thus critical for India to meet its water-sharing treaty obligations vis-à-vis Bangladesh. The flash floods that ravaged India's Himachal Pradesh and Arunachal Pradesh states between 2000 and 2005 were linked to the unannounced releases from rain-swollen Chinese dams and barrages.

The Brahmaputra is a huge attraction for China's dam program because this river's cross-border annual discharge of 165.4 billion cubic meters into India is greater than the combined transboundary flows of the three key rivers running from the Tibetan plateau to Southeast Asia—the Mekong, the Salween, and the Irrawaddy. An officially blessed book published in 2005, *Tibet's Waters Will Save China,* openly championed the northward rerouting of the mighty Brahmaputra, although it is unclear whether this idea is technically feasible. As China gradually moves its dam building on the Brahmaputra from the upper reaches to the river's lower water-rich Great Bend—the area where the Brahmaputra makes a U-turn around the Himalayas to enter India, forming the world's longest and steepest canyon in the process—it is expected to embark on Mekong-style mega-dams.

More fundamentally, China's new focus on building dams in its southwest carries transnational safety concerns because this is an earthquake-prone region. Indeed, some Chinese scientists blamed the massive 2008 earthquake that struck the Tibetan Plateau's eastern rim, killing 87,000 people, mainly in Sichuan Province, on the newly constructed Zipingpu Dam, located beside a seismic fault. The weight of the water impounded in the 156-meter-high dam's massive reservoir was said to have triggered severe tectonic stresses, or what scientists call reservoir-triggered seismicity (RTS). China's southwest is an area of high seismic activity because it sits on the fault line where the Indian Plate collides against the Eurasian Plate.

To be sure, China, despite its riparian dominance in Asia, faces important water challenges internally. Although China's average renewable water resources are 2,051 cubic meters per capita annually, the figure is just 700 cubic meters in its water-stressed north, home to nearly half the country's population. The intrastate disparity in water availability is compounded by the fact that the largely parched north serves as the country's agricultural and industrial heartland. This has contributed to serious surface-water pollution and the steady depletion of groundwater resources in the north.

Yet such is its fixation on supply-side measures that China is to spend a staggering $290 billion under its current five-year plan on water-related infrastructure projects, including dams. At a time when dam building has run into growing grassroots opposition in Asian democracies like Japan, South Korea, and India, China will remain the nucleus of the world's dam projects. Significantly, China is also the global leader in exporting dams.

While the dams China is building in Africa and Latin America are largely designed to supply the energy for its mineral-resource extraction and processing, many of the dam projects in Southeast Asia financed and undertaken by Chinese state-run firms are intended to generate electricity for export to China's own market. Indeed, China is demonstrating that it has no qualms about building dams in disputed territories, such as Pakistan-administered Kashmir, or in areas torn by ethnic separatism, like northern Myanmar. At home, by embarking on a series of dams in its ethnic-minority-populated borderlands, China is seeking to appropriate river waters before they cross its frontiers, thereby exacerbating ethnic tensions through the submergence of land and displacement of residents.

China's overseas dam projects have drawn attention to their mounting environmental and human costs. For example, work on the Myitsone Dam—the biggest of the seven dam projects in Myanmar sponsored by China to import electricity—instigated new disputes and fighting, ending a 17-year ceasefire between the Kachin Independence Army and government forces, before authorities shocked Beijing by suspending the project in late 2011. The bold action set the stage for Myanmar's own transformation from military rule and a virtual Chinese client state to a country that has opened its doors to political and economic reform, attracting global investors and the first-ever visit by a U.S. president. The question haunting Chinese policymakers today is, "Who lost Burma?"

As for China's dam projects at home, the countries likely to bear the brunt of the Chinese thirst for power and control over transboundary waters are those located farthest downstream on rivers like the Brahmaputra, the Mekong, and the Ili: Bangladesh, whose future is threatened by climate and environmental change; Vietnam, a rice bowl of Asia; and Kazakhstan, which boasts 17,000 natural lakes but whose own overexploitation of water resources has already dried up 8,000 small lakes.

Whereas the Brahmaputra is the largest source of freshwater for Bangladesh, Vietnam is located downstream on two rivers flowing in from the edge of the Tibetan plateau: the Red River, the main watercourse of northern Vietnam; and the Mekong, the principal river of southern Vietnam. China's water appropriations from the Ili threaten to turn Kazakhstan's largest lake—Balkhash, spread over 18,000 square kilometers—into another Aral Sea, which has become the symbol of human-made environmental disaster. Diversion of water for irrigation from the Ili Basin already "has led to ecological problems in the region, notably the drying up of small lakes."

At a time when upstream Chinese dams have helped stir popular passions in Vietnam, Laos, Cambodia, and Thailand, the U.S. has sought to diplomatically cash in on downstream concerns by launching the Lower Mekong Initiative, or LMI. The U.S.-sponsored LMI—seeking to promote integrated cooperation among Cambodia, Laos, Thailand, and Vietnam in the areas of environment, education, health, and infrastructure—emphasizes sustainable hydropower development and natural resource management, including improving institutional capacity to address connected transnational issues. The LMI, however, cannot obscure the imperative to build institutionalized cooperative arrangements involving all the Mekong basin states, including China. One U.S. official has urged Beijing to overcome its loathing of institutionalized water cooperation and join the Mekong River Commission, which was set up in 1995 to foster integrated and sustainable management of basin resources. The situation in the basin has also been roiled by Laotian and Cambodian plans to build dams on the Mekong, including with Chinese financial and technical aid. Laos, which wants to become the "battery" of Southeast Asia by selling electricity to its neighbours, has courted regional controversy by starting work on the 1,260-megawatt Xayaburi (Sayabouly) Dam and unveiling a plan to build the smaller 260-megawatt Don Sahong Dam near its iconic Khone Falls area in the south, just before the river enters Cambodia. Environmentalists have warned that the Xayaburi Dam, which Laos began constructing over its neighbours' objections, posed a potential threat to the survival of the wild population of the Mekong giant catfish.

India

Another zone of water discord centers on India, which has multiple riparian identities. It is the uppermost riparian on some rivers that originate on its territory, such as the Chenab and the Jhelum, which flow to Pakistan, and the Teesta, which drains a part of northern Bangladesh. India is the mid-riparian on the Brahmaputra and the main Indus stream. And India is the lowermost riparian on the rivers that begin in Tibet and flow southward via Nepal to empty into the Ganges Basin, such as the Karnali, the Gandak, and the Kosi (Arun). Besides India, few other states in Asia fall in all the three categories—upper, middle, and lower riparian. Indeed, such is India's geographical spread that it has a direct stake in all the important river basins in South Asia.

Because of its mottled riparian status, India is potentially affected by water-related actions of states located upstream—China, Nepal, and Bhutan—while its own actions can carry a cross-border impact on Pakistan or Bangladesh. No nation is more vulnerable to China's re-engineering of transboundary flows than India because it alone receives nearly half of all river waters that leave Chinese territory. A total of 718 billion cubic meters of surface water flows out of Chinese territory yearly, of which 48.33% runs directly into India. (Some additional Tibetan waters also flow to India via Nepal.) Bangladesh, on the other hand, has one of the world's highest dependency ratios with regard to cross-border inflows, receiving 91.3% of its water from India, although a sizable portion of that water originates in Tibet.

India confronts a deepening water crisis, which is more acute than China's. Yet India's per capita capacity to store water for dry-season release (200 cubic meters yearly) is one of the world's lowest; indeed, it is 11 times lower than China's (2,200 cubic meters). The 2030 Water Resources Group—a consortium of private social-sector organizations providing insights into worldwide water issues—has a dire warning for India: the country is likely to face a 50% deficit between water demand and supply by 2030. India's own agencies say it must nearly double its annual grain production to more than 450 million tons by 2050 to meet the demands of increasing prosperity and a growing population, or risk becoming a major food importer—a development that will disrupt the already tight international food markets. The growing water shortages also threaten to slow Indian economic growth and fuel social tensions.

With water increasingly at the center of interprovincial feuds in India, the country's Supreme Court has struggled for years to settle water-related lawsuits, with several of the parties returning to litigate on new grounds. Plans for large water projects in India, meanwhile, have run into stiff opposition from influential nongovernment organizations (NGOs), so that it has become increasingly difficult to build a large dam, blighting the promise of hydropower. Proof of this was the federal government's 2010 decision to abandon three dam projects on the Bhagirathi River, a Ganges tributary, including one that was already half-built, with authorities having spent $139 million on construction work and ordered equipment worth $288 million.

Yet, seeking to exercise the right of prior appropriation on transnational rivers, the Indian government has since 2012 approved the construction of several dams for electric-power generation in the Himalayan states of Arunachal Pradesh, Sikkim, Uttarakhand, and Jammu and Kashmir. They include the Tawang (800 megawatt), Tato (700 megawatt), Subansiri Upper (1,800 megawatt), and Teesta (520 megawatt) projects. Cost and time overruns are common problems in every dam project in India. But given the growing grassroots power of NGOs in blocking dam building, it is unclear which of the newly approved projects will be completed and in what time frame.

In truth, India demonstrates that dams and democracy normally don't go well together. Whereas China continues to build giant dams and reroute rivers, trumpeting these projects as symbols of its engineering prowess, the public pressures generated by India's democracy act as a brake on ambitious water projects that displace many people or flood vast areas. For example, while India's river-linking plan remains in the realm of fantasy, China's similar program began transferring water domestically through the Eastern Route by 2013.

Still, given the growing gap between Asian water demand and supply, water disputes are almost as rife between India and its neighbours as they are between China and its neighbours. There are, however, two key differences. One, India has water pacts with all its riparian neighbours other than China. And two, its water-sharing treaties with Bangladesh and Pakistan contain dispute-settlement mechanisms.

The Indus Treaty, according to a 2011 majority staff report prepared for the U.S. Senate Foreign Relations Committee, is "considered the world's most successful water treaty, having remained relatively intact for 50 years and having withstood four Indo-Pakistani wars." Yet this treaty has not been able to stop bilateral water disputes from surfacing and embittering relations. The treaty, however, contains elaborate provisions to resolve differences or disputes through the appointment of a neutral international expert or a court of arbitration. These mechanisms help to moderate disagreements, ensuring that they do not escalate to conflict.

Still, the reality is that water shortages have become acute in Pakistan, which maintains one of Asia's highest population-growth rates. The total quantum of cross-border flows into Pakistan from India has not materially changed over the years, in spite of genuine concerns over the impact of global warming. The inflows include an average of 167.2 billion cubic meters yearly from the three large rivers reserved for Pakistan under the Indus Treaty, plus 11.1

billion cubic meters in bonus waters that run across the border from the three smaller rivers set aside for India's use. So, Pakistan's effective share, according to the U.N., adds up to 85.9% of the 207.6 billion cubic meters in total yearly flows of the six Indus-system rivers. In other words, Pakistan's share of transboundary waters is greater than that of Egypt, another state located farthest downstream on a major international river system.

But with Pakistan's per capita water availability falling in proportion to its population expansion, the country has since the 1980s gone from being a water-sufficient country to becoming a water-stressed one. It is now headed toward acute water scarcity. India's own portion of the Indus Basin is reeling under growing water stress, with the deficit between water supply and demand estimated at 52%. Both Pakistan and India thus face difficult choices on water that are likely to be compounded by climate change, including the accelerated thawing of glaciers—a significant source of meltwaters for the major rivers, particularly the Indus and the Brahmaputra. Dealing with the challenges demands greater bilateral water cooperation, which hinges on improved India-Pakistan relations.

Low-lying Bangladesh, for its part, has too much water during the annual four-month monsoon, when large parts of the deltaic country become inundated, and too little in the dry season, which runs from early spring to early summer. Bangladesh's annual per capita water availability averages 8,252 cubic meters—or more than five times that of India—but the major interseasonal variations, which are larger than that in any other South Asian country, and the limited storage capacity of its aquifers, make its water situation difficult.

India's 1996 Ganges water-sharing treaty with Bangladesh, which ended protracted acrimony over the diversion of water by India's Farakka Barrage, guarantees the downstream state specific cross-border flows in the critical dry season—a new principle in international water relations. This provision means that even if the river's flows were to diminish due to reasons beyond India's control—such as climate change or the planned Chinese damming of a key Ganges tributary, the Arun (also known as the Kosi) that contributes significantly to downstream Ganges water levels—India would still be obligated to supply Bangladesh with 34,060 cubic feet of water per second of time (cusecs) on average in the dry season, as stipulated by the treaty. Bangladesh's share of downstream flows is about 50%.

The Ganges Treaty, by and large, has been smoothly implemented, but new disagreements have flared over smaller river basins shared by Bangladesh and India, especially over New Delhi's proposed revival of a long-dormant multipurpose dam project, Tipaimukh, in remote Manipur State bordering Myanmar. Located 210 kilometers upstream from the Bangladesh border on the Barak River and designed to control floods, improve river navigation, and generate 1,500 megawatts of hydropower, the Tipaimukh Dam had been held up for years by grassroots concerns on the Indian side over displacement and submergence. To help resolve bilateral differences over this plan, India has arranged tours for Bangladeshi officials and lawmakers to the project site and supplied the design and other technical details.

Separately, Bangladesh wants India to reserve for it about half of the waters of the Teesta River, which originates in the Himalayan Indian state of Sikkim and ultimately merges with the Brahmaputra in the Bangladeshi delta. The draft text of the proposed Teesta Treaty has been under discussion since at least 2010, and the two countries would have signed the agreement in 2013 but for the opposition of the government of India's West Bengal State, for whose northern part the Teesta serves as the lifeline. Many believe that it is only a matter of time before this agreement is signed, a development that will end the long global absence of a new water-sharing treaty since 2002, when Syria and Lebanon agreed on a sharing formula on their small border river El-Kaber.

Two other South Asian states, Nepal and Bhutan, sit on vast untapped Himalayan hydropower reserves. Nepal, which remains in danger of becoming a failed state, holds up to 83,000 megawatts of potential hydropower reserves, yet it produces less than 1,000 megawatts of electricity for its 32 million citizens from all sources of energy and actually imports power from India. Several water treaties underpin the India-Nepal relationship, but the pacts have been particularly controversial in upstream Nepal, where many seem to believe that they are loaded in India's favor. The two neighbours thus have made slow progress on bilateral water collaboration, with Nepal recently turning to China for dam construction. The Bhutan-India water relationship, by contrast, has flourished through joint, small-scale hydropower projects, with electricity exports swelling Bhutanese coffers.

If the already difficult water situation on the Indian subcontinent is to be prevented from deteriorating, much greater interstate and intrastate cooperation is needed. This is one of the world's most-densely populated and thirstiest regions. Yet it is wracked by complex water challenges that are set to become more difficult due to demographic and economic expansion and global warming. This region has virtually the same land area as Central Asia, but a population that is more than 18 times larger. Its water resources are barely six times greater than those of Central Asia. In global terms, the countries of South Asia account for about 22% of the world's population, but make do with barely 8.3% of the global water resources.

CONCLUSION: FROM COMPETITION TO COOPERATION

The situation in Asia—the hub of global water challenges—shows that water can be fashioned into a hidden political weapon by various means, including the denial or delayed transfer of hydrological data, and that a powerful state can wield the water weapon irrespective of whether it is located upstream or downstream. In a diplomatic or economic sense, water wars are already being waged between riparian neighbours in several of Asia's subregions. With a number of Asian nations jockeying to control transnational water resources, even as they demand transparency and the sharing of information about their neighbours' hydroengineering projects, sharpening water competition could provoke greater tensions and conflict.

Such competition actually underscores Asia's broader challenges, which threaten its continued rise. To be sure, the ongoing global power shifts are primarily linked to Asia's economic rise, the speed and scale of which have been phenomenal. But Asia faces major constraints. It must cope with entrenched territorial and maritime disputes; harmful historical legacies that weigh down its most important interstate relationships; increasingly fervent nationalism; growing religious extremism; and sharpening competition over water, energy, and other resources.

Moreover, Asia's political integration lags behind its economic integration and, to compound matters, it has no overarching security framework. One central concern is that, unlike Europe's bloody wars of the first half of the 20th century, which made war there unthinkable until the advent of the Ukraine crisis recently, the wars in Asia in the second half of the 20th century only accentuated bitter rivalries. Several interstate wars have been fought in Asia since 1950, when both the Korean War and the annexation of Tibet started, without resolving the underlying disputes. Given the significant role that natural resources have historically played in global strategic relations—including instigating conflict—Asia's increasingly murky resource geopolitics threatens to exacerbate existing interstate tensions.

Water-sharing disputes have become common across Asia. Measures taken by one nation or province to augment its water supply or storage capacity often threaten to adversely affect downstream basins, thereby stoking political or ethnic tensions. To compound matters, governmental or commercial decisions on where to set up new manufacturing or energy plants are increasingly being influenced by local availability of adequate water resources. Attempts to set up water-intensive energy or manufacturing plants in already water-stressed areas have provoked strong local protests, including violent confrontations with police.

Today, it has become virtually impossible to set up nuclear power plants along freshwater bodies in Asia, the center of the so-called global nuclear renaissance. These water-guzzling plants perforce have to be erected along coastlines so that they can rely on seawater for their operations. Yet the 2011 Fukushima disaster has served as a warning of the vulnerability of seaside nuclear facilities to extreme weather events, which are likely to become more common in an increasingly global-warming-driven environment. Meanwhile, the proliferation of new dam projects highlights the continuing Asian efforts to engineer potential solutions to the water crisis via traditional supply-side approaches when the imperative is instead to adopt smart water management.

Against this background, the big question is: how can the struggle for water be prevented from becoming a tipping point for overt conflict? Strategic competition over natural resources will continue to shape Asia's security dynamics, yet the associated risks could be moderated if Asia's leaders were to establish norms and institutions aimed at building rules-based cooperation. Unfortunately, little progress has been made in this direction, as underlined by the absence of institutionalized cooperation in the vast majority of transnational river basins.

Averting water wars demands rule-based cooperation, water sharing, uninterrupted data flow, and dispute-settlement mechanisms. Transparency, collaboration, and sharing are the building blocks of water peace. Asia also needs new market mechanisms, public-private partnerships, innovative practices and technologies, conservation, and astute management to advance adaptation and affordable solutions and thereby open the path to a more sustainable and peaceful environment to safeguard its continued rise.

Asian economies must focus on three specific areas to mitigate their water crisis. One is achieving greater water-use efficiency and productivity, especially by controlling profligate agricultural practices. Another is using new clean-water technologies to open up nontraditional supply sources, including desalinated ocean and brackish water and recycled wastewater. The third is expanding and enhancing water infrastructure to correct regional and seasonal imbalances in water availability, and to harvest rainwater, which can be an additional supply source to help ease shortages. Improving water-supply management calls for abandoning the business-as-usual outlook and embracing unconventional approaches.

Renewed efforts are also needed to try and co-opt China in basin-level institutions. Without China's active participation in water institutions, it will not be possible to transform Asian competition into cooperation. Only water institutions involving all important co-riparians can make headway to regulate inter-country competition, help balance the rights and obligations of co-basin states, and promote sustainable practices. If China were to accept rule-based cooperation, it would have to strike a balance between its right to harness transnational water resources for its development and a corresponding obligation (embedded in customary international law and the 1997 United Nations Convention) not to cause palpable harm to any co-riparian state.

A balance between rights and obligations indeed is at the heart of how to achieve harmonious, rule-based relations between co-basin states. To be sure, any water arrangement's comparative benefits and burdens should be such that the advantages outweigh the duties and responsibilities, or else the state that sees itself as a loser may walk out of discussions or fail to comply with its obligations. China must be persuaded that its diplomatic and economic interests would be better served by joining forward-looking institutionalized cooperation. Beijing will need considerable convincing, of course, if it is to participate in any basin-level framework centered on compromise, coordination, and collaboration. If China insists on staying on its current unilateralist course, the risk is not only that it will define and implement its water interests in ways irreconcilable with those of its co-riparian states, but also that prospects for a rule-based order in Asia could perish forever.

The dirty little secret about bilateral or multilateral water cooperation in any basin *is that it is* really more about *politics* than about *law*. Without improved inter-country relations and better trust, Asia's hydropolitics will remain grating. Strained political relations in most of Asia's subregions make an Asia-wide security structure or more effective resource cooperation difficult to achieve. Connected with this is the overarching challenge for Asian countries to eliminate the baggage of history that is preventing them from charting a more stable and peaceful future. Unassuaged historical grievances have constricted diplomatic space for building political accommodation and reconciliation. Asian states must find ways to overcome their histories of antagonism to build cooperation. As a Russian proverb warns, "Forget the past and lose an eye; dwell on the past and lose both eyes."

CHINA-INDIA CLASH OVER CHINESE CLAIMS TO TIBETAN WATER

Sharpening Asian competition over energy resources, driven in part by high growth rates in gross domestic product and in part by mercantilist attempts to lock up supplies, has obscured another danger: Water shortages in much of Asia are beginning to threaten rapid economic modernization, prompting the building of upstream projects on international rivers. If water geopolitics were to spur interstate tensions through reduced water flows to neighboring states, the Asian renaissance could stall.

Water has emerged as a key issue that could determine whether Asia is headed toward mutually beneficial cooperation or deleterious interstate competition. No country could influence that direction more than China, which controls the Tibetan plateau – the source of most major rivers of Asia.

Tibet's vast glaciers and high altitude have endowed it with the world's greatest river systems. Its river waters are a lifeline to the world's two most-populous states – China and India – as well as to Bangladesh, Myanmar, Bhutan, Nepal, Cambodia, Pakistan, Laos, Thailand and Vietnam. These countries make up 47 percent of the global population. Yet Asia is a water-deficient continent. Although home to more than half of the human population, Asia has less fresh water – 3,920 cubic meters per person – than any continent besides Antarctica.

The looming struggle over water resources in Asia has been underscored by the spread of irrigated farming, water-intensive industries (from steel to paper making) and a growing middle class seeking high water-consuming comforts like washing machines and dishwashers. Household water consumption in Asia is rising rapidly, according to a 2006 U.N. report, but such is the water paucity that not many Asians can aspire to the lifestyle of Americans, who daily use 400 liters per person, or more than 2.5 times the average in Asia.

The specter of water wars in Asia is also being highlighted by climate change and environmental degradation in the form of shrinking forests and swamps, which foster a cycle of chronic flooding and droughts through the depletion of nature's water storage and absorption cover. The Himalayan snow melt that feeds Asia's great rivers could be damagingly accelerated by global warming.

While intrastate water-sharing disputes have become rife in several Asian countries — from India and Pakistan to Southeast Asia and China — it is the potential interstate conflict over river-water resources that should be of greater concern. This concern arises from Chinese attempts to dam or redirect the southward flow of river waters from the Tibetan plateau, where major rivers originate, including the Indus, the Mekong, the Yangtze, the Yellow, the Salween, the Brahmaputra, the Karnali and the Sutlej. Among Asia's mighty rivers, only the Ganges starts from the Indian side of the Himalayas.

The lopsided availability of water within some nations (abundant in some areas but deficient in others) has given rise to grand ideas — from linking rivers in India to diverting the fast-flowing Brahmaputra northward to feed the arid areas in the Chinese heartland.

As water woes have been aggravated in its north due to environmentally unsustainable intensive farming, China has increasingly turned its attention to the bounteous water reserves that the Tibetan plateau holds. It has dammed rivers, not just to produce hydropower but also to channel waters for irrigation and other purposes, and is currently toying with massive interbasin and inter-river water-transfer projects.

After building two dams upstream, China is building at least three more on the Mekong, inflaming passions in Vietnam, Laos, Cambodia and Thailand. Several Chinese projects in west-central Tibet bearing on river-water flows into India, but Beijing is loath to share information.

Following flash floods in India's northern Himachal Pradesh state, however, China agreed in 2005 to supply New Delhi data on any abnormal rise or fall in the upstream level of the Sutlej

River, on which it has built a barrage. Discussions are on to persuade it to share flood-control data during the monsoon season on two Brahmaputra tributaries, Lohit and Yarlongng Tsangpo, as it has done since 2002 on the Brahmaputra River, which it has dammed at several places upstream.

The 10 major watersheds formed by the Himalayas and Tibetan highlands spread out river waters far and wide in Asia. Control over the 2.5 million-square-km Tibetan plateau gives China tremendous leverage, besides access to vast natural resources. Having extensively contaminated its own major rivers through unbridled industrialization, China now threatens the ecological viability of river systems tied to South and Southeast Asia in its bid to meet its thirst for Water and energy. Tibet, comprises approximately one-fourth of China's land mass today, since 1950 giving China a contiguous frontier with India, Myanmar, Bhutan and Nepal. Tibet traditionally encompassed the regions of the central plateau, Kham and Amdo. After annexing Tibet, China separated Amdo (the present Dalai Lama's birthplace) as the new Qinghai province, made the central plateau and eastern Kham the Tibet Autonomous Region, and merged the remaining parts of Tibet into the Chinese provinces of Sichuan, Yunnan and Gansu.

The traditional Tibet is not just a distinct cultural entity but also a natural plateau, the future of whose water reserves is tied to ecological conservation. As China's hunger for primary commodities has grown, so too has its exploitation of Tibet's resources. And as water woes have intensified in several major Chinese cities, a group of ex-officials have championed the northward rerouting of the waters of the Brahmaputra in a book titled "Tibet's Waters Will Save China."

Large hydro projects and reckless exploitation of mineral resources already threaten Tibet's fragile ecosystems, with ore tailings beginning to contaminate water sources. Unmindful of the environmental impact of such activities in pristine areas, China has now embarked on constructing a 108-km paved road to Mount Everest, located along the Tibet-Nepal frontier. This highway is part of China's plan to reinforce its claims on Tibet by taking the Olympic torch to the peak of the world's tallest mountain before the 2008 Beijing Games. As in the past, no country is going to be more affected by Chinese plans and projects in Tibet than India. The new $6.2 billion Gormo-Lhasa railway, for example, has significantly augmented China's rapid military-deployment capability against India just when Beijing is becoming increasingly assertive in its claims on Indian territories. This hardline stance, in the midst of intense negotiations to resolve the 4,057-km Indo-Tibetan border, is no less incongruous than Beijing's disinclination to set up, as agreed during its president's state visit to New Delhi last November, a joint expert-level mechanism on interstate river waters.

The Qinghai Tibet Railway

Contrast China's reluctance to establish a mechanism intended for mere "interaction and cooperation" on hydrological data with New Delhi's consideration toward downstream Pakistan, reflected both in the 1960 Indus Waters Treaty (which reserves 56 percent of the catchment flow for Pakistan) and the more recent acceptance of World Bank arbitration over the Baglihar Dam project in Indian Kashmir.

No Indian project has sought to reroute or diminish trans-border water flows, yet Pakistan insists on a say in the structural design of projects upstream in India. New Delhi permits Pakistani officials to inspect such projects. By contrast, Beijing drags its feet on setting up an innocuous interaction mechanism. Would China, under any arrangement, let Indian officials inspect its projects in Tibet or accept, if a dispute arose, third-party adjudication?

If anything, China seems intent on aggressively pursuing projects and employing water as a weapon. The idea of a Great South-North Water Transfer Project diverting river waters cascading from the Tibetan highlands has the backing of President Hu Jintao.

The Chinese ambition to channel the Brahmaputra waters to the parched Yellow River has been whetted by what Beijing touts as its engineering feat in building the giant $25 billion Three Gorges Dam project, which has officially displaced a staggering 1.2 million citizens. While China's water resources minister told a Hong Kong University meeting last October that, in his personal opinion, the idea to divert waters seems not viable, the director of the Yellow River Water Conservancy Committee said publicly that the mega-plan enjoys official sanction and may begin by 2010.

The Brahmaputra (Yarlong Tsangpo to Tibetans) originates near Mount Kailash and, before entering India, flows eastward in Tibet for 2,200 km at an average height of 4,000 meters, making it the world's highest major river. When two other tributaries merge with it, the Brahmaputra becomes as wide as 10 km in India before flowing into Bangladesh.

The first phase of China's South-North Project calls for building 300 km of tunnels and channels to draw waters from the Jinsha, Yalong and Dadu rivers, on the eastern rim of the Tibetan plateau. Only in the second phase would the Brahmaputra waters be directed northward. In fact, Beijing has identified the bend where the Brahmaputra forms the world's longest and deepest canyon just before entering India as holding the largest untapped reserves for meeting its water and energy needs.

While some doubts do persist in Beijing over the economic feasibility of channeling Tibetan waters northward, the mammoth diversion of the Brahmaputra could begin as water shortages become more acute in the Chinese mainland and the current $1.2 trillion foreign-exchange hoard brims over. The mega-rerouting would constitute the declaration of a water war on lower-riparian India and Bangladesh.

WATER HEGEMONY: EXAMINING CHINA'S HYDRO-BEHAVIOUR

China's "peaceful rise", a phrase propounded with crafty ease by Chinese officials and scholars since 2003, has always intrigued the outside world. The 'rise of China' has become near conventional wisdom amongst IR scholars and Chinese experts resulting in a large number of high-quality work examining China's rise and its implications for the international system. The inquiry continues. The questions remain familiar almost now rhetorical: How will China behave as it rises? Will it be responsible and act cooperatively or as it gains military muscle and economic power be confrontationist thereby creating challenges and threats?

The paper queries China's hydro-behaviour and looks at its actions on the Brahamaputra (Yarlung Tsangpo) and the Mekong (Lancang) to infer certain hegemonic tendencies. Through the course of the paper and the analysis that follows, it can, with some understanding, be concluded that China's policies on the transboundary rivers does not indicate to the 'peaceful' nature of its rise. In fact, there seems to be a great deal of 'hydro-arrogance', 'hydro-aggression' and 'hydro-egoism'. There are indicators that confirm to this and the paper will delve into it specifically. One strong pointer is China's hydrobehaviour towards Tibet. The hydro-relevance of Tibet suggests that it is the lifeline of China. This frames Beijing's maximalist orientation towards harnessing the water resources and therefore dams and diversions are engineering process towards mitigating its food and energy requirements and overcoming its uneven distribution of water.

Large shifts of water from Tibet will continuously form part of China's development plans – it's an unquestionable necessity but also has strategic significance as the Tibetan plateau is the source of Asia's 10 major river system meandering to 11 countries that includes the Indus, Sutlej, Brahmaputra, Irrawady, Salween and Mekong. About 2 billion people stretching from Afghanistan to the Ganga-Meghna-Brahmaputra basin in South Asia to the Mekong in the Southeast depend on the rivers. The reason for China's intransigence on Tibet is clear – water. Tibet's vast water resources is key to sustaining China's northwest region, revitalising its deserts and the Yellow river itself, as well as being crucial to its Himalayan Strategy. China's need and the water requirements of the other down riparian countries sets up a contesting and conflicting situation often prompting analysts to say that 'China's thirst will leave others thirsty'.

China's rise not being peaceful can have various connotations. In relation to water issues, given its enormous requirement, China will be far less accommodative and in the realist sense "guardian of its own security and independence". This makes China a "rational egoist" interested in its own utility as well as a "defensive positionalist" firm in maintaining relative capabilities. Therefore one needs to continuously inquire the impact of China's actions particularly on the peripheral states which it always considers as being rivals.

In the regional context China's ascendancy has far reaching significance than from a Western perspective that views China's rise as a challenge to a 'Western-dominated international society'. Some of the Western writings, particular the English School, are largely pessimistic about China's ability to "continue rising peacefully". Others more specifically argue that the peaceful rise in the next 30-years will be challenged by domestic reforms and cracks will emerge as China transits from a command to a market economy. These arguments are well circulated and contested and make the debate on China's rise fascinating.

Like it or not, China does matter. It is home to a 1/4th of the world's population but finds itself with disproportionately less arable land, water and oil. Its economy while galloping at a pace that is undoubtedly impressive has left a telling impact on the environment. There are limits to China's resources that can match its ability to be self-sufficient in food. Being food secure equally means optimising the water resources. A hungry China is equally a thirsty China. It is a compelling reminder that no engagement with China can afford to ignore its resource dilemmas.

NATURE OF TRANSBOUNDARY RIVERS

Transboundary rivers originating from, flowing through and draining into territorially defined boundaries are a significant part of the freshwater biome, contributing roughly 60 per cent of world's freshwater excluding the Antarctica. There are about 260 river basins home to 40 per cent of the world population with roughly 145 sharing agreements/treaties in existence. Clearly the rivers make the international system positively busy with an array of cooperation and shared benefits. However, rivers display a peculiar tendency that can be referred to as the 'unsettlement of the settled'. Water relations can never be permanently settled since flows in river are not constant. The flows in turn are determined by seasonal variations and usage particularly those that are non-consumptive in nature. Also, interventions and diversions on rivers impact flow. Political relations therefore can easily swing according to the changing quantitative and qualitative nature of the river.

Varied interpretations on the use of river have resulted in differing claims between riparian countries. 'Limited Territorial Sovereignty', however, allows each riparian state to use the flow of the shared rivers within its territory provided such utilization does not impinge on the rights of the co-riparian. that nations are entitled to "reasonable share of water". But since there is no legal-binding international treaty on water sharing, riparian relations will remain hostage to individual states' current needs and future requirements. As major parts of the globe experience high-level of water-stress, riparian relations will get contentious.

While rivers are visible yet they are not transparent. This relates to the difficulty in monitoring and measuring the flows and as such the lack of knowledge prompts suspicion and creates conflictual positions. Since rivers physically link upstream and downstream users, knowledge can also be 'constructed' to suit the riparian state interest. The possession or capture and control of water resources can result in aggressive tendencies and can readily translate into power and dominance. Water thus can assume hegemonic attribution.

POWER AND HEGEMONY

The paper coneptualises the role of hegemony and power in transboundary water to understand the power asymmetries and the hegemonic nature of transboundary water relations. Steven Lukes' study on power is a common tool of analysis in understanding state's behaviour. Some studies have already applied power and hegemony to transboundary water particularly while analysing the hydro-relations between Turkey and Syria on the Tigris and Euphrates and Ethiopia vis-à-vis Egypt on the Nile.

Power is not easy to define and highly contested. It is "less about what power is than about what power does." Lukes description of three dimensions of power is interesting when approached through water. The first form of power being the state's military and economic superiority or 'structural power' also referred to as 'hard power'. It can be reasoned that states riparian position and its control of water can fall under structural power. Here the hydro-hegemon can employ structural power in a coercive way. The second form of power refers to setting the agenda, dictating the discussion and ability to shift the goal post. The stronger party gives very little choice or option to the weaker party. This is referred to as the 'bargaining power'. The third form of power occurs when the hegemon takes the initiative of depoliticising the issue and becomes a kind of a guarantor and regulator of affairs, a 'dean' or 'guide' so to speak. This is referred to as 'ideational power' or 'psychological power'. Mark Zietoun and Jeron Warner describe hydro-hegemony as "hegemony at the river-basin level achieved through water resource control strategies such as resource capture, integration and containment. The strategies are executed through an array of tactics (e.g. coercion-pressure, treaties, knowledge construction, etc.) that are enabled by the exploitation of existing power asymmetries within a weak international institutional context." Eventually all international river basins are determined by 'who gets how much water, how and why?'

China's continued water development, now witnessing a rapid pace with successive interventions on the rivers, is in pursuant of its internal compulsions and therefore self-driven. It, however, does not find it necessary to take into consideration the concerns of its downstream neighbours. China's upper riparian position gives it the hydrological advantage to use and control the waters the way it wills. This allows for enormous power (structural). Power also determines who the hegemon is. Recently, Wen Jiabao in an interview to Malaysian and Indonesian media stressed on the fact that China would never seek hegemony when it becomes a developed country. Such statement of calm and assurance is typical of China and Wen is the perfect PR man. However, one cannot discount China's deception and dismiss the fact that it will not strive to become a regional hegemon (domination).

China's effort to dominate Asia has to be understood from two important features of Asia: continental and maritime. To be a true hegemon, China will have to dominate over both the continental and the maritime. It's continental domination, first having filled the space left by the collapse of the Soviet Union its prime continental challenger, is now solidly secure with the control of the waters of the Tibet. China's maritime dominance continues to be challenged by countervailing powers like the US in Asia's littoral and India in the Indian Ocean. It can be argued here that China's continental hegemony is predominantly hydro-hegemony. With roughly 10 major rivers flowing out of China's territory to 11 countries and none coming in, it's a resource dominance of unimaginable proportion. With such control, what can China do? First, its disproportionate water hold gives it the capacity to coerce the weaker riparian. As a hydro-hegemon it can set and dictate the agenda for all riparian. It can also determine the knowledge that is included and exclude the hydrological information by ensuring that any information used enhances the hegemon's case and not that of a weaker party contestation.

CHINESE CIVILIZATION AND WATER MANAGEMENT

Chinese civilization like many of the early civilization flourished around the mighty river systems of the Yellow and the Yangtze. These great rivers also accompanied with it widespread deluge and destruction, "...rising to the heavens with their swell." While the society respected water as nature's gift it also acknowledged its destructive force. The history of Chinese civilization in many ways is a history of hydraulic engineering, canal building and water conservation. Modern day projects such as the Three Gorges and the SNWP (South-to-North Water Project) carry a distinct Chinese tradition of taming the rivers which goes back to nearly 5000 years when Yu the Great of the Xia Dynasty (2205 BC) also referred to as Da Yu (Mighty Yu) dredged the vast floodplains of ancient China. Legend has it that Yu created Sanmenxia (now a city in western Henan province of central China) by cutting the Longman mountain into three ridges with a divine battle axe to control the floods of the Yellow river. Yu's period symbolized the beginnings of Chinese water projects and water control. The Great Yu's control of the floods is cast as 'courage' and 'struggle' of the labouring people against the elements of nature. Looked from a Chinese political philosophy, it bears a certain class imprint and thus part of the popular political consciousness.

Some of the most famous water projects of ancient China include the Dujiangyan Irrigation System, the Ling Canal and the Grand Canal. The Dujiangyan Irrigation System, built in 3 century BC on the Min river, a major tributary of the Yangtze, is regarded as the oldest water project in the world and listed as a UN World Heritage Site. It still serves the Chengdu inhabitants. Li Bing who built the project acquired a mythic status representing mans struggle against the forces of nature and its ultimate triumph. Bing left behind a legacy of water planners and builders who are revered and commemorated in China. The Ling Canal and the Grand Canal represents engineering feats of connecting rivers. The Ling Canal completed in 214 BC is probably one of the oldest canals in the world linking the Xiang and Li rivers both tributaries of the Yangtze. The Grand Canal built over 2000 years ago and still functioning, is an engineering marvel that connected the rivers Hai, Yellow, the Huai, the Yangtze and the Qiantang to form a great aquatic artery from north to south with a total length of 1794 km running from Hangzhou to Beijing. It is also interesting that China's recently revived political direction of building 'a harmonious society', 'harmony with nature' and a 'harmonious world', all Confucian concept, does not comply with its current water projects. It seems that for China the challenge is not just ultimate environmental security, but immediate and medium-term survival.

Thirsty China: Overview of the water resources

According to the Water Resource Ministry, the total amount of water resources in China in 2007 was 2469.6 billion m^3, of which the surface water resources were 2,376.4 billion m^3. The figures become very interesting when we observe that the amount of water that flowed into Chinese territory from outside was only 15.7 billion m^3. In comparison, the water that flowed out of the territory was 569.9 billion m^3. Also to note is the fact that the water that flowed into the boundary rivers was 67.4 billion m^3 and water that flowed into seas was 1,435.3 billion m^3. China has much in total volume of water resources but less in per capita volume. The available water resources per capita was 1,869 m^3 in average. What is to be noted is that the total amount of water resources is decreasing. The amount of total water supply in 2007 was 578.9 billion m^3, of which surface water was 470.4 billion m^3 (81.2 per cent) and groundwater 105.8 billion m^3 (18.3 per cent).

China is expected to face 25 per cent supply gap for projected water demand by 2030 with two-thirds of its cities already facing difficulty in accessing water. Having put in place the structures as part of its strategic objective, China in December 2010 made a decision to accelerate reform and development of water resources, known as the No.1 Document in 2011. The document focuses on three 'red lines': over-exploitation, usage efficiency, pollution.

These facts suggest that China is water insecure and its insecurity primarily relates to the disproportionate availability or uneven distribution of waters within its territory – the majority of which is in the south (Tibet) with the north and west excessively water stressed. The region south of the Yangtze river, which accounts for roughly 36 per cent of Chinese territory, has 81 per cent of water resources. The territories north of the Yangtze, where much of water is required, make up 64 per cent but have a meager 19 per cent of water capacity.

Without Tibet, China's hydrological supremacy would be overturned from being entirely water-independent to water-dependent. Had it not been for Tibet, China would not have been the world's most independent riparian country. In fact Beijing's total control over Tibet in effect is the 'total' control of the water resources. 'Absolute territorial sovereignty' over the waters gives an added strategic sharpness to China's regional approach. The classic lines, *"He who holds Tibet dominates the Himalayan piedmont; he who dominates the Himalayan piedmont, threatens the Indian subcontinent; and he who threatens the Indian subcontinent may well have ail of South-East Asia within his reach, and all of Asia,"*

China has no significant bilateral riparian treaties on any water allocation or water utilization, an indication of it being hydro-hegemonic. Its Water Resource Ministry website, however, states "...that China has built cooperation relationships with more than 60 countries, and signed water cooperation agreements and memorandum of understanding with 40 countries." In fact, China was one of the three countries that did not approve of the 1997

UN Convention on the Law of the Non-Navigational Uses of International Waterways.

In order to overcome this hydrological unevenness, projects like the 'south-to-north water diversion', first proposed by Chairman Mao in 1952 to ease water shortages in cities like Beijing and Tianjin, is a national priority. In fact Mao had made a seemingly innocent remark: "the south has a lot of water, the north little...if possible, it is OK to lend a little water." Since then it has prompted a breed of Chinese leadership who think hydrologically. Many of the top leadership today are hydraulic engineers and technocrats including Hu Jintao and Wen Jiabao.

The south-to-north project which started in December 2002 was designed to take water from China's largest river, the Yangtze, to the arid northern regions. It is expected to be completed by 2050 and would eventually divert about 44.8 billion cubic meter of water to the north annually. The northward-bound water has three routes - an eastern route, a middle route and a western route. The project started with the construction of the *eastern route* in 2002. The construction of the *middle route* followed in 2003 which will come into service after 2014's flood season. It is expected to handle 9.5 billion cubic meters of water annually. By the end of 2010, 115 billion Yuan had been spent and 40 projects were started making a new annual record. The *western route* is controversial owing to political and strategic ramification for China's riparian neighbours particularly on the Mekong and the Brahamaputra. However, in spite the sensitivity, China has not stated that it will not go ahead with the western route. Though still in the planning stage, it involves working in the Qinghai-Tibet Plateau (3,000m–5,000m above sea level). Once completed in 2050, the western route project will bring 4 billion cubic metres of water from the Tongtian, Yarlung and Dadu rivers across 500km to northwest China.

More than anything else, the water shortage becomes an impediment to China's goal of meeting food production and questions the leadership claims to self-sufficiency in food grains. Water deficiency, prolonged drought and below average rainfall in the nine provinces (including the six major wheat producing provinces) of the northern and eastern region have resulted in a surge of grain imports not experienced in the last 15 years. Reduced self-sufficiency is dangerous for a country with a population as large as China and therefore its search for water becomes an unending imperative often desperate and aggressive.

Electricity is equally crucial in China's economic development. With a GDP growing at the rate of over 10 per cent a year, China's energy requirement is projected to increase by 150 per cent by 2020. Its ever increasing demand for energy requires it to look for various sources. While resource rich in coal and a net importer of oil, both climate unfriendly, China is compelled to develop its hydroelectricity as a clean and renewable source. China has already half of the world's large dams including the Three Gorges. Its exploitable hydropower is estimated to be around 378GW with an annual power supply of 1.92 trillion KWh. Huge hydroelectricity projects for energy and water diversion schemes for food sufficiency are strategic measures to China's growth path.

ON THE YARLUNG TSANGPO/BRAHMAPUTRA

China has been successful in damming the Yarlung Tsangpo on November 12, 2010. The 510 MW Zangmu hydroelectricity power station being built on the middle reaches of the Yarlung between the counties of Sangri and Gyaca is equivalent to the entire existing hydropower generating capacity in Tibet. As a long-term objective of capturing the flow, China has ensured that no free flowing rivers exist in Asia. Yan Zhiyong, general manager of China Hydropower Engineering Consulting, has been quoted as saying: "By about 2020 most of China's hydropower projects outside of Tibet will have been completed, and the industry's focus will shift to the Jinsha, Lancang, the upper reaches of the Nujiang river and the Yarlung." The riparian dynamics is set to get far more contentious and controversial with greater nervousness among the lower riparian.

Studies carried out by the Chinese Academy of Sciences' put the Yarlung hydropower potential second only to the Yangtze but the highest in terms of power-generating potential per unit of length. The hydropower development is expected to lead to a development boom with increased activities in mining and rapid growth in road and railways. The Zangmu dam marks a beginning of a new era in Chinese engineering and construction capability.

It was only in the last decade that the Chinese leadership has focused its attention on river development plan in Tibet. Earlier it was low-key and mostly about Tibetan self-sufficiency. But with new studies revealing larger hydropower potential of 114 gigawatts on the Yarlung basin including a possibility of 38-gigawatt hydropower facility at the Great Bend in Medog county (equal in power to the Three Gorges), the Chinese leaders have now a water mine to exploit. Chinese hydro-obsession as seen in the Three Gorges will drive mega projects on the Yarlung. Small-to-medium hydro power stations do not excite the Chinese leaders. Many 40-50 MW project on the Yarlung were not carried out because of river-silt issue and displacement concerns. The hydropower plans on the Yarlung comes at a time when other infrastructural development has taken place or will soon be completed. By 2012 the electricity grid in Tibet will be connected to the national grid through Qinghai. The Qinghai-Tibet railway has now made it possible to move materials for building large dams on the Yarlung. The Chinese now have a clear policy direction on the Yarlung and with energy supply becoming ever more pressured, the time and condition is ripe to develop the rich hydropower resources of Tibet and a no-holds-bar approach to taking total and complete political control of Tibet.

The most disturbing and controversial project is the Shoutian or "reverse flow" Canal, announced by Jiang Zemin in 1999 as the "xibu da kaifa" (the Great Western Extraction). The plan proposes to transport 206 billion m3 of water from the Yarlung Tsangpo (Brahamaputra) or roughly 33 per cent of the flow into the Yellow river and then supplied to the northwestern part of China. The fact that these great transfers and projects have been conceived by the Chinese army – the brainchild of Guo Kai a general in the PLA – adds to some misperception of military design though it cannot be doubted that such projects are "from a supply first mentality", that ensures supplying water for heightened food production.

Guo Ki inspired Li Ling's book *How Tibet's Water Will Save China,* detailing the Shoutian Canal as the solution to chronic water shortages in China's dry north and northwest. The plan proposes: "a dam at Shoumatan Point will back up water that will plunge 2,000m through 15km of tunnels near Dagmo and discharge through 26 of the world's biggest turbines into a tributary rejoining the riverbed and reservoir of the storage dam north of Medog. At twice the capacity of Three Gorge's, the 40GW pumped storage facility will be the world's largest hydroelectric facility. After diverting the original 33 per cent, the volume of returned water determines residual river flow from the holding dam."

Over the years, China's great technology leap in the area of water development has given it strategic width in the region. While it is easy to damn the dams, however convincing the argument is, such structures and the benefits accrued is an attraction for development. China's expertise and knowledge on dam building helps to enhance its power and influence and importantly weaken lower riparian coalition.

On the Mekong/Lancang

On the Mekong, China is only a dialogue partner in the Mekong River Commission (MRC), which was formed by the concerns of four lower-riparian countries – Laos, Cambodia, Thailand and Vietnam in 1995. 22 per cent of the river is located in China and withdraws 26 per cent of the waters annually from the Lancang (Mekong). Though China's non-binding participation in the Mekong basin has increased, it is unthinkable that it will join MRC as an active member. Sitting on the sideline and being non-committal to any formal arrangement gives China the power to observe and comment without any binding role or responsibility. Moreso, China's hydropower development on the Lancang (Mekong) is typically based on little information and no transparency. China plans 15 dams on the river of which at least two will be of mega-size. The Xiaowan dam is to be completed in 2012 and will be the second only to Three Gorges. Clearly the dams will have widespread impact on the down riparian states. Also, the western route of the 'south-to-north' diversion project involves diverting water from the upper Lancang to the Yangtze river. The Mekong lower riparian countries remain suspicious of China's power game and upstream hydroelectricity projects. China as the upper riparian player would like the water debate in the lower Mekong basin to be intensified between the lower riparian states just as it likes the water debate in Pakistan and Bangladesh to be directed and contested with India, without highlighting its own hydroelectricity plans either on the Indus or the Yarlung Tsangpo or the Lancang. For China not being transparent on its dams is a ploy, despite the fact that under international law countries downstream of a river are entitled to be fully informed. China's dams and water diversions are important components of its hydro-hegemony. On the one hand it can be an effective bargaining tool when dealing with countries like India with whom it has testy political relations. On the other hand, hydro-diplomacy through partnership on dam construction and infrastructural development helps it to widen and deepen its influence and weaken lower riparian coalition.

Out of the 15 dams planned, the Chinese have started work on eight dams on its territory, the Chinese companies have also started constructing two hydroelectricity dams in Cambodia, one of the downstream basin countries. Lower riparian countries like Cambodia have much to lose by being too critical of China's dam construction, and would rather receive billions of dollars from China into the country's infrastructure. China's expertise and knowledge on hydrology and dam construction helps to enhance its power. Laos hydro-power potential is the highest in the lower Mekong basin states. Sensing that the Chinese dams are unstoppable, the government plans to build a series of 9 dams including the Xayaburi. With dams flow controversies and discord is going to intensify. The Xayaburi brings in direct conflict with Vietnam and Laos over fear of low flow and sediment. Vietnam is the world's leading rice producer and hence the concern is pitched high. Thailand has a larger stake in the Mekong basin in the sense of being the lead country in initiating the MRC, which was also signed in Bangkok. As the prime mover of this much lauded river cooperation amongst the lower riparians, Thailand would like to facilitate sustainable development and to follow the principle of 'equitable utilization'.

The dam race will leave behind a trail unending consequences with China conducting the philharmonic on the upper reaches.

China's dam-centric approach has an underlying message that these engineering feats are essential to the livelihood of millions of people. China's uncompromising position on dams and diversion will only result in a dam spree in the lower riparian countries.

COUNTER HYDRO-HEGEMONY STRATEGY

Power asymmetry is a fact of realpolitik but it need not be completely subjugating. Counter-hegemonic tactics and strategies can turn a disadvantaged riparian party into a position where it can change the rules of the game or bring in a level of parity. However, dealing with a superior riparian player requires a thought-through approach. China's hegemonic path is currently 'dominance by coercion'. In the next 30-years it would aspire to be a regional leader buttressed by authority and respect. Also it must be noted that China has been successful in effectively mixing 'cohesion and compliance' with 'attraction and intimidation', what Gramsci called "a mix of force and consent".

To counter-balance China's hydro-hegemony, it is critically important to understand its intentions and accordingly frame policies that are not reactive but perceptive. For one, China understands it supreme riparian position, another it frames it strategically. India, given its power parity is the rightful counter-balancer in spite its position being a lower riparian. A parallel can be drawn to Ethiopian counter-hegemonic strategies against Egyptian hegemony on the Nile.

A typical recourse is to advocate the principles of international water law, however non-binding they are. Raising concerns through such norms alerts and sensitises the international community in spite the fact that issues of 'equitable utilisation' and 'limited sovereignty' are always difficult and uncomfortable to agree upon. The principle of 'information exchange, notification and consultation' is crucially important with China given the nature of the dams and water diversions. For example, withholding data on the flows of the rivers or plans to build storages or dams or projects that divert water comes under the 'no harm rules'. India's own water sharing structures with its neighbours– Pakistan and Bangladesh– are quite exceptional and takes due consideration of the 'no harm rules'. There is a high moral ground here that India can take but for that it has to shirk off its defensive stance over China's water development on the Tibetan rivers for which India also has a rightful use.

Importantly, India is not one-river downstream with China. This makes India's riparian relations with China exceptional and critical. India is multi-river dependent on the Brahmaputra on the east and the Indus and the Sutlej on the west. The Ganga which originates in India has nine tributaries joining it from Nepal, three of which Karnali, Gạndaki and Kosi arise in Tibet. Some figures indicate that about 354 BCM of water flow into India from the Tibet of which 131 BCM is accounted for in the Brahmaputra (the low-end figure is 78.10 BCM). It is important for India to draw China into a dialogue on water issues and consistently raise hydrological concerns at bilateral meetings. But critically for India is the fact that it has to articulate its middle riparian position to change the perception in the neighbourhood that India is a 'water hegemon'.

A perceptive response that India should undertake is to increase its storage capacity. Water storage per person (in cubic meter) in India is about 200. The US has roughly 6000 and China almost 2500. India needs to strengthen its storage capacity to a reasonable and sustainable level based on proper environmental impact assessment and not entering into a dam race with China on the Yarlung/Brahamaputra. This is important, as India needs to take into consideration the concerns of Bangladesh. India's counter diplomacy should be to isolate China as an unreasonable upper riparian at the regional and global level.

Any counter strategy with China has to be well nuanced and not always framed in the legalistic sense. Some would argue that India should play the power game through managing and engaging China. This holds significant political value when dealing with China on the Tibetan water resources. By raising the question, however contesting it might be, that should China alone be the stakeholder to the waters in Tibet, gives India the opportunity re-consider its Tibet policy. Rajiv Sikri notes: "India could state that it considers Tibet, as an autonomous region, to be a part of the territory of the People's Republic of China – the implication being that it is only if Tibet is a truly autonomous region that India recognises it as a part of China." If China wants to keep its relationship with India adversarial then India should keep its Tibet policy ambiguous. Sujit Dutta says: "India's repeated reiteration that Tibet is a part of China has not helped to clinch the territorial bargain. There has neither been corresponding reciprocity from China nor has it helped in building trust. India thus needs to nuance its current strategy."

Tibet has also to be seen from an ecological perspective and the glacial melting has added new concerns and challenges. There are crucial sustainability and ecological issues that can potentially affect millions of people downstream. Raising water resources in Tibet as a 'commons' would draw international attention and possibly prompt China into a water dialogue with the downstream countries on ways to preserve and share the benefits of the waters of Tibet.

It needs to be remembered that China has a strong environmental constituency with activists, scientists and journalists, despite odds, sensitising local people and authorities to ecological concerns. Tibet's ecology has been a key issue for civil society and powerful environmental groups like the International Union for Conservation of Nature (IUCN) to campaign for Tibet as a vulnerable area to be protected from rampant resource exploitation. In fact in 2003, a 7.1 million hectare in Yunnan province, where upper reaches of the Yangtze, Lancang and Nujiang run parallel was declared a World Heritage in 2003. Interestingly, China has ratified the Convention on the Protection of World Cultural and Natural Heritage which was adopted by the UNESCO in 1972.

Conclusion

China's upper riparian position and its enormous domestic requirement gives water a strategic characteristic in the region and as such different level of trust and mistrust; cooperation and misperception are seen. China values water and its utilisation as fundamental to its development; the greatest achievement being to lift more than 400 million people out of abject poverty in three decades through economic growth at breakneck speed. It will need to continue with that and therefore will continue wanting water. China perceives its peripheral states as potential rivals. Stability in the region would significantly depend on the stable supply of water. Suggesting the Tibetan rivers, as 'commons', is clearly anathema for the Chinese leadership. In a realist perspective, China's water development approach in Tibet is unilateral giving little space for dialogue and accommodation and bound to affect downstream riparian both in terms of water flow and ecological consideration. A coalition of lower riparian coming together specifically to draw China into a water dialogue is conceivable in spite the fact that many of them have a strategic partnership with China.

In brief, China's privileged riparian position gives it enormous strategic latitude by deploying structural power in a coercive mode. Also it can use power over the bargaining process to greater effect during times of negotiations. China can also use its power to force through contentious issues; to firm up deals (as in dams) and to impose ideas for example that its water predicament is reasonable and uncompromising.

8

Water Scarcity and the Threat of Water Wars in South Asia

South Asia is known for many wonderful and beautiful things such as its varied cultures, languages, religions, landscapes and peoples but above all it is known for its volatility and sudden outbreaks of violence and often brutal and destructive conflicts. The Indian subcontinent, as it was once known, was partitioned on the basis of religion in 1947 according to the concept of the two-nation theory. Since then several wars have been fought over territory, sovereignty and in one case for independence which eventually led to the emergence of Bangladesh in 1971 as an independent nation-state. As things now stand the next war in the South Asia region could well be over water. This appears almost inevitable unless India adopts a more accommodative attitude towards its neighbour's claims for reasonable and equitable water sharing rights. Recent history has, however, suggested quite the opposite with New Delhi ignoring the just demands of Bangladesh which as the lower riparian nation is wholly dependant for its survival on the regular and sustained flow of water coming through India from the Himalayas.

Since 1971 Bangladesh has generally adopted a defensive attitude in its relations with its large neighbour in recognition of the economic and military might of India. However, if New Delhi continues with its policy of draining the life blood of Bangladesh it is more than likely that this small but populous nation would be forced to take on a more assertive role in its relations with India and in realizing its just demands for water, as well as in addition to other contentious bilateral issues, could ultimately lead to conflict in the coming decade. Policy makers in Bangladesh are yet to wake up to this reality but as a new generation of leaders emerge faced with the calamitous consequences of the large scale withdrawal and diversion of water by India they may have few choices but to confront New Delhi in a more aggressive and confrontational manner. This may appear at first glance to be highly unlikely but with millions displaced by desertification and the numerous other adverse effects (some of which has wrongly been attributed to climate change to distract world attention to the actual causes of environmental damage in Bangladesh) of the Indian water withdrawal policy such a scenario cannot be easily dismissed. Fueling this growing animosity would be decades of mistrust caused by an arrogant and duplicitous policy devised and practiced by India's politicians and diplomats in their dealings with Bangladesh.

BACKGROUND TO WATER SHARING DISPUTES

The very geographical location of Bangladesh makes it the lowest riparian country of more than 50 trans-boundary rivers. The waters of the Ganges, Brahmaputra and other trans-boundary rivers have been sustaining the life and living of millions of Bangladeshis. Without these waters, the livelihood of millions of Bangladeshis would come under severe stress. Unfortunately, since independence, Bangladesh has been observing with great concern, the gradual reduction of the dry season flows of the Ganges, Teesta and many other trans-boundary rivers due to anthropogenic interventions across the borders – primarily by India. Since its independence in 1947, India has made intensive efforts to harness and develop the water resources in the Ganges basin. The data indicates that Indianow has several dozen large barrages and other diversionary structures operating in the basin which are capable of diverting 100,000 cusec flows from the Ganges and its different tributaries. Moreover, India has constructed more than 400 major, medium and small storage dams in the basin area. Of these, the major storage reservoirs have a total capacity of 2221 billion cubic feet or 63 billion cubic meters (BCM). Bangladesh itself could not embark upon any such major development of the waters of the trans-boundary rivers including the Ganges in the face of uncertainties of its dry season availability from across the border. Moreover, the flat terrain of Bangladesh does not allow any storage of excess monsoon waters for use during the dry season and such projects would in any case be extortionately exorbitant for the country at its present stage of development and with its limited financial resources.

The consequences for Bangladesh of India's policy of diversion and withdrawal of water have been both dramatic and devastating. Upstream diversion of the precious dry season flows of the Ganges has adversely affected the hydrology, river morphology, agriculture, domestic and municipal water supply, fishery, forestry, wildlife, industry, navigation, public health and biodiversity in large areas of Bangladesh dependent on the Ganges water. Western analysts have been duped into believing that these negative environmental affects are caused by climate change that will in a few decades result in the rise of sea waters that will inundate large areas of the country. However, the actual cause of increased salinity in the south-western region of Bangladesh has been India's diversion and withdrawal of water which allows ingress of sea water from the Bay of Bengal due to the reduced natural fresh water flows in the opposite direction during the dry season. Another extremely serious but indirect consequence of this water diversion policy is the contamination of ground water with arsenic. With the reduction of water from India millions in Bangladesh are now forced to access ground water which if pumped continuously over a prolonged period assists a chemical reaction that oxidizes naturally occurring arseno-pyrites deep in the soil resulting in the release of arsenic into the water – a process which may properly described as almost akin to mass poisoning. This consequential alarming degradation of the environment and water supply in south-western Bangladesh has already forced thousands to leave in quest of survival elsewhere. In the face of deteriorating human health, reduced economic productivity and loss of amenities, life and living in this part of Bangladesh people are becoming increasingly vulnerable, insecure and resentful. These are probably the prime causes of conflict between states if history is to be any guide.

THE FARAKKA BARRAGE PROJECT AND DIVERSION OF THE GANGES WATER

If we leave aside the period between 1947-1971 when Bangladesh was called East Pakistan and considered by India as a hostile entity the likelihood of agreement on water sharing was obviously limited. However, it was during this period that Indian diplomacy became a byword for duplicity and this approach was to continue in its relations with Bangladesh after it obtained independence from Pakistan with the help of the Indian military – which in hindsight had very little to do with altruism or kind hearted generosity and more to do with Indian geo-strategic imperatives. In any case, it was on October 29, 1951 that the thenPakistan government drew the attention of the Indian authorities to the report of a scheme for diverting large amounts of dry season flow of the Ganges. Four months later, on 8 March, 1952 India replied that the project was only under preliminary investigation and described Pakistan's concern over probable effects as purely hypothetical. Again on May 22, 1953 India reassured Pakistan that the Farraka and Gandak projects (a tributary of the Ganges) were still being investigated and India would appreciate cooperative development of the water resources of the Ganges. Nine years after the issue was first mooted the Government of India announced that it was going ahead with the plan to build a barrage across the River Ganges at Farraka and Pakistan was formally informed. Talks took place occasionally between 1961 and 1970 but real negotiation and consultations did not. By 1970India completed construction of the Farraka Barrage. The 24 mile feeder canal was, however, not yet ready.

While the Indian government's behaviour towards Pakistan during this 19 year period (1951-1970) is explicable on the grounds that both nations were inherently inimical towards each other having just fought two wars within just thirty years it is still not explainable why India would adopt the same negotiating tactics towards the new nation of Bangladesh which it had recently assisted in its liberation war? I have provided my own theory in my book 'The India Doctrine' where I draw attention to India's policy of domination over South Asia and an underlying resentment over the 1947 partition which seemingly allows Indian policy makers to ignore the just grievances of its smaller neighbours and not merely in the area of water sharing but including the whole array of bilateral issues that now bedevil interstate relations in the region.

After Bangladesh gained independence in 1971 relations with India gradually deteriorated and this was reflected in negotiations between the countries over water sharing rights. The Governments of India and Bangladesh decided in March 1972 to set up the Indo-Bangladesh Joint Rivers Commission (JRC). One of the major functions of the JRC was to maintain liaison between the participating countries in order to ensure the most effective joint efforts in maximizing the benefits from common river systems to both the countries. The question of sharing the water of the Ganges was, however, kept out of the purview of the JRC, to be settled at the level of Prime Ministers. In this regard, many in Bangladesh felt at the time that the Awami League government of Sheikh Mujibur Rahman was too compliant and would easily buckle to Indian demands which actually turned out to be the case. The Prime Minister of India and Bangladesh met in New Delhi in May 1974 and discussed amongst other things, the Ganges issue. Following this meeting, there was a Joint Declaration on May 16, 1974, wherein they observed that during the periods of minimum flow in the Ganges, there might not be enough water and, therefore, the fair weather (dry season) flow of the Ganges in the lean months would have to be augmented to meet the needs of Calcutta port and to fulfill requirement of Bangladesh. They also agreed that the best means of augmentation through optimum utilization of the water resources of the region available to the two countries should be studied by the Joint Rivers Commission. The two sides expressed their determination that before the Farakka project is commissioned; they would arrive at a mutually acceptable allocation of the water available during the periods of minimum flow in the Ganges. The JRC accordingly took up the issue of augmentation of the Ganges flows but was unable to reach any agreement.

At a subsequent minister level meeting in April 1975 the Indian side proposed a test-run of the feeder canal of the Farakka

Barrage for a limited period during that dry season. On good faith, Bangladesh agreed to India's request and allowed it to operate the feeder canal with varying discharges in ten-day periods from April 21 to May 31, 1975, ensuring the continuance of the remaining flows to Bangladesh. Although India was supposed to divert limited quantities of water from the Ganges for the said test-run up to May 31, 1975, it continued withdrawals from Farakka to the full capacity of the feeder canal during the dry season of 1976 without entering into any understanding or agreement on sharing the flows despite Bangladesh's repeated requests. The consequences of India's actions had been tragic. The unilateral Indian withdrawals throughout the dry seasons of 1976 caused a marked reduction in the dry season Ganges flows in Bangladesh. This sudden change in the flow pattern caused an alarming situation in the south western region of Bangladesh.

To cut a long story short, Bangladesh repeatedly requested India to stop the unilateral withdrawals but this bore little fruit. Bangladesh then took the issue to the United Nations in 1976 and the General Assembly urged both sides to seek an immediate solution. Between 1977 and 1988 Bangladesh and India signed several temporary agreements but no permanent understanding could be reached. Between 1988 and 1996 there was no instrument for sharing the dry season Ganges flows between the two countries. In the absence of any agreement, India again started unilateral withdrawals from Farakka. It was not until the Awami League returned to power in 1996 in Bangladesh under the leadership of Sheikh Hasina (daughter of the slain leader Sheikh Mujibur Rahman) that a treaty between the countries was signed on the sharing of the Ganges Water at Farakka. This treaty has not been viewed favourably in Bangladesh as it was felt to be a subservient arrangement without the usual safeguards and guarantees and contrary to norms of international law. It appears these apprehensions were well founded as recent reports suggest that the quantity of water flowing down from the Farakka point has been declining due to the withdrawal of water by India through various canals in violation of the water sharing agreement.

The treaty is now under legal challenge in the Supreme Court of Bangladesh on the following grounds amongst others –

1. That Bangladesh has been receiving lesser amounts of flows at Farakka as its share compared to the quanta it should be receiving as agreed between the contracting parties set out in the schedule contained in Annexure II of the Treaty.
2. The instruments signed by Bangladesh and India do not provide entitlement to the former to participate or to become party to negotiations on any water course or in any consultations thereof e.g. Bangladesh cannot participate in the bilateral negotiation between India and Nepal which aim to implement projects on major tributaries of the Ganges river emanating from the Nepalese territory like the Pancheswar and Saptkosi High Dam Projects.
3. Over the last three decades the Bangladesh government has repeatedly requestedIndia for upstream hydro-meteorological data of the Ganges, Brahamputra and other rivers. The Indian side has declined to supply or exchange such upstream data and information. The 1996 treaty and other Indo-Bangladesh agreements are totally silent about the provisioning of this information.
4. India either unilaterally or bilaterally with Nepal and Bhutan are undertaking planned measures for harnessing and regulating water resources of the Ganges, Brahmaputra, Meghna and some of their tributaries without informing or providing notification to the downstream riparian country of those rivers which is Bangladesh.
5. The 1996 Treaty and other Indo-Bangladesh do not provide for any third-party arbitration on settlement of disputes.

These are only a few of the grounds that are claimed by the petitioner to be in contravention of customary international law and in particular the provisions of the 1997 UN Convention on the Law of the Non-Navigational Uses of International Watercourses and the Berlin Rules on Water Resources which both contain internationally accepted safeguards and guarantees that were omitted from the 1996 treaty. In particular, India's withdrawal of waters in an unreasonable and inequitable manner and the terms of the 1996 treaty appear to be in violation of Articles 7,8,13,17,29,56,57,58,59,60,68,72 and 73 of the Berlin Rules but most importantly and significantly Article 12 which states –

1. Basin States shall in their respective territories manage the waters of an international drainage basin in an equitable and reasonable manner having due regard for the obligation not to cause significant harm to other basin States.
2. In particular, basin States shall develop and use the waters of the basin in order to attain the optimal and sustainable use thereof and benefits therefrom, taking into account the interests of other basin States, consistent with adequate protection of the waters.

And Article 16 which provides – Basin States, in managing the waters of an international drainage basin, shall refrain from and prevent acts or omissions within their territory that cause significant harm to another basin State having due regard for the right of each basin State to make equitable and reasonable use of the waters.

Regardless of the outcome of the case, relations between Bangladesh and India are likely to deteriorate as agreement on water sharing in an equitable and reasonable manner appear a distant and forlorn prospect making conflict a more likely scenario. In some respects, a low level conflict has already begun as there are frequent and bloody skirmishes between the two countries border security forces and occasionally fighting has occurred over construction of groins and spurs on the Indian side intended to divert the course of rivers so that they encroach further into Bangladesh territory while supplementing the Indian side.

RIVER LINKING PROJECT

If the Farakka Barrage dispute had been the only bone of contention between the two countries then some minimum resolution to the dispute may have been forthcoming but with India (in total disregard of the environmental harm that would be sustained byBangladesh) now undertaking the massive River Linking Project (RLP) a further serious deterioration in relations is inevitable. Quite astonishingly, the RLP concept was conceived not by an expert committee or by the relevant government department but instead by the Indian Supreme Court which ruled (in relation to a Public Interest Litigation hearing) that there should be interlinking of rivers to offset drought and flooding in various parts of the country. Justice Kirpal set a 10 year deadline for implementation of the project. A brief six-page order passed on October 31, 2002 formed the basis on which the Indian government set up a high powered task force which devised a Perspective Plan comprising two components –

1. Peninsular Rivers Development; and
2. Himalayan Rivers Development

The Peninsular Rivers Component envisages the inter-linking of several major rivers at several different points along their course. The Himalayan Rivers Component which poses more serious difficulties for Bangladesh envisages construction of storages on the principal tributaries of the Ganges and the Brahmaputra in India, Nepal and Bhutan. Also, canal systems are to be inter-linked to transfer surplus flows of the eastern tributaries of the Ganges to the West apart from linking the (main) Brahmaputra and its tributaries with the Ganges and the Ganges with Mahanadi.

The effect of the RLP on Bangladesh has been variously described as devastating, catastrophic and also causing incalculable and irreparable damage to the country's environment and ecological balance. This unfortunately is not mere exaggeration since the Brahmaputra and the Ganges provides more than 85% of the total surface water available in Bangladesh during the dry season. Of the two, the Brahmaputra provides 67% of the water. The diversion and withdrawal of these waters under the RLP would constitute a similar proposition to Bangladesh as the Iraqi WMD program did (under the Saddam Hussain regime) for the United States and the United Kingdom. In the present context the threat to Bangladesh is not hypothetical.

In the face of this looming crisis the Government of Bangladesh has already lodged protests to the Government of India expressing serious concern over the RLP and has urged India to refrain from implementation of the plan. The Government has also communicated Bangladesh's serious concern over the Indian plan to the World Bank and Asian Development Bank and requested them to desist from providing any support toIndia relating to this plan. The matter was also raised during several meetings of the JRC where India was urged to desist from such a move without the consent of Bangladesh. It appears, however, that the Indian political leadership is committed to go ahead with this plan at the cost of its neighbours. The feeling is intensifying in the minds of the general public in Bangladesh against the Indian plan and their voice of protest is growing louder with the passage of time.

Considering that the Farraka Barrage and the RLP are only two of the many projects being undertaken by the Indian Government to divert and withdraw waters from the common rivers indicates that water sharing disputes with Bangladesh will progressively increase and naturally lead to growing tensions between the countries. The other major disputes on water sharing now include the Teesta, Feni, Meghna, Mahananda, Monu, Khowai, Gumti, Muhuri and Kodla Rivers and also construction of the Tipaimukh Dam in Manipur district of India. This last mentioned project has had the effect of eroding a large portion of Sylhet district in Bangladesh with almost 5000 acres drifting towards the Indian side following erosion of the riverbanks due to an artificial change in the course of the rivers Surma and Kushiara. All these water sharing disputes and the continued disregard for the concerns expressed by Bangladesh about these projects and the continuation of diversion and withdrawal of water in an unreasonable and inequitable manner is being viewed as an attack on the sovereignty of the country which if not restrained and outstanding issues settled amicably could lead to conflict in the coming decades.

ASSESSING THE SINO-INDIAN WATER DISPUTE

Two thirsty regional powers, each on one side of a mountain range covered by steadily shrinking glaciers; a more quintessential example of a zero-sum game would be hard to imagine. While relations between China and India have historically been tense, the precious water reserves of the Himalaya might well form the prelude to a new era of hostility. Indian news media and think tank experts have warned that China will erect several dams on the headwaters of mighty rivers like the Brahmaputra, the Ganges and the Indus. "The project," warns Brahma Chellaney of the

Center for Policy Research in New Delhi, "implies environmental devastation of India's northeastern plains and eastern Bangladesh and would thus be akin to a declaration of water war..."1 Pundits like Chellaney have even maintained that China is determined to exploit its riparian dominance and fashion water as a political weapon against India.

This is not the first time that China and India have locked horns over water resources originating in the Himalayas. In 1962, tensions over the disputed boundary and Chinese infrastructure projects in Aksai Chin escalated into a brief border war. Many Indian strategists have approached the Tibetan plateau as if they were looking up against the walls of a fortress, uncertain about the aspirations of its rulers in Beijing. "The Himalayas have been regarded as an impenetrable barrier against any threat from the north," wrote Sardar Patel, the iron fist of the first Indian cabinet, in a letter to Prime Minister Jawaharlal Nehru in 1950. "In our calculations we shall now have to reckon with communist China in the north and in the northeast, a communist China which has definite ambitions and aims and which does not, in any way, seem friendly disposed towards us."

India was well aware of the fact that whoever con- trolled that geographic bastion also controlled India's lifelines. Nehru pointed at the great strategic value of the water resources of the Himalayas. "For my part, I attach probably most importance to the development of our big schemes—river valley schemes—than to anything else. I think it is out of those that new wealth is going to flow into this country," he stated in front of the Indian parliament; "When I see a map of India and I look at the Himalayan range, I think of the vast power concentrated there, which is not being used, and which could be used, and which really could transform the whole of India with exceeding rapidity if it were properly utilized." Sixty years later, it seems that relations have come full circle, with China mulling over water diversion plans that India considers a threat and leaders on both sides being pressured not to make compromises on the national interest.

The Sino-Indian water dispute is an important case on which to judge whether Asia's two juggernauts will be able to manage conflicting interests and avoid sliding into a downward spiral of rivalry that could destabilize the entire region. It allows us to test whether global challenges like climate change prompt states to work together to protect common goods, or whether environmental threats compel states to stand firm and grab the largest possible share of shrinking natural resources.

It also permits us to clarify the awkward balance between nationalism and inter- dependence; in this case, two countries relying on the same water reserves. This paper seeks to contribute to the debate about self-restraint in the behavior of Asia's rising powers—self-restraint that will be vital if Asia's emerging protagonists are to steer clear of the traditional tragic dynamics of power transition. I start this paper with a concise overview of the water dispute between China and India and then discuss the status of Chinese projects to divert water from the Himalayan rivers. I argue that most of India's alarmist claims have been overblown. There is no evidence yet that Chinese projects constitute an imminent threat to India's water security. However, as I will show in this paper, continued restraint by China cannot be taken for granted. Articles and interviews with Chinese experts make clear that while there are a growing number of arguments in favour of a cautious approach, hardliners are emboldened by India's own water nationalism.

The State Of Play

China and India's long-term development will increasingly depend on the availability of water. From 1999 to 2008, the volume of internal renewable water resources decreased from 2,220 to 2,092 cubic meters per capita in China and from 1,762 to 1,631 cubic meters per capita in India, positioning them among the countries with the lowest per capita reserve base. In the last decade, China and India have been plagued by drought and shortages of drinkable water. Not surprisingly then, new options are being considered to tap the Himalayan rivers to ease water needs. At the same time, many studies have forecasted that those rivers could run dry as a consequence of melting glaciers. Lester Brown, a renowned environmentalist, insists that water shortages in the two countries present the largest threat to food security humanity has ever faced. Both Chinese and Indian political leaders seem to recognize this. In 1998, then Chinese vice prime minister Wen Jiabao was reported as saying that the "survival of the Chinese nation" was threatened by the country's shortage of water. In 2007, Prime Minister Manmohan Singh remarked, "Dry land agriculture, changing climate and water scarcity are the new challenges we are facing... given the threat of climate change and global warming, we face the real prospect of reduced supply of water. This threat is of particular concern to us in India as we have, since times immemorial, depended on glaciers for our water supply in this part of our sub-continent."

India depends on rivers that originate in China for one third of its renewable water supplies. Yet, what initially sparked fear in India about China's management of the Himalayan rivers was not water shortage, but deadly flash floods. In 2000, heavy monsoon rains caused the Brahmaputra River to burst its banks, inundating large swaths of land in the Indian northeast and leaving millions homeless. While ineffective water management and deforestation were identified as important causes, India's then ruling Bharatiya Janata Party claimed that India should demand compensation from China, arguing that a landslide on the Chinese side of the Brahmaputra River lay at the origin of the floods. Earlier that year, the agriculture minister had posited that flash floods in the Siang River in Arunachal Pradesh were the consequence of problems with Chinese dams. In 2002, after a series of talks, India and China inked a memorandum for provision of hydrological information on the Brahmaputra River during the flood season, with new memoranda following in 2005 and 2008.

While rumors about Chinese plans to divert the water of the Brahmaputra have circulated since 1996, it took almost a decade for them to become a major issue in the Indian public and political debate. In 2003, *Rediff* journalist Claude Arpi wrote a long article about the potential megaprojects on the upper stream of the Brahmaputra. "The massive diversion of the river to China's northwest would have even more devastating consequences," he concluded. "North India and Bangladesh would be starved of their lifeline. Nutrient-rich sediments that enrich the soil of these regions would be held back in the reservoir instead of reaching the river's delta. Millions would be affected and a water war could ensue." In 2004, a popular Indian magazine, *Outlook India*, published a story about the consequences of the 1962 war. "The Chinese deliberately created floods on the Brahmaputra in Arunachal not too long ago," the author asserted. "There is every reason to believe China will proceed with diverting water, ignoring India's objections." The 2006 Chinese National Defense White Paper added to this suspicion by noting that the People's Armed Police had contributed to twenty-one key national construction projects, including the Qinghai-Tibet Railway and the South-North Water Diversion Project.

By 2006, members of the Indian parliament started questioning the cabinet about Chinese diversion projects on the Sutlej and the Yarlung Zangbo, the upper stream of the Brahmaputra. In the meantime, local governments had also become more active in raising their concerns to the national level. The government of Arunachal Pradesh pressured Prime Minister Manmohan Singh to persuade Beijing to halt its plans to drain water away from the Brahmaputra. The Assam government formed an expert committee to study Chinese dams in Tibet. "Large-scale diversion of water would adversely hit the state's economy and could even lead to environmental problems and affecting the surface water table in the Indian north- east," Chief Minister of Assam Tarun Gogol stated.

While China had lived up to the stipulations of the 2002 memorandum by providing Delhi with hydro- logical information, and had agreed to "take measures for controlled release of accumulated water," and "ensure protection and rational use of water resources in the trans-Himalayan rivers," it refused to communicate about major dam construction projects in Tibet. Indian experts also complained that Beijing was not willing to consider a water-sharing treaty.

An obvious reason for India to be concerned about the management of the Yarlung-Brahmaputra is its dependence on the river for agriculture in the northeast of the country. Indian farming remains a very vulnerable sector that is prone to overcultivation and frequent environmental hazards. Significant reduction in the Brahmaputra's discharge is expected to produce social instability. Some Indian experts also warn that it could severely affect neighboring Bangladesh, adding to problems of poverty, migration and violence. Indian pundits believe that major dam projects could give China more strategic leverage over India and that the growing Chinese presence in Tibet resulting from large-scale projects might further reduce the mountain province's role as strategic buffer.

TAPPING THE ASIAN WATER TOWER

How far has China advanced with its plans to tap into the Asian water tower? Hitherto, China's main project has been the construction of a large dam on the Brahmaputra River in Zangmu, less than 200 kilometers from the Indian border. Even after the Indian government had asked for clarification and Indian intelligence services had released satellite images of the site, it was several months into the project before the Chinese foreign ministry officially acknowledged its existence. Indian analysts believe four more dams have been planned in the middle reaches of the Brahmaputra. Indeed, 2010 satellite images show that at least four construction sites have been developed in the vicinity of Zangmu. China has stressed that the purpose of these facilities is to generate electricity and that, because of the slope of the river, it will not be necessary to store water in large reservoirs. Another *fait accompli* caught both India and Pakistan unaware: 2009 media reports presented evidence of a large Chinese dam on a tributary of the Indus River near Shiquanhe, less than one hundred kilometers from Jammu and Kashmir. But here as well, the main use of the facility is power generation, not water diversion.

Even though those hydropower plants might not affect transboundary rivers as much as would large water diversion projects, India assumes that if China did not bother to communicate about the former, it would also not take Delhi's concerns seriously should it launch major diversion schemes. Furthermore, the fact that Beijing denied the possibility of channelling water away from rivers like the Brahmaputra while its experts continued to develop blueprints for large programs indicates for many Indian spectators that Beijing's true intentions are being hidden. Commenting on China's promise to behave responsibly in the management of transboundary rivers, the *Times of India* skeptically remarked, "Whereas India will celebrate the improved trust quotient with China, in reality, it cannot make a huge hue and cry over these projects of an upper riparian state."

Indeed, there is plenty of evidence that China continues to study its options for funnelling water away from the Himalayas to the economic centers along the coast and the vast arid tracts of land in the west. In 2002, after decades of research and bureaucratic wrestling, the state council approved the South-North Water Diversion Project (Nanshui beidiao gongcheng). One leg of this project concerns the upgrading of the Grand Canal between Hangzhou and Beijing. The second route connects the Yangtze river to Beijing. The third is expected to divert water from rivers in Tibet and Yunnan to the Yellow River. Though only one branch of this western route (xixian gongcheng), the diversion of the Brahmaputra has been the subject of most debate. Initial plans were developed in the late eighties, supported mainly by the military establishment. The military in turn managed to mobilize the Chinese People's Political Consultative Conference, the country's supreme political advisory body. In 1997, He Zuoxiu, a scientist and member of the Consultative Conference, claimed that the western route could increase China's arable land by an estimated 133 million hectares, which would resolve China's agricultural problems and provide employment for 160 million people. "All in all, implementing this project would end unemployment in China and provide enough food for every Chinese," he stated. In 1999, experts from the prestigious China Academy of Science, the State Development Planning Commission, the Ministry of Water Resources and the Ministry of Forestry and Land Resources carried out a joint field survey.

In October 2000, after listening to the expedition's report, General Zhao Nanqi, deputy chairman of the ninth Consultative Conference and a former president of the Academy of Military Sciences, stated "Even if we do not begin this water diversion project, the next generation will. Sooner or later it will be done." Prior to becoming vice premier, Wen Jiabao declared, "In the 21st century, the construction of large dams will play a key role in exploiting China's water resources, controlling floods and droughts, and pushing the national economy and the country's modernization forward." In 2003, a feasibility study was carried out on new water projects in Tibet, which, according to the Yellow River Water Conservancy Committee director Li Guoyin, was essential because the Yellow River was being exhausted by growing demand in western China. In 2005, Guo Kai, a senior researcher with the organization, was invited to Zhongnanhai to present his ideas on the western route. The same year, Li Ling, an officer from the second artillery corps, published the widely read book *Saving China Through Water From Tibet* (Xizang zhi shui jiu Zhongguo), which listed various causes and options for tapping the Yarlung.

A first option for the western route is to build a dam on the Great Bend of the Yarlung near to Longbai, 30 kilometers from Arunachal Pradesh. At the Great Bend the river flows through a gorge between two mountains and then descends almost 2,500 meters as it makes its bend. After this curve, which is also known as the Shuomatan Point, the river enters into Arunachal Pradesh and crosses the Assam Valley. Damming the Yarlung at the Great Bend would generate power half the capacity of the Three Gorges Dam. The Great Bend is also the starting point of the corridor proposed by water nationalists such as Guo Kai and Li Ning. The water from the Yarlung could be collected into a large reservoir near to the Lajia Gorge and subsequently channelled to the Yellow River or the Qinghai Lake. From the Qinghai Lake, water would be supplied to Gaxan Nur in Inner Mongolia, Urumqi in Xinjiang, and the Tarim Desert. This is referred to as the Shuotian canal project (Shuotian yunhe fangan). The entire project, with water corridors running to the Qinghai Lake and the Yellow River, would have a capacity of 50 to 200 billion cubic meters of water per year, or up to 6,000 cubic meters per second, which is as much as one-third of the Brahmaputra's total average annual discharge. With an estimated cost of $25 billion, the Shuotian canal is a project of superlatives, involving the construction of a dam of 300 meters high, tunnels 56 kilometers long and dikes extending for hundreds of kilometers.

But these proposals have also been criticized. In 2000, Minister of Water Resources and supporter of the Three Gorges Dam Qian Zhengying told the state council that developing the western route was technically and economically impossible. This concern was echoed by his successor, Wang Shusheng, who derided proposals from experts like Guo Kai as purely unprofessional and unscientific. He argued that all dikes and existing projects along the Yellow River would be washed away. Wang also posited that storing water in the Qinghai Lake could contaminate it with salt water. In a 2006 article, Qing Hui, an economic historian, listed various social and environmental reasons why river diversion plans were "nonsense." Wang Weiluo, a land planning expert, stressed that excessive development of river projects, single-minded pursuit of economic growth, the destruction of virgin forests, and especially the destruction of the Tibetan plateau were the largest contributing factors to the country's droughts and floods. That year, the Chinese Academy of Engineering published a study on the sustainable development of China's water resources that questioned the logic of feeding the Yellow River with water from other rivers. The report posited that most farming around the Yellow River was located uphill, which would make it very expensive to use the river's water for irrigation. Moreover, the western route could lead to major changes in vegetation. In the past, concerns expressed by Tibetans and by Chinese environmentalists had an influence on the decisionmaking process. In 2006, for example, a dam project on the Tibetan Lake Megoe Tso was cancelled after enduring protests. For the same reason, the Ministry of Environmental Protection suspended the construction of the Ludila and Longkaikou hydropower stations on the Jinsha River. "We need adequate scientific research and plans to decide where to build them so people can benefit to the full extent," summarized a professor at the China Institute of Water Resources and Hydropower Research in the *Global Times.*

This has not tempered the enthusiasm of proponents of large-scale water diversion programs. An article in the *People's Daily* explained that plans were being delayed, but certainly not cancelled. For many in the older generation, which is represented by opinion leaders like Guo Kai, Li Ling and He. Zuoxiu, projects like the western route are a matter of subjugating nature to the interest of the nation. "Man need not revere nature," He Zuoxiu famously declared. "Sometimes it is necessary to destroy the environment and ecology a bit or trans- form nature in the interests of human beings." In an interview with *China Daily*, He explained that "To really protect the environment there, the locals must escape from poverty to prosperity." This economy-first dictum has also been highlighted by local officials: "We haven't got any hydropower stations set up along big rivers like the Brahmaputra, but in the future we will consider setting them up on these sites," said Baima Wangdui, director of the Tibetan water resources department (Xizang Shuili Bumen). "Tibet is rich in water resources and has good potential for setting up more hydropower stations and with the economic development of Tibet we need more resources." At the occasion of the groundbreaking of the Zangmu Dam, Hao Peng, the deputy secretary of the Communist Party in Tibet, posited that the exploitation of Tibetan rivers was a very urgent task. Expectedly, this reasoning is supported by large influential construction companies. "Tibet's resources will be converted into economic advantage," maintained Yan Zhiyong, the general manager of China Hydropower Engineering Consulting Group. "The major technical constraints on damming the Yarlung Tsangpo have been over- come."

The India Dimension

In the last few years, Chinese experts and journalists have become more interested in the development of India. Books and papers have proliferated on the border conflict, the competition for energy, Delhi's growing ties with the United States and Indian military modernization. The dispute over Tibetan water resources has not yet emerged as an important topic in this debate. Influential

journals on Indian affairs like *Nanya Yanjiu* and *Nanya Yanjiu Jikan* have only published two studies on the Sino-Indian water dispute. In Chinese news media, the wrangling over transboundary rivers remained a fairly minor issue compared to American president Barack Obama's visit to India or Chinese involvement in infrastructure projects in the Pakistani part of Kashmir. Like Chinese discussions about the feasibility and desirability of the western route, the debate about the management of international rivers has by no means matured. Still, in spite of the limited sources available, some important approaches to the Sino-Indian water dispute can be distilled.

A growing group of experts insist that China has to display restraint and moderation if it is to avoid the costs of a water war. Remarkably, Jiang Wenlai of the Chinese Academy of Agricultural Sciences has stated that China itself may lie at the root of many problems. "No doubt China's water problem is serious, very serious even in particular regions, but Chinese scholars tend to exaggerate China's water problem... and consciously or unconsciously contribute to the China water threat theory... We should stress our problems, but we should also stress our protection and management achievements." He stated that safeguarding China's interests should not exclude the equitable distribution of water resources and argued that what mattered most was more efficient usage and international consultation. In a 2007 book on international rivers, Wang Zhijian complained that China had a lack of understanding of international water problems and that this affected strategic thinking at the level of national and local governments.

In this regard, some experts call for more transparency. Lou Chunhao, a South Asia watcher at the China Institute of Contemporary International Relations, a government think tank, suggests that China strengthen cooperation with India on a data monitoring system to alleviate India's worries about possible environmental changes. This view is shared by Ma Jun, director of the Institute of Public and Environmental Affairs in Beijing: "We are not clear about the environmental impacts of the Zangmu hydropower station at present, because the environmental impact assessment report has not been accessible to the public for some reason."

Growing awareness of the perils of new water disputes has also emerged from various initiatives that were launched to discuss and study the importance of transboundary water reserves. In 2006, Tsinghua University established its Centre for Cross-border Rivers, Water and Ecological Security to explore options for the rational use of transboundary water resources. Similar projects were set up at the Universities of Yunnan, Wuhan and Hohai. In 2007, the Geographical Society of China started a research group on regional cooperation on cross-border river basins. The Ministry of Water Resources established a Department of International Cooperation to provide guidance on international economic and technical cooperation, issues related to transboundary rivers and the formulation of policies for management of international rivers, as well as to coordinate negotiation activities. Within the Ministry of Foreign Affairs, the Department of Boundary and Ocean Affairs was mandated to negotiate the management of international rivers.

More attention has also been paid to the development of guidelines to manage international rivers. Ma Bo, a scholar at Fudan University, stated that the Helsinki Rules on cross-border water management could be a starting point for China's policies: Only through fair and reasonable rights can countries guarantee the peaceful exploitation of water resources. Experts like Ma have also proposed joint exploitation and the establishment of more effective consultation mechanisms.

On the other hand, it has been argued that the impact on India of diverting Tibetan rivers would be modest. Commenting on the Zangmu dam, a senior engineer of the company that was in charge of its construction stated, "The river will not be stopped during construction. After it comes into operation, the river water will flow downstream through water turbines and sluices. So the water volume downstream will not be reduced." It has also been argued that even if China embarks on a water diversion program, this could never be the main cause of falling river levels in India because up to eighty percent of the waters of the Brahmaputra are collected from tributaries on the Indian side of the McMahon Line, the unofficial border. Indian experts riposte that these tributaries depend on unpredictable rainfall during the monsoon season, to which Chinese scholars respond that this precipitation could become a more significant source of water than the glaciers on the upper stream because the latter are shrinking rapidly as a consequence of global warming. Their Indian counterparts in turn warn that it is exactly this rainfall on the southern slopes of the Himalayas that is becoming unpredictable as a consequence of climate change, and that the threat of severe drought in years with weaker monsoons makes it important for India to secure a part of the water that comes from the Chinese side of the Himalayas. Ding Yifan, a researcher at the Development Research Centre of the state council, told the *Global Times* that the pros of building the dam still outweighed the cons, saying that "Any mega-projects in China are likely to arouse controversy. Most projects proceed as planned and prove beneficial in the long run."

Here we arrive at the crux of the problem. Demand for water in both countries is growing and climate change makes the flow of the Himalayan rivers uncertain. Several Chinese scholars describe this conundrum as a security dilemma and assume that tensions will be almost inevitable because governments in both countries are under strong pressure to fulfil national needs, and that each measure to do so might be perceived by neighboring countries as a threat. Lan Jianxue, an India specialist at the China Institute for International Studies, a government think tank, points out that internal disputes over water are likely to prompt governments to stand strong on external water disputes. He expects that the shrinking of the Himalayan glaciers will turn the Ganges, the Yangtze River and other rivers into seasonal flows, making water security a matter of food security and, hence, political security. Zhang Boting, the deputy general secretary of the China Society for Hydropower Engineering, goes further: "We should build a hydropower plant...as soon as possible because it is a great policy to protect our territory from Indian invasion and to increase China's capacity for carbon reduction."

Some scholars argue that existing international norms on transboundary rivers do not require China to show restraint in exploiting them; rather, those standards permit China to claim a much larger share. Feng Yan of Yunnan University explains that China utilizes less than 5 percent of the rivers flowing from the Himalayas to neighboring countries. Lan insists that the fair use principle in the Helsinki Rules implies that China should be able to go substantially beyond its current usage ratio. "China should follow the principle of absolute territorial sovereignty," Lan argues, "which means that a country has an unlimited right to use the resources within its territory." Sun Shihai, a prominent India specialist at the China Academy of Social Sciences, said that China should not accept that India "ben[t] international rules into its advantage" to try to restrict the reasonable development of China's water resources.

Another argument suggests that India and others are deliberately exaggerating the Chinese water threat. For example, Lan wrote that the Tibetan government in exile was creating political hype about Chinese dams to pressure Beijing and to win international support for their cause. He referred to a new strategic action plan, which was passed at the fifth International Conference of Tibet Support Groups held in Brussels in 2007, which urged China to conserve the Tibetan environment and protect the most important source of water in Asia. Lan also emphasized that India itself had been diverting water from the Brahmaputra and in this way caused "incalculable economic and environmental losses" in Bangladesh and threatened "the survival of the Bengali people." Another expert, Liu Siwei, specifically points to India's plans to divert water from the Brahmaputra to the Ganges, which he says would affect the "environment and survival of a hundred million people in Bangladesh." He goes on to describe how India is cutting off rivers to Pakistan, threatening the "agricultural hinterland of Punjab province where farmers found that the surface water and groundwater clearly had been sinking." Feng Yan claims that India is tarred with the same brush as China because its own diversion program covers dozens of rivers that are important to Bangladesh. According to her, India continues to ignore the needs of down-stream countries, regardless of its water-sharing treaties with Pakistan (1960) and Bangladesh (1996). "It is the Indian government that caused competition for water with neighbouring countries," said Feng. In an interview with the *Global Times*, National Defence University professor Meng Xiangqing stated that foreign media were fueling the water disputes in order to contain China and curtail its rapid development.

A widely circulated article in a Sichuan newspaper commented that India has been trying to build up international pressure in order to force China to sign humiliating international treaties and to limit its reasonable utilization and development of Tibetan water resources. One journalist even went so far as to claim that Indian dam projects could lead to the flooding of large parts of Chinese territory, including the Tibetan Autonomous Region and Arunachal Pradesh. As Arunachal Pradesh is controlled by India but claimed by China, this argument clearly shows how the water dispute can be linked to the longstanding territorial conflict.

The dispute over rivers seems to be pushing China and India toward a new phase in their complicated relationship. Though Indian suspicions may be premature given that Beijing has yet to green light major diversion projects in Tibet, the degree to which China and India take each other's interests into account will have a decisive impact on the prospects for stability in Asia. That China has agreed to share data on major rivers with India and that there is recognition by Chinese scholars of the need for more arrangements to manage transboundary rivers are encouraging signs. Additionally, studies that focus on international guidelines as they relate to water disputes, though still limited in number, appear to be on the rise.

Bibliography

Ali Ihsan: *Water as an Element of Cooperation and Development in the Middle East*, Ankara, Ayna Publications, 1994.

Alka Rani : *Aquatic Plants for the Waste Water Treatment*, Daya, Delhi, 2004.

Ashok Jaitly: *Troubled Waters: Climate Change, Hydropolitics, and Transboundary Resources*. Stimson Centre, Washington, DC, 2009.

Bhaskara, Harry: *Ending the Daily Water Chore In Against All Odds*, Panos Publications. London. 1989

Brahma Chellaney: *Water, Peace, and War: Confronting the Global Water Crisis*, Lanham, MD: Rowman & Littlefield, 2013.

Cecilia Tortajada: *Appraising Sustainable Development: Water Management and Environmental Challenges*, Oxford University Press, Delhi, 2005.

Conway, D.: *Climate Change and Water Resources in the Nile Basin*, London, University of London, 1993.

Darwish, Adel: *Water Wars: Coming Conflicts in the Middle East*, London, Victor Gollancz, 1999.

Falkenmark, Malin: *Rural Water Supply and Health: The need for a New Strategy*, Scandinavian Institute of African Studies. Uppsala. 1982.

Gideon Fishelson: *Water and Peace: Water Resources and the Arab-Israeli Peace Process*, Westport, CT, Praeger, 1993.

Gupta K.R. : *Water Crisis in India*, Atlantic Pub, Delhi, 2008.

Gupta, R. : *Analysis of Water Distribution Networks*, Narosa, Delhi, 2011.

Hoekstra, A. Y. and A. K. Chapagain: *Globalization of Water: Sharing the Planet's Freshwater Resources*, Oxford: Blackwell, 2008

Husain, Ahmad : *Environment and Water Resource Management*, Sumit Enterprises, Delhi, 2006.

James J.: *Water Atlas of the United States*, Port Washington, NY, 1973.

Jha.B.H.: *Diversion of the Brahmaputra: Myth or Reality?* Institute for Defence Studies and Analysis: New Delhi, 2011.

Jun.M: *Defending Water Security, 2001.*

Kruvant, W.J.: *People, Energy, and Pollution*, Cambridge, Ballinger Publishing, 1975.

Kugelman M.: *Water: Asia's New Battleground*, News Security Beat, 2011.

Lloyd Myers : *Handbook of Water Harvesting*, Washington D.C.: U.S. Dept. of Agriculture, Agricultural Research Service, 1983

Mahajan Gautam : *Evaluation and Development of Ground Water*, APH, Delhi, 2008.

McGarry, M.G.: *Matching Water Supply Technology to the Needs and Resources of Developing Countries*, United Nations. New York. 1987

Nageswara, Rao K. : *Water Resources Management : Realities and Challenges*, New Century Publication, Delhi, 2006.

Nissen-Petersen, E. : *Rainwater Catchment Systems for Domestic Supply: Design, Construction and Implementation*, London, U.K.: IT Publications, 1999.

Patrizio Warren: *Developing Participatory and Integrated Watershed Management*, Daya for FAO, Delhi, 2001.

Peter G.: *Water and Sanitation: Economic and Sociological Perspectives* Academic Press. Orlando. 1984.

Ram Kumar : *Geography of Water Resources*, Rawat, Delhi, 2008.

Rao K. Nageswara : *Water Resources Management : Realities and Challenges*, New Century Publication, Delhi, 2006.

Sutter. R.G: *Chinese Foreign Relations: Power and Policy Since the Cold War*. Plymouth, Rowman and Littlefield Publishers, 2010.

Index

❑❑❑